This is a novel, fascinating, and fundamental contributi[...] soundly and realistically, the contemporary practice of ps[...] including the social dimension in its cultural, historical, political, and ecological aspects that classical theories had actively ignored. It is necessary not only for those who have a psychoanalytical perspective of our modern world, but also for other professionals dealing with mental health.

Carlos D. Nemirovsky, MD, President of the Buenos
Aires Psychoanalytic Association.
Author of *Winnicott and Kohut on Intersubjectivity
and Complex Disorders* (Routledge, 2020)

This book broadens our analytic insight by avoiding unilateral and uniform thinking and integrating information from several authors, cultures, and sciences, including the English, Latin-American, French, and Portuguese contributions to psychoanalysis and group analysis, as well as sociological, cultural, religious, and political perspectives, and biology and neuroscience. This is a courageous and important contribution to the never-ending search for the truth about the Human Being.

Isaura Manso Neto, MD, President of the Portuguese
Society of Group Analysis. Author of *The Portuguese
School of Group Analysis* (Routledge, 2020)

The authors critically review the contributions and limitations of psychoanalysis and link this to the novel view of group analysis, in its British school of S H Foulkes and the Latin-American one of Enrique Pichon-Rivière. Their approach is integrative, and they introduce the term 'gossamer', already used in botany for the networks of plants and trees that interconnect, to illuminate how these various centres of theory and practice articulate and fuse, thus paving the way for the development of a new paradigm of the human being. This is a major conceptual achievement that should be seriously considered.

Malcolm Pines, MD, psychoanalyst and group and analyst.
Former President of the Group-Analytic Society.
Author of *Circular Reflections* and a forthcoming
book of *Selected Papers* by Routledge.

In this marriage of true minds, Juan Tubert-Oklander and Reyna Hernández-Tubert espouse and embody 'a new paradigm of the human being', grounded in holistic thinking and analogical hermeneutics, which transcends dichotomies and shows the perennially oscillating figure and ground relation of individual and collective phenomena. A profound, passionate, erudite, soaring summa analytica.

Peter L. Rudnytsky, PhD, University of Florida and Chicago
Psychoanalytic Institute. Author of *Formulated Experiences:
Hidden Realities and Emergent Meanings from
Shakespeare to Fromm* (Routledge, 2019).

Psychoanalysis, Group Analysis, and Beyond

Psychoanalysis, Group Analysis, and Beyond presents an important new paradigm in psychoanalysis and group analysis, presenting the individual and the group as elements of a wider whole and taking socio-political and cultural contexts into account.

Juan Tubert-Oklander and Reyna Hernández-Tubert explore the contributions of group analysis to this new perspective, which suggests a holistic conception of the respective status and nature of what the common-sense view of the world conceives as the individual and the community. Part I presents thoughts on the 'gelding' of psychoanalysis, focuses on the limitations of classical psychoanalysis, and elaborates on key topics including epistemology, inclusion and exclusion, culture, and the real. Part II considers the reincorporation of what had formerly been excluded, through the theory and practice of group analysis. Finally, Part III bridges the gap, presenting several approaches to the building of the new paradigm that is so sorely needed.

Psychoanalysis, Group Analysis, and Beyond will be of great interest to group analysts, psychoanalysts, and psychotherapists in practice and in training, as well as other professionals specializing in group work.

Juan Tubert-Oklander, MD, PhD, is a psychoanalyst, group analyst, and marriage and family psychotherapist, who was born, studied medicine, and was trained as a group therapist in Buenos Aires, Argentina. He has lived and worked in private practice in Mexico City since 1976, where he was trained in adult and child psychoanalysis, now being a Mexican citizen. He is the author of numerous papers and book chapters, published in Spanish, English, Italian, French, Portuguese, Czech, Hebrew, and Chinese. He is the co-author, with Reyna Hernández-Tubert, of *Operative Groups: The Latin-American Approach to Group Analysis* (2004) and the author of *Theory of Psychoanalytical Practice: A Relational Process Approach* (2013) and *The One and the Many: Relational Psychoanalysis and Group Analysis* (2014), as well as several books in Spanish. He is Full Member of the Argentine Psychoanalytic Association and the International Psychoanalytical Association, Honorary Member of the Group-Analytic Society International, and Member of the International Association of Relational Psychoanalysis and Psychotherapy. He is Professor in the Master's Degree Course of Psychoanalytic Psychotherapy and Professor and Coordinator of the Doctorate of Psychoanalysis and Group Analysis at the Marista University of Merida.

Reyna Hernández-Tubert, MD, PhD, is a Mexican psychiatrist, child and adolescent psychiatrist, psychoanalyst, group analyst, and marriage and family therapist, living and practising in Mexico City. She is the author of numerous papers and book chapters, published in Spanish, English, Italian, and French. She is the co-author, with Juan Tubert-Oklander, of *Operative Groups: The Latin-American Approach to Group Analysis* (2004). She is Full Member of the Argentine Psychoanalytic Association, the International Psychoanalytical Association, and the Group-Analytic Society International, and Member of the International Association of Relational Psychoanalysis and Psychotherapy. She is Professor in the Master's Degree Course of Psychoanalytic Psychotherapy and the Doctorate of Psychoanalysis and Group Analysis at the Marista University of Merida.

The New International Library of Group Analysis (NILGA)

Series Editor: Earl Hopper

Drawing on the seminal ideas of British, European and American group analysts, psychoanalysts, social psychologists and social scientists, the books in this series focus on the study of small and large groups, organisations and other social systems, and on the study of the transpersonal and transgenerational sociality of human nature. NILGA books will be required reading for the members of professional organisations in the field of group analysis, psychoanalysis, and related social sciences. They will be indispensable for the "formation" of students of psychotherapy, whether they are mainly interested in clinical work with patients or in consultancy to teams and organisational clients within the private and public sectors.

Recent titles in the series include

The Portuguese School of Group Analysis
Towards a Unified and Integrated Approach to Theory Research and Clinical Work
Edited by Isaura Manso Neto and Margarida França

Richard M. Billow's Selected Papers on Psychoanalysis and Group Process
Changing Our Minds
Edited by Tzachi Slonim

Addressing Challenging Moments in Psychotherapy
Clinical Wisdom for Working with Individuals, Groups and Couples
Edited by Jerome S. Gans

Psychoanalysis, Group Analysis, and Beyond
Towards a New Paradigm of the Human Being
Juan Tubert-Oklander and Reyna Hernández-Tubert

For more information about this series, please visit: https://www.routledge.com/The-New-International-Library-of-Group-Analysis/book-series/KARNNILGA

Psychoanalysis, Group Analysis, and Beyond

Towards a New Paradigm of the Human Being

Juan Tubert-Oklander and Reyna Hernández-Tubert

Routledge
Taylor & Francis Group

LONDON AND NEW YORK

First published 2022
by Routledge
2 Park Square, Milton Park, Abingdon, Oxon OX14 4RN

and by Routledge
605 Third Avenue, New York, NY 10158

Routledge is an imprint of the Taylor & Francis Group, an informa business

British Library Cataloguing-in-Publication Data
A catalogue record for this book is available from the British Library

Library of Congress Cataloging-in-Publication Data
Names: Tubert-Oklander, Juan, author. | Hernández de Tubert, Reyna, author.
Title: Psychoanalysis, group analysis, and beyond : towards a new paradigm of
the human being / Juan Tubert-Oklander and Reyna Hernández-Tubert.
Description: Milton Park, Abingdon, Oxon ; New York, NY : Routledge, 2022. |
Series: The new international library of group analysis
Identifiers: LCCN 2021013568 | ISBN 9780367151331 (hardback) |
ISBN 9780367151362 (paperback) | ISBN 9780429055287 (ebook)
Subjects: LCSH: Psychoanalysis. | Group psychoanalysis. | Subconsciousness.
Classification: LCC BF173 .T838 2022 | DDC 150.19/5—dc23
LC record available at https://lccn.loc.gov/2021013568

ISBN: 978-0-367-15133-1 (hbk)
ISBN: 978-0-367-15136-2 (pbk)
ISBN: 978-0-429-05528-7 (ebk)

DOI: 10.4324/9780429055287

Typeset in Times New Roman
by Apex CoVantage, LLC

*For our grandchildren
Aurora Regina,
who was born with this book,
Isabella and Rodrigo,
who were with us while it was written.*

Contents

Acknowledgements

Several chapters have been published previously, in either English or Spanish. We thank the editors and publishers for authorizing their reproduction in this volume.

Juan Tubert-Oklander, Mauricio Beuchot Puente, and Torres Editores for Chapter 1, published in the book *Ciencia mestiza: Hermenéutica analógica y psicoanálisis*.

Charles Levin and the Canadian Psychoanalytic Society for Chapters 2 and 13, published in the *Canadian Journal of Psychoanalysis*.

Dieter Nietzgen and Sage Publications for Chapters 9, 10, 11, 12, and 15, published in *Group Analysis*.

Susana Vinocur Fischbein and the Argentine Psychoanalytic Association for Chapter 5, published in *Revista de Psicoanálisis*.

Gabriela Legorreta and Lawrence J. Brown, and Routledge – Taylor & Francis Group for Chapter 7, published in the book *On Freud's 'Formulations on the Two Principles of Mental Functioning'*.

Peter Zelaskowski and the Group-Analytic Society, for Appendix IV.

Chapters 3, 4, 6, 8, and 16 and Appendices I, II, and III have not been previously published.

Foreword

This collection of essays in psychoanalysis and group analysis is a product of the particularly creative intellectual and professional partnership of Juan Tubert-Oklander and Reyna Hernández-Tubert, from Argentina and Mexico, respectively, but now living and working in Mexico. They have been married for many decades, and have produced several children and grandchildren as well as a body of literature, which has become influential both theoretically and clinically in South America, North America, and in Europe. They have succeeded in introducing to an English-speaking readership the work of psychoanalysts such as Enrique Pichon-Rivière and José Bleger, contributing to the fields of relational psychoanalysis and group analysis, and forging suggestive links and bonds with the work of René Kaës in France, Malcolm Pines in England, and with that of several members of the next generation of group analysts throughout Europe.

I have especially appreciated their willingness to engage with the core intellectual problems of our professions. I have rarely known and worked with colleagues who have so fully understood my own general approach to the study of socially unconscious processes, and my attempts to integrate sociology and psychoanalysis within group analysis. I feel privileged to have had the opportunity to discuss with them their ideas and perspectives. I have been stimulated by their passion for and commitment to our work.

Juan and Reyna have become determined to go 'beyond' the paradigms of contemporary psychoanalysis and group analysis, and to transcend our professional and intellectual horizons. However, I wonder if we are ready and able to find new models and frames of reference that will be as fecund as the one that we have established, and that has in so many ways only just begun to bear fruit. It is so difficult to work with and love our imperfect object, especially in the context of its multitude of cultures, languages, lineages, and ethnicities, not to mention its profound complexities. Nonetheless, I am convinced that this book will become a landmark in our attempts to make clinical use of our appreciation of the sociality of human nature and the nature of human sociality in the global human group and in each individual member of it.

I truly believe that the beauty and erudition of these essays will richly compensate us for an inevitable degree of envy of the partnership of the authors of them. This book will be of lasting value to students and colleagues alike. The list of references is in itself especially useful.

Earl Hopper

Series Editor
February 2021

Introduction

Juan Tubert-Oklander and Reyna
Hernández-Tubert

Orthodox psychoanalysis has traditionally had an anti-environmental bias. Psychoanalysis was defined as the study and treatment of the inner unconscious mental processes of the individual and their corresponding ideational contents. Hence, any reference to actual relationships with real human beings or to the social, cultural, historical, political, or ecological context was deemed to be 'merely external and conscious', 'non-analytical', or even 'anti-analytical'. And those who dared defy this unwritten injunction were either ignored or sternly criticised, or even expelled from the institutionalised psychoanalytic community.

This generated much discredit for psychoanalysis in many quarters, such as many branches of philosophy, the social sciences, and the Humanities, in which it was seen as a reactionary practice and ideology that ignored or actively denied the impact of social facts and the most urgent social and political problems, thus upholding the maintenance of the status quo.

This is rather surprising, since psychoanalysis started by exploring the pathogenic effects of distorted interpersonal relationships, particularly with a child's adult caretakers, and has shown, along its history, a potential for social criticism. Something obviously happened to our discipline that hampered its development in those directions, quite apart from all its great accomplishments in the enquiry of inner life.

This major restriction of the developmental potential of psychoanalysis – which has all too frequently been imposed by political means or personal attacks – may be described as the maiming (or even gelding) of psychoanalysis. In any case, it is a sickness, and as such it requires a cure.

Nonetheless, and in spite of many spontaneous attempts at healing, curing a disease starts by establishing its nature and aetiology. Hence, the first part of the book – called 'The gelding of psychoanalysis' – will be devoted to the task of exploring the forms and causes of this bizarre phenomenon.

There are quite a few reasons for this restriction, and they may be described as *metaphysical, ontological, epistemological, historical, socio-political, ideological,* and *emotional.*

The *metaphysical* reason is Freud's commitment to materialistic metaphysics. This is the assumption that underlies most of the current scientistic conception of

DOI: 10.4324/9780429055287-1

the world, as well as its common-sense version, that only matter and energy are 'real'. Hence, the only possible real basis for mental phenomena is to be found in the human brain or, at least, in the individual organism. So, any interpersonal, group, or social occurrences are mere epiphenomena of neural individual events, mental constructions that cannot be considered 'real'.

The *ontological* reason is the very idea of the Cartesian subject that, although it was relativised by the psychoanalytic demonstration that it cannot be limited to consciousness, still underlies Freud's theoretical thought, which takes as the point of departure of human development an isolated individual that has yet to discover the world.

The *epistemological* reason is Freud's deep conviction that Science is the only possible source of reliable knowledge – and by this he meant natural science, which he believed to be the only valid one. Hence, his project was that psychoanalysis should become yet another natural science, as respectable as physics or chemistry, and he envisioned that in the future 'all our provisional ideas in psychology will presumably someday be based on an organic substructure' (Freud, 1914c, p. 78). This implied an utter oblivion of the hermeneutic approach of the Humanities, which is indispensable for a full understanding of personal and social processes. This belief is shared by a great part of the psychoanalytic community, particularly in the English-speaking world. Hence, their virulent attacks on those psychoanalysts, like James Home (1966), who dared question the scientific nature and status of psychoanalysis.

The *historical*, which should perhaps be called 'psycho-historical', determinant is the fact that Freud's original traumatic theory of neurosis – quite inadequately named the 'seduction theory', a veritable euphemism for paedophilic sexual abuse! – was interpersonal and environmental, and implied a severe social criticism, but was abruptly abandoned by its author in 1897. There is no real record of his reason for this unexpected turn but, ever since, Freud and his circle first, and the subsequent generations of orthodox psychoanalysts after them, have had a violent rejection of any attempt – such as Ferenczi's (1933) – to revive the traumatic theory of neuroses, or even to include environmental – interpersonal, social, cultural, political, or ecological – factors in the psychoanalytic understanding and interpretation. The underlying motivations are clearly an expression of the following items in this list.

The *socio-political* reason relates to the maintenance of social order. Freud's original traumatic theory of neuroses affirmed that the cause of these disturbances was to be found in the parents' and other caretaking adults' abuse of their charges. But, acknowledging that adults abused children opened the door to recognising other abuses of authority against the weak and powerless that are supposed to be cared for, such as teachers on students, doctors on patients, analysts on analysands, and – Heaven forbid! – the authorities on the people. In other words, it implied a stern criticism of social authority. No wonder that the young Freud received the most violent, irrational, and slanderous attacks from his colleagues and decent society when he publicly posed such ideas. But the fact that, thirty-five years after recanting them, Freud and his circle imposed similar attacks on Ferenczi's effort to salvage and revamp the traumatic theory strongly suggests that the urge to defend and preserve the bases of social authority was the underlying unconscious motivation of their rejection of such theory, as well as of any attempt to include the social and political context in the psychoanalytic enquiry and theory.

The *ideological* reason is to be found in Freud's conception of the world and society. As Erich Fromm (1958) stated, Freud was no revolutionary, from the political point of view, but a rebel. This means that he fought against the unfairness of being left out of the positions of power and prestige, which he craved, but did not question the hierarchical structure of society. Indeed, he was rather conservative in this respect. He was quite willing to question the sexual mores of society, but not its power structure. He was part of an uprising middle class, and so were most of the members of the succeeding generations of analysts. On the contrary, most of the analytic thinkers who questioned this principle of authority and included the socio-political dimension – like Wilhelm Reich and Otto Fenichel – had a left-wing ideology.

Finally, the *emotional* reason corresponds to an aspect of Freud's biography that is not usually considered. As a youngster, he intended to overcome the social limitations imposed on him by society's antisemitism, by studying law and following a political career. After he became disillusioned with this project and replaced it by the ambition to become a great scientist, he maintained an antipolitical bias for the rest of his life (Pines, 1989). This undoubtedly affected his interpretation of social conflicts, which he reduced to the intrapsychic dimension of the Oedipal conflict (Schorske, 1974).

These are, as far as we can establish, the many reasons for the systematic exclusion of the socio-political dimension from the orthodox version of the theory and practice of psychoanalysis. Nonetheless, there have been many attempts to redress this unnecessary limitation.

One well-known instance of such attempts has been the interpersonal and culturalist approach to psychoanalysis, initiated by Harry Stack Sullivan, Erich Fromm, Frieda Fromm-Reichmann, Karen Horney, and Clara Thompson, and further developed in the William Alanson White Institute. Another one has been the relational trend in psychoanalysis, initiated by Sándor Ferenczi and continued in the work and ideas of the British Independents, Heinz Kohut' Self Psychology, and the contemporary school of Relational Psychoanalysis. But there has been another, more radical approach to the enquiry and treatment of the social dimension of human existence, one that is not usually considered within the interpersonal and relational traditions, albeit it partially overlaps and is quite compatible with them. This is the tradition of Group Analysis.

Group Analysis is not the same thing as psychoanalytic group psychotherapy. The latter is just the application of unmodified psychoanalytic theories and techniques, derived from the experience of bi-personal psychoanalytic treatments, to the treatment of individual patients in groups. Group analysis, on the other hand, approaches the task of conducting groups, whether therapeutic or non-therapeutic, with an analytic attitude and generates new concepts and techniques, which are specific to the group situation, derived from the group-analytic experience, just as psychoanalysis has done on the basis of the bi-personal psychoanalytic experience. It also includes and uses not only those psychoanalytic concepts that are applicable to the group-analytic situation, but also those of the Social Sciences and the Humanities. Such integrative approach to the study of human affairs provides a new way of conceiving the analytic endeavour initiated by Sigmund Freud. This is presented in Part II of the book, called 'A fresh look'.

Group analysis started independently, in the late 1930s and early 1940s, in two quite separate places: in Britain, in the work of S. H. Foulkes (1948, 1964a, 1990), and in Argentina, in that of Enrique Pichon-Rivière (1971a, 1971b, 1979; Losso, Setton, & Scharff, 2017; Scharff, 2017; Tubert-Oklander, 2017b; Tubert-Oklander & Hernández de Tubert, 2004). Foulkes coined the name 'group analysis', and it has been since identified with the Group-Analytic Society he founded. Pichon-Rivière, on the other hand, called his theory and practice of group conduction 'operative groups', but, in spite of some minor differences in their respective conceptions, it can fairly be said that they represent two versions of one and the same endeavour (Tubert-Oklander & Hernández-Tubert, 2014a [Chapter 9]).

The fundamental characteristic of this common conception is the rejection of the individual paradigm, which affirms that only individuals are 'real', and of the alleged opposition between 'individuals' and 'groups'. Both Foulkes and Pichon-Rivière assumed that human life is unitary and that 'individual', 'group', and 'society' are mere abstractions, constructed by a tendency of our cognitive processes to extract an aspect of a complex whole, in order to be able to think it through. The result is therefore a figure-ground relation, which can and should be reversed over and over again in order to get a glimpse of the nature of the whole. Such holistic theory and practice are characteristic of the group-analytic approach, which thus opens the way for a full inclusion of relational and social facts in our analyses.

Consequently, psychoanalysis and group-analysis are no longer in opposition to each other, but turn out to be two aspects and perspectives of the wider field of *analysis*, which was inaugurated by Sigmund Freud. But this point of view requires a major revamping of our theories, in order to bridge the gap between a perspective that starts from the assumption of the isolated individual and another one that affirms the primary and essential relational and social nature of the human being.

Both perspectives have their assets and their liabilities. Individualistic theories, such as Freud's metapsychology, which take as their starting point the existence of an isolated subject, are very good for studying and accounting for a person's intimate experiences and inner processes, but are at a loss when trying to explain what happens between people – that is, relationships and interpersonal processes – and the nature and functioning of collective entities, such as groups, institutions, communities, and society-at-large – that is, transpersonal processes – and their impact on individuals. Similarly, those collectivistic theories that affirm the primary and essential relational and social nature of human beings are most proficient at describing and explaining interpersonal and transpersonal processes, but are quite unable to account for the intimate feeling of I-ness and agency that constitutes the individual subject. Obviously, it is not a question of choosing one of these two perspectives, but of transcending their dilemmatic opposition.

What we need is a new paradigm of the human being, a holistic conception of the respective status and nature of what the common-sense view of the world conceives as the individual and the community, and this is what group analysis provides. S. H. Foulkes introduced his concept of the group and social *matrix*, conceived as

> the hypothetical web of communication and relationship in a given group. It is the common shared ground which ultimately determines the meaning and significance of all events and upon which all communications and interpretations, verbal and nonverbal, rest.
>
> (Foulkes, 1964b, p. 292)

The individual personality is embedded in, surrounded, contained, pervaded, and determined by this gossamer network, which is a living and ever-evolving entity, and it is continuous with it, because the individual also has a matricial organisation.

In the same vein, Pichon-Rivière (1979) has coined his concept of *vínculo* – a Spanish term that has been alternatively translated as 'link' or 'bond'. The bond (link) is a highly complex structure that includes the subject, the object (which is really another subject), their mutual relationship, and the whole group, institutional, historical, cultural, ideological, social, political, physical, and ecological context. It is essentially dynamic and evolutive, displaying a perpetual interchange between 'inner' and 'outer'. There is, therefore, a basic unity between individual, group, their social and political contexts, and the non-human environment.

We are truly in need of a new paradigm of the human being, to replace the dilemmatic opposition of 'individual' and 'collective' (Tubert-Oklander, 2014), and this is the subject of the various chapters included in Part III, called 'Bridging the gap'.

The structure of the book is therefore basically dialectical, following the Hegelian triad of *thesis-antithesis-synthesis*. Part I – 'The gelding of psychoanalysis' – focuses on the limitations of classical psychoanalysis, which led to the exclusion of the interpersonal and socio-political environment. Part II – 'A fresh look' – deals with the reincorporation of what had been excluded, through the theory and practice of group analysis. And Part III – 'Bridging the gap' – displays several approaches to the building of the new paradigm we so sorely need. This is, of course, a major task that can only be realised by a multi-disciplinary community of thinkers, and not only by analysts, whether psychoanalysts or group analysts. But, in any case, the contribution of our professional perspective and knowledge is bound to be a significant part of this collective effort that is already on its way, from many quarters.

On the other hand, this three-part division is mainly pedagogical and related to the main formal subject of each chapter, but all of them include in their arguments the various elements of this dialectic, which is mirrored in the overall structure of the book.

One final caveat is that, even though each chapter bears the name of its main author, all our writings of the past twenty-seven years have been the result of an ongoing dialogue and shared effort. The formal authorship depended, in each case, on the circumstances of the presentation or publication of each text and on our personal penchant for specific subjects – theoretical and epistemological for Juan, social and political for Reyna, and clinical for both.

The dates included in the chapter titles are not intended as reference calls, but as a contextual information given in order to help the reader, if he or she so wishes, to follow the chronological evolution of our thought.

We trust that this new effort may be of use for our community of colleagues and students, and also, on account of its socio-political theme, that it may be of interest to students of the social sciences and the Humanities, as well as the general public, since it responds to an urgent and pressing need to introduce a new way of thinking about the relation between the person and the community. Our contemporary society, based on the individual paradigm, has fallen prey to a conception of life as a ruthless cannibalistic competition that endangers the very survival of Humankind, and the collectivistic ideologies that emerged during the Twentieth Century came into similar dead ends. Hence, the need for a radical change in our assumptions and habits of thinking and relating, and in this we believe that analysis has much to offer to society.

Mexico City, February 2021.

Part I

The gelding of psychoanalysis

Chapter 1

Freud's contradictions and the hybrid nature of psychoanalysis (2008–2020)

Juan Tubert-Oklander

When we began our work together, both of us had been feeling for quite some time that there was a major contradiction between the practice and the theory of psychoanalysis. This contradiction stemmed from an original duality in the thinking and practice of the creator of our discipline, a split that ran deep into his personality, thinking, feeling, values, and actions. It was obvious to us that the practice of analysis – both psychoanalysis and group-analysis – was based on an intimate, intense, and highly personal relation, and that the analytic dialogue was a shared attempt to make sense of the patients' life experiences and of the shared experiences generated by the analytic encounter. Consequently, it was obvious to us that analysis was an interpretative practice – 'an art of interpretation which takes on the task of, as it were, extracting the pure metal of the repressed thoughts from the ore of the unintentional ideas', as Freud (1904a, p. 252) rightly put it – but the theory he developed to account for his therapeutic experiences, observations, and discoveries intended to be strictly causal, in the model of the natural sciences, and we felt that there was no way in which these two aspects of psychoanalysis could ever fit together.

We tackled this problem in many ways over the years, looking for elements for thinking it through in literature, philosophy, linguistics, and semantics, but we still lacked a more precise language in which to formulate our ideas on the matter. Fortunately, in 2005, we met the Mexican philosopher Mauricio Beuchot, who was the author of a novel philosophical proposal of what he called 'Analogical Hermeneutics' (Beuchot, 1997). This was the beginning of a long-time dialogue and collaboration among us, which eventually led to Juan and Mauricio co-writing a book in Spanish called **Hybrid Science: Psychoanalysis and Analogical Hermeneutics** *(Tubert-Oklander & Beuchot Puente, 2008).[1] The present chapter is a revised and updated version of Chapter II of that book (Tubert-Oklander, 2008a).*

Which Freud are we talking about?

In the first chapter of our book together, called 'The presence of hermeneutics in Freud's epistemological discourse', Mauricio Beuchot Puente (2008) expounded,

DOI: 10.4324/9780429055287-3

with utmost clarity, his conviction that Freud's psychoanalytical method was, from the very beginning, both hermeneutical and relational. It was *hermeneutical*, because his research strategy was based on the interpretation of the hidden meanings that lay beyond the patients' manifest expressions, and it was *relational*, because the whole procedure was necessarily based on the emotional and dialogic bond that ensued between therapist and patient.

However, Beuchot does not fail to point out the existence of major contradictions in Freud, who intended that psychoanalysis should abide by the epistemological criteria of Nineteenth Century natural science, just as his creation was setting the bases for the need for a new epistemology, which would emerge during the Twentieth Century and put an end to the Cartesian dissociation between mind, body, and heart, as well as between subject and object (Tubert-Oklander, 2000).

This is indeed a delicate matter. The psychoanalytic movement emerged and evolved as an ideological movement, comparable to a religious or political organisation, rather than a scientific one. Hence, its founder became something of a cult figure, an icon, or even an idol, of psychoanalysis (Tubert-Oklander, 2009–2014), and his *Complete Works* are frequently read and studied, not as the indispensable historical context for a better understanding of contemporary psychoanalysis or as a fount of possible ideas to be critically analysed, but as the unquestionable source of psychoanalytic truth. Consequently, many original psychoanalytic authors have felt obliged to reinterpret Freud, to make him say what they are actually thinking, rather than acknowledging – both internally and publicly – the divergence, or even incompatibility, of the new ideas they are putting forward with his.[2]

It is quite obvious that the previous statement, about the contradiction between Freud's scientific ideals and the very nature of the discipline he created, is bound to generate an intense criticism from two quite different quarters. On the one hand, those who share his particular epistemological stance, which conceives psychoanalysis as a natural science, will affirm, on the basis of a selection of Freudian quotes, that this was the founder's explicit project, so that any attempt to assert that it has, or should have, a different epistemological status is utterly untenable.

On the other, those who conceive psychoanalysis as something totally different from and incompatible with positivistic science will show us, from a different but similarly sized selection of quotes, a hermeneutic Freud, who practiced what Wilhelm Dilthey (1883) called a *Geistewissenschaft*, a Human Science or Science of the Spirit that has an access to knowledge that differs from that of the *Naturwissenschaften*, the Natural Sciences. Of course, Freud would not have accepted such proposition, but they conceive this humanistic or romantic side of his work and thought as the 'true Freud', who has been distorted by his orthodox following. In this 'either-or' situation, nobody seems to like a position like mine, which tries to acknowledge the existence of such a deep contradiction and find a way to transcend it.

The basic flaw in such arguments is that they both insist on taking an author's thought as if it were, or had to be, unitary and consistent. Freud, just as all of us, had all sorts of unacknowledged inconsistencies and conflicts. In particular, there is an essential incompatibility between the characteristics of the novel field of enquiry he had opened and the new discipline he was creating, on the one hand, and the scientific ideal to which he wished to abide, on the other.

The problem is that epistemology always comes one or several steps behind science. True scientists are daring enquirers who pose all sorts of questions and problems, moved by deep worries, derived from living experience, that unsettle their spirit. These they strive to answer, using the means at their disposal, and, when these fail, they manage to devise new ways of tackling them. The epistemologist beholds, astonished, these accomplishments and tries to account for them, by inventing theoretical models that might shed light on what the scientist has actually done. If one of these models turns out to be particularly convincing, he might be tempted to formulate it normatively, as 'that what scientists are supposed to do'. And such formulations may become the Law for a certain community of researchers.

Most scientists try to abide by the more prestigious epistemological models in their community at the time, and they do get results that way, but always within the limits of the existing paradigm.[3] At least, until the inconsistencies and proliferation of unexplained findings in their shared work bring about a crisis in their discipline and force some of them to devise new ways to deal with it. Those few thinkers who then dare to formulate some radically new questions, thus creating a new paradigm, are obliged to go beyond the limits of what is already known and develop a novel approach that they themselves do not fully understand. This unleashes a deep crisis, in themselves and in their community, which is what Thomas S. Kuhn (1962) calls a 'scientific revolution'. The new and the old paradigm coexist for some time, thus generating much strife and bitterness among colleagues, which in the end subsides with the death of those who had been reared in the old set of assumptions.

That is the moment when these original thinkers feel lonely and lost in a darkness they only manage to illuminate partially, by means of the light they themselves generate, when they may turn, hopefully, to the models received from their teachers, without being fully aware that their own work is demolishing them into obsolescence. Such was the case of Freud.

If we accept this conception of the function of epistemology as an enquiry into the methods, findings, and theories developed by actual scientists, instead of seeing it as a normative discipline, it is obvious that Freud could not fully understand the revolutionary consequences of his discovery – the unconscious – and his creation – psychoanalysis – for overcoming the model of thought in which he had been reared and to which he aspired as an ideal. As I once wrote (Tubert-Oklander, 2000), Freud was a psychoanalyst of the Twentieth Century, who operated with Nineteenth Century epistemology; it is our turn to do Twenty-first Century psychoanalysis, leaning on the Twentieth Century epistemology.

Epistemology-in-use and affirmed epistemology

The epistemologist Abraham Kaplan (1964) distinguishes between what he calls 'logic-in-use' and 'reconstructed logic', and this he explains in the following terms:

> [S]cientists and philosophers use a logic – they have a cognitive style which is more or less logical – and some of them also formulate it explicitly. I call the former the *logic-in-use*, and the latter the *reconstructed logic*. We can no more take them to be identical or even assume an exact correspondence between them, than we can in the case of the decline of Rome and Gibbon's account of it, a patient's fever and his physician's explanation of it.
>
> (p. 8)

This is the fundamental principle: *the map is not the territory*, as Alfred Korzybski (1941) said in his famous aphorism. The symbol is not the thing symbolised, the portrait is not the person depicted, the representation is not the thing represented, and Freud's logical reconstruction of his practice differs significantly from what he actually did. Moreover, I think it fails to do justice to the utter revolutionary character of his creation.

But, just as we can distinguish between the way in which a person actually thinks and the way in which he believes he thinks, we can also do it between the epistemology that underlies how a scientist actually works and how he theorises about his results, and the ideal epistemological model he aspires to attain, either on account of its prestige within his community or the subjective value it has for him. It is also quite frequent, for a researcher who is not quite sure about what he is doing – as a result of its novelty or because it conflicts with what he has learnt in his training – to strive to affirm that his work is strictly based on the generally accepted principles, in an attempt to feel legitimised, in the eyes of both his colleagues and his own. I shall therefore call the unstated principles that underlie his revolutionary work his *epistemology-in-use* and that other pre-existent model he feels should rule his enquiry his *affirmed epistemology*.

Freud's epistemology-in-use is, precisely, the one described by Beuchot. It is unquestionable that, in his clinical practice, he strictly adheres to the principle of looking for hidden meanings, rather than causes. Consequently, his approach to phenomena such as dreams, parapraxes, or neurotic symptoms is clearly interpretative, not explicative.

As Charles Rycroft (1966) pointed out,

> In some aspects of his work Freud saw this himself clearly. His most famous work he entitled *The Interpretation of Dreams* [1900a] not *The Cause of Dreams* and his chapter on symptoms in his *Introductory Lectures* [1916–1917] is called *The Sense of Symptoms*.
>
> (p. 13)

There, Freud says,

> Thus neurotic symptoms have a sense, like parapraxes and dreams, and, like
> them, have a connection with the life of those who produce them [pp. 257–
> 258][. . . And then he adds] I have shown you, then, on the basis of two chosen
> examples, that neurotic symptoms have a sense, like parapraxes and dreams,
> and that they have an intimate connection with the patient's experiences.
>
> (p. 269)

However, since his field of enquiry includes not only neurotic symptoms, parapraxes, and dreams, but also all other behaviour, purposive or spontaneous, and
the subject's relations with others, including the analyst, we may well affirm
that *for Freud, every human expression is always meaningful*. Besides, his discovery of the unconscious dimension of human existence leads him to formulate
the hypothesis that, although all expression or behaviour may or may not have a
conscious meaning for its agent, it never fails to have a meaning (or set of meanings) that is unknown to him and can only be accessed by means of inferences –
that is, an interpretative work. In other words, *all human manifestations are
subject to interpretation since they express meanings that are not immediately
accessible*.

This hermeneutic perspective is particularly clear in Freud's (1904a) third-
person presentation of his method in 'Freud's psycho-analytic procedure', in
which he writes,

> Freud has developed on this basis an art of interpretation which takes on the
> task of, as it were, *extracting the pure metal of the repressed thoughts from
> the ore of the unintentional ideas.* . . . The details of this technique of interpre-
> tation or translation have not yet been published by Freud. According to indi-
> cations he has given, they comprise a number of rules, reached empirically,
> of how the unconscious material may be reconstructed from the associations,
> directions on how to know what it means when the patient's ideas cease to
> flow, and experiences of the most important typical resistances that arise in
> the course of such treatments.
>
> (p. 252, my italics)

This quotation shows that not only he is aware that he is doing a hermeneutic
job, but also what kind of theory of interpretation he holds. The assumption that
interpretation consists in 'extracting the pure metal of the repressed thoughts
from the ore of the unintentional ideas' implies that the hidden meaning that is
to be unveiled is pre-existent to the interpretative act and that all that is needed
is to extract it from its deceptive manifest appearance, by means of an adequate
technique. In such a positivistic univocal theory, interpretation should be strictly
objective, by excluding or minimising the participation of the interpreter's
subjectivity.[4]

Nonetheless, what we know of Freud's concrete practice, through both his numerous clinical examples and the testimony of his former patients, suggests a quite different way of working. It is clear that, although he never mentions Dilthey in his writings and he surely would not have shared his conception of the Sciences of the Spirit, Freud systematically used that operation called *Verstehen* (Dilthey, 1883), that is, empathic comprehension through identification, 'putting oneself in the other person's shoes', at least as a source of a possible understanding, if not of validation. He even went as far as using his own fantasies, remembrances, or associations as sources for interpretation[5] – a most unusual position for a staunch believer in objectivity!

This is in sharp contrast with Freud's affirmed epistemology, which was the positivistic conception of the natural sciences. Humanistic-minded psychoanalysts, particularly those identified with French psychoanalysis, will most probably take exception at this statement about his conception, which would not be objectionable to most English-speaking psychoanalysts, reared in the empiricist tradition. But let us see some textual quotations in which Freud clearly expresses his scientific creed.

> *Psycho-Analysis an Empirical Science.* – Psycho-analysis is not, like philosophies, a system starting out from a few sharply defined basic concepts, seeking to grasp the whole universe with the help of these and, once it is completed, having no room for fresh discoveries or better understanding.[6] On the contrary, it keeps close to the facts in its field of study, seeks to solve the immediate problems of observation, gropes its way forward by the help of experience, is always incomplete and always ready to correct or modify its theories. There is no incongruity (any more than in the case of physics or chemistry) if its most general concepts lack clarity and if its postulates are provisional; it leaves their more precise definition to the results of future work.
>
> (Freud, 1923a, pp. 253–254)

Up to this point, Freud seems to be only saying that psychoanalysis is not a general philosophical system – a *Weltanschauung* or Conception of the World, such as that of Hegel – but an empirical science, inasmuch it is based on experience.[7] Even his comparison with physics or chemistry does not go beyond affirming that all these disciplines are not based on the unquestioned application of their general principles or axioms, but on checking their provisional hypotheses against experience. This would seem to be unobjectionable but let us see another quotation: 'Psycho-analysis is a part of the mental science of psychology. It is also described as 'depth psychology' . . . Psychology, too, is a natural science. What else can it be?' (Freud, 1940a, p. 282).

Here the author goes beyond his previous statements, since he affirms that psychology – and, consequently, psychoanalysis, which is nothing but 'depth psychology' – is not only an empirical science, but also a natural science, and that it could not be anything else. And this is not, as some would claim, an early position that was later superseded by his discoveries, but the expression of Freud's lifelong conviction that natural science is the only path to knowledge, as shown in this last quotation, which was written in 1938, one year before his death.

This implies a wholesale rejection of Dilthey's distinction between the Natural Sciences and the Sciences of the Spirit, which Freud must have known, although he never mentions it.[8] Consequently, for him there is only one kind of science, which is empirical, rational, and natural.

He further develops this idea in Lecture XXXV of his *New Introductory Lectures on Psycho-Analysis* (Freud, 1933a), called 'The question of a *Weltanschauung*'. There he reaffirms that psychoanalysis '[being] a specialist science, a branch of psychology – a depth-psychology or psychology of the unconscious – . . . is quite unfit to construct a *Weltanschauung* of its own: it must accept the scientific one' (p. 158). Then he offers a very precise definition of what he considers this scientific conception of the world to be:

> But the *Weltanschauung* of science already departs noticeably from our definition [of a *Weltanschauung* as 'an intellectual construction which solves all the problems of our existence uniformly on the basis of one overriding hypothesis, which, accordingly, leaves no question unanswered and in which everything that interests us finds its fixed place']. It is true that it too assumes the uniformity of the explanation of the universe; but it does so only as a programme, the fulfilment of which is relegated to the future. Apart from this it is marked by negative characteristics, by its limitation to what is at the moment knowable and by its sharp rejection of certain elements that are alien to it. It asserts that *there are no sources of knowledge of the universe other than the intellectual working-over of carefully scrutinized observations – in other words, what we call research – and alongside of it no knowledge derived from revelation, intuition or divination.*
>
> (pp. 158–159, my italics)

Here he passes from his previous epistemological assertions about the scientific method, to a wider gnoseological stance about the very possibility of knowledge: science (and this means for him only natural science) is the only source of reliable knowledge, so that neither religion, nor art or philosophy may be considered as such. So, he is upholding the positivist conception of knowledge, and based on the ontological principle of materialistic metaphysics, as can be readily seen in the following quotation: 'we must recollect that all our provisional ideas in psychology will presumably some day be based on an organic substructure' (Freud, 1914c, p. 78).

This is a clear manifestation of Freud's conviction: only the material is real, so that any scientific statement should eventually be referred to its physical foundation, which represents the deepest level of reality. This is nothing but an affirmation of materialistic metaphysics and of the belief that all sciences will in the end be reduced to physics, this being the reductionism he had learned from his teachers in his medical studies.

One may well think that such categorical assertions have nothing to do with the Freudian discovery, and it is effectively so: they actually reflect the unexamined, unquestioned, and never abandoned beliefs of a 'pre-Freudian Freud'. This is said by Abraham Kaplan (1964), in a humorous vein,

> There are behavioural scientists whose claim that 'ultimately' what they are asserting is derivable from the laws of physics or biology is rather like the profligate's assurance that eventually he will come into a large inheritance; but the creditors are scarcely to be blamed for insisting on 'a little something on account'. Freud was convinced that his findings would sooner or later be formulable on a strictly biological basis; it was not, however, his materialistic metaphysics that gave his work importance, but the significance of his findings in their own terms. It may well be that the psychologist can derive the whole of his discipline from neurology, biochemistry, and the rest; it is not destructive scepticism but productive pragmatism to say, 'I'd like to see him do it!'
>
> (p. 125)

In sum, I believe I have shown the presence in Freud of two radically different and contradictory ways of thinking. A large part of his work may be seen as an attempt to avoid becoming conscious of this contradiction, thus allowing these two views to coexist without entering into a conflict. This is the mental mechanism (which I would rather call a 'defensive strategy') he named 'splitting' (*Spaltung*), when describing its function in the mental functioning of perversions (Freud, 1940b).

There have also been some attempts to integrate these two apparently incompatible positions, by means of an analogical reading of Freudian metapsychology, as we will discuss in the next section.

Having it both ways

From the beginning of his enquiry of the human mind, Freud felt the need to develop a new scientific theory of mind, which would differ significantly from the one held by psychology at the time, since it would be centred on the description and explanation of what goes on beyond consciousness. That is why he invented the term 'metapsychology', meaning a theory of what is beyond the psychology of consciousness. This idea is even previous to his *The Interpretation of Dreams* (1900a), as can be seen in the following fragment of a letter to his friend Wilhelm Fliess, of March 10, 1898,

> It seems to me that the theory of wish fulfilment [as the cause of dreams] has brought *only the psychological solution and not the biological – or, rather, metapsychical – one.* (I am going to ask you seriously, by the way, *whether I*

may use the name metapsychology for my psychology that leads behind consciousness.) Biologically, dream life seems to me to derive entirely from the residues of the prehistoric period of life (between the ages of one and three) – the same period which is the source of the unconscious and alone contains the aetiology of all the psychoneuroses, the period normally characterized by an amnesia analogous to hysterical amnesia.

(Freud, 1898, my italics)

Two things are clear in this quotation: that metapsychology is a psychology that goes beyond consciousness and that it is a biological psychology, or even something indistinguishable from biology. What does this mean? That for the author these have a different epistemological status. Psychology (of consciousness) is based on *intentions*, understood as the mental representation of a final goal that is to be reached – hence, a teleological explanation, which is not considered to be scientific. Metapsychology, on the other hand, on account of its biological character – that is, scientific – studies the material causes of psychological phenomena and provides causal explanations. On the psychological level of analysis, one may well resort, like Dilthey, to an empathic understanding of intentions, but on the metapsychological level – which would be the only truly scientific one – strict causal explanations are required.[9]

As Freud intended that the discipline he created should develop as a science – and hence, a natural science, which is the only science he recognised – it was only logical for him to conceive its deepest and basic theoretical level as a biological science. This was the basis of his stubborn insistence in the fundamental importance of instinctual drives, in general, and sexuality, in particular, to fully account for human mental life. Without this firm anchoring on biology, he feared that psychoanalysis might lose its footing and abandon the field of science, falling into mysticism – what he called 'occultism'. A most interesting illustration of this attitude can be found in Carl Gustav Jung's (1961) report of a conversation he had with Freud in Vienna, in 1910,

I can still recall vividly how Freud said to me, 'My dear Jung, promise me never to abandon the sexual theory. That is the most essential thing of all. You see, we must make a dogma of it, an unshakable bulwark'. He said that to me with great emotion, the tone of a father saying, 'And promise me this one thing, my dear son: that you will go to church every Sunday'. In some astonishment I asked him, 'A bulwark – against what?' which he replied, 'Against the black tide of mud' – and here hesitated for a moment, then added – 'Of occultism'. First of all, it was the words 'bulwark' and 'dogma' that alarmed me; for a dogma, that is to say, an undisputable confession of faith is set up only when the aim is to suppress doubts once and for all. But that no longer has anything to do with scientific judgment; only with a personal power drive.

(p. 150)

Apart from Jung's interpretation of what he deemed to be an extraordinary emotional investment that Freud laid on his sexual theory, there is no doubt that the latter considered it to be the foundation of his theoretical understanding of the human being. And, although there must have been unconscious motivations for this – as there are for any human act – there also was, as I have already argued, an epistemological need, derived from his model of science and the theory of knowledge he worked with.

Freud wrote his first metapsychological text in 1895, but he only sent it to Fliess, and he showed no interest in publishing it. He even destroyed his manuscript, and we only know it from a copy kept by his friend, which was recovered by Marie Bonaparte and finally published in 1950. It is known under the name of 'A project for a scientific psychology' (Freud, 1950a). Here, the author strives to develop a theoretical model of the mind as an apparatus composed of parts, which includes a *structural* element – which he calls 'neurons' – and a *dynamic* one – which he calls 'quantity' or '$Q\eta$'. Starting from these assumptions, he describes the organisation and the relations between the structures he postulates and the displacements of quantity – that is, energy – that activate them.

In this theoretical work, Freud is extremely precise in his definitions, as can be seen in his brief 'Introduction' to this text,

> *The intention is to furnish a psychology that shall be a natural science*: that is, to represent psychical processes as quantitatively determinate states of specifiable material particles, thus making those processes perspicuous and free from contradiction. Two principal ideas are involved: (1) What distinguishes activity from rest is to be regarded as Q, subject to the general laws of motion. (2) The neurones are to be taken as the material particles.
>
> (p. 295, my italics)

It is quite obvious in this quotation that Freud clearly upholds the positivistic conception of science, conceived as the only science, and the materialistic metaphysics as its base. There appears to be no place, for him, for Dilthey's Sciences of Spirit. Mauricio Beuchot (1985) specifies this in his meticulous study of the *Project*:

> In terms of this frame, Freud strives to structure psychology as a natural science. This would allow mental processes to cease having the abstract and equivocal character they received in the *Geisteswissenschaften* [Sciences of the Spirit], in the 'humanistic' line of thought, and finally acquire a concrete and unequivocal character, as things are treated in the *Naturwissenschaften* [Sciences of Nature], in the 'scientistic' or 'positivistic' perspective. It may even be said that, *even if this distinction already existed in Freud's time, he does not assign it any importance, it does not appear in his writings, he has no need for it, since for him natural science is the whole of science and, if psychology is to have scientific status, it must be structured as a natural science.*
>
> (p. 13, my translation, my italics)

But beyond this epistemological problem lurks a metaphysical substratum. The two concepts introduced at the very beginning of the *Project* – 'neurons' and 'quantity' – correspond exactly to the Newtonian conception of the Universe, as a gigantic space populated by *pieces of inert matter*, called *objects*, which are set in motion, stopped if they are moving, accelerated, deformed, or destroyed by *forces* that act on them, and whose collection is referred to by the mass noun *energy*. In the Newtonian scheme, matter has both structure and mass, but is inert, while energy lacks both, but is dynamic in itself.

It is quite obvious, when reading the *Project*, that its author was attempting to apply to the field of mental phenomena the general laws of physics established by Newton. Consequently, the dynamic principle of his theory – the equivalent of Newton's 'energy' – was defined as 'a quantity subject to the general laws of motion', while the structural element – called 'neurons' – should necessarily be inert, unless a force acted on them. This theory-building strategy leaned both on his ontological conviction – materialistic metaphysics, which holds that only matter and energy are 'real' – and on his epistemological position – physicalist positivism, which claims that all other sciences will eventually be reduced to the solid language of physics, taken as the paradigm of all science.

Nonetheless, things are not so simple. Beuchot has shown that the *Project* can be read in two different but complementary ways. On a first level, it is a quasi-neurophysiological theory of mind, the kind of psychology that can be conceived by a neurologist, albeit a neurologist of genius. But there is also a second, deeper level, which hints at a hermeneutical and profoundly humanistic theory of mind, which announces the incipient psychoanalyst.

In the first level, Freud places himself, consciously and purposively, within the field of the positivistic science of his time. Nonetheless, his theory-building strategy already implies going beyond it. From such science, he retains its 'epistemological direction [through] the use of two main lines: the concordance or adaptation of thoughts to facts and the concordance or adaptation of thoughts to thoughts – hypothetical induction and theoretical construction' (Beuchot, 1985, p. 29, my translation).

In hermeneutical terms, the method that Freud received from his teachers consisted in respecting both the *sense* – the logical concordance between the various thoughts or hypotheses – and the *reference* – checking the hypotheses against the observable reality.[10]

But, in the actual task of theory building, Freud gives more importance to the former than to the latter. He thus appears to us as a theoretical genius who, starting from some initial premises, identifies some necessary mental functions, postulates the existence of certain structures that may sustain them, and then checks the concordance between all these hypotheses, in order to attain consistency in the theory. His weakest point is, therefore, the paucity of empirical testing of his hypotheses, albeit he tests them indirectly through their analogical application to the clinical situations he is discovering.

In spite of these novel epistemological aspects, theory on this first level is still a biological and functionalist theory of a 'mental apparatus', comparable to the various systems constructed by physiological theorisation and experimentation, rather than a true psychology. It should be noted that the *Project* has been an object of attention for some neurophysiologists and neuropsychologists, who have found striking coincidences between Freud's proposals and recent advances in neurosciences (for instance, Pribram & Gill, 1976).

While, on the first level of interpretation, Freud appears as an avant-garde neuroscientist, on the second level he seems to be a hermeneut *malgré lui*. In this reading, he appears as a most unusual investigator, who embarks on passionate flights of imagination, which go much further than anything conceived by the science, the epistemology, and the philosophy of his time. Of course, most of the time he would not have recognised himself in this description, so at odds with his ideal of scientific rationality.

Nonetheless, at some moments, he exhibits a striking intuition about the real nature of the intellectual work he was carrying out. For instance, at the time he was writing the *Project*, he writes to his friend Fliess, on May 25, 1895, the following description of his state of mind,

> A man like me cannot live without a hobbyhorse, without a consuming passion, without – in Schiller's words – a tyrant. I have found one. In its service I know no limits. It is psychology, which has always been my distant, beckoning goal, and which now, since I have come upon the problem of neuroses, has drawn so much nearer. I am tormented by two aims: *to examine what shape the theory of mental functioning takes if one introduces quantitative considerations, a sort of economics of nerve forces*; and, second, *to peel off from psychopathology a gain for normal psychology*. Actually, a satisfactory general conception of neuropsychotic disturbances is impossible if one cannot link it with clear assumptions about normal mental processes. *During the past weeks I have devoted every free minute to such work; have spent the hours of the night from eleven to two with such fantasizing, interpreting, and guessing*, and invariably stopped only when somewhere I came up against an absurdity or when I actually and seriously overworked, so that I had no interest left in my daily medical activities. It will still be a long time before you can ask me about results.
>
> (Freud, 1895, p. 129, my italics)

How distant is this passionate frenzy, this nocturnal activity, from the detached, rational, moderate, and neutral – we might say 'diurnal' – attitude that is prescribed for scientists in the positivistic tradition! And how different is this effort to 'fantasise, interpret, and guess' from his dictum that 'there are no sources of knowledge of the universe other than the intellectual working-over of carefully scrutinized observations – in other words, what we call research – and alongside of it no knowledge derived from revelation, intuition or divination'! (Freud, 1933a, p. 159).

Nevertheless, this deeply romantic vein of Freud does not break away from the scientific tradition, since he stops his creative frenzy when he 'comes up against an absurdity', be it on account of the incompatibility of his new ideas with his previous knowledge, hypotheses, or convictions, or of not checking with his own empirical observations. And he neither abandons the attempt to follow a methodical approach, since his point of departure is a foundational assumption – the quantitative approach, which should be 'subject to the general laws of motion' – and a methodological hypothesis – that the path to knowledge of normal psychology goes through the study of psychopathology and that the understanding of the latter requires to be based on the principles of the former.[11]

Nonetheless, Freud's method of 'fantasising' fully introduces us to the field of hermeneutics – and, particularly, analogical hermeneutics – since it implies complete freedom for the investigator to imagine – we might even say, to dream – multiple alternative interpretations, based on guesswork or intuition, but without relinquishing the need to compare and test, that is, the rigour of science. The result is a hybrid of science, philosophy, art, and daydreaming, which is very difficult to place in our ordinary schemas.

The conclusion is that the *Project* – and, hence, the whole metapsychology that derives from it – has two contrasting readings: a first *metonymic* level, in which it appears as a more neurophysiological than psychological theory, and a second *metaphoric* one, in which the former should be read as an analogical model of an invisible psychological organisation, whose dynamics it aims to clarify.

In sum, Freud was not fully either the rigorous, rational, and positive scientist he wished to believe he was, nor the unleashed poet or mystic he feared to be. On the contrary, he was a human being who presented, like all of us, these two different facets, in that state of unstable equilibrium we call 'life', and this is what he sought to reflect in the theory and practice he invented. Consequently, psychoanalysis also turned out to be an indefinable and non-classifiable product of the human spirit, a hybrid entity that escapes from all the ordinary schemas we are accustomed to use in thinking. And this is what we have set out to explore.

Postscript (2020)

The original Spanish version of this chapter was written and published in 2008 (Tubert-Oklander, 2008a). Recently, when I revised and translated this text, I had some doubts about the English version of the title of Section 3. In Spanish, it was named as '*Navegando entre dos aguas*' – literally, 'navigating between two waters' – an idiom that means trying to be in two places at the same time, usually emphasising non-commitment or inability to choose. But how should I translate it into English? The options were: 'having a foot in two camps', 'serving two masters', 'falling between two stools', and 'having it both ways'. I discarded the first three, because they emphasise the inability or unwillingness to commit or choose, or the impossibility of standing in the middle between two incompatible positions. The fourth one was more interesting, on account of its ambiguous connotation. It could be used to either emphasise the contradiction and the impossibility of a third option (as in the expression 'you can't have it both ways') or suggest the possibility of transcending the apparent opposition. So, I kept it.

But this made me reflect on what was my own position on the matter, both at the time of writing the original text and now that I was editing and translating it. The chapter begins, from its very title, by posing a sharp contrast between two Freuds: the positive natural scientist and the romantic, and perhaps mystic, hermeneut. This suggests that we must choose between them, that there is no middle third. But, towards the end of the chapter (precisely in the third section), there is the proposal that *we do not have to choose*, that psychoanalysis is a hybrid and ambiguous being, a product of the mestization between scientific and humanistic thinking, rationalism and romanticism, causal explanations and hermeneutic interpretation. This is what Beuchot (1997) calls an 'analogic middle' or what Gregory Bateson (1979) names 'an appropriate synchrony or harmony between rigor and imagination' (p. 236).

Of course, my doubts about translation are revealing a certain ambivalence in me about the matter. My rigorous, rational part (what Freud, 1900a, called the 'secondary process') decries the contradictions in Freud and in psychoanalytic theory, while my romantic imaginative side (the 'primary process') says, 'Why not?'[12] And I am in the task of negotiating this paradox, just like everyone else, and this is really the subject of this book.

I think I was helped in solving my translation conundrum by the fact that my friend Peter L. Rudnytsky (2019) used the expression 'having it both ways' as the name of a section of the Introduction to his new book *Formulated Experiences: Hidden Realities and Emergent Meanings from Shakespeare to Fromm*.[13] His whole book is a plea for an analogic middle (though he does not call it that way), in which he argues that 'it can be "both/and" rather than "either/or" when it comes to hidden realities and emergent meanings' (p. 23).

Of course, the opposition between 'either/or' and 'both/and' thinking has been stressed in recent years by relational psychoanalysts (Aron, 1996). It is also the theme of our next chapter.

Notes

1 See Appendix I for a brief presentation of Analogical Hermeneutics.
2 One major example of this is Jacques Lacan (1966), one great innovative psychoanalytic thinker who always claimed that he was only expounding the 'true Freud'. On the other hand, W. Ronald D. Fairbairn (1952) minced no words in clarifying that he thought that some of Freud's basic concepts were simply wrong and that he was suggesting an alternative view (Clarke & Scharff, 2014; Tubert-Oklander, 2018). This brought him quite a few criticisms.
3 A paradigm is a mostly tacit agreement among the members of a community of scientists about what exists and what does not, what sort of problems can (or should) be formulated, how they should be tackled, what to observe and how, in what language should their findings be described, evaluated, and explained, what sort of theories can be constructed in order to make sense of all this, and how to distinguish the good theories from the bad or not-so-good ones (Kuhn, 1962). The process of becoming a

member of such a community demands that the candidate learn, incorporate, and identify with this normative set of assumptions, until it becomes a second nature for him or her. Those who fail in this task are summarily excluded from the community. This is particularly so in the case of psychoanalytic organisations.

4 In Beuchot's (1997) presentation of his Analogical Hermeneutics, he shows that there have always been three different forms of hermeneutics, depending on their attitude towards the relation between text and interpretation. These are *univocality*, *equivocality*, and *analogism*. *Univocality* assumes that, for any given text, there is one and only one true interpretation, so that all others are false. This is the positivistic view. *Equivocality* claims, on the contrary, that for every text there are innumerable possible interpretations, which all have a similar value, so that there is no way for choosing one of them over the others, apart from personal taste and practical convenience. This is the basis of relativism. Finally, *analogism* – a term derived from 'Analogy', which in Greek means 'proportion' or 'fair measure' – poses that there may be various possible interpretations for any given text, but not infinite, and that not all of them are equivalent, since some of them are better, others are not so good, many are poor, and some are just bad. Nonetheless, there may be a few alternative valid interpretations for that text, each focusing on a different aspect, as seen from a disparate perspective. (More about this may be found in my book *The One and the Many: Relational Psychoanalysis and Group Analysis* (Tubert-Oklander, 2014) and in Appendix I of this book.)

5 This he did, for instance, in his interpretation of the well-known 'Sappho dream', which he called 'A lovely dream' (Freud, 1900a, pp. 285–289). There he based his interpretation of a patient's dream on his own spontaneous recollection of an episode in Alphonse Daudet's novel *Sappho*. He says about this that he 'did not expect to find [his] guess at an interpretation justified' (p. 286). Nonetheless, he made it and, to his astonishment, the patient replied that the interpretation 'fitted in very well with a piece he had seen at the theatre the evening before', and it proved to be consistent with and clarifying for his present conflict, as seen in the subsequent analysis of the dream.

6 This is the basis of his utter rejection of *Weltanschauungen* (Conceptions of the World) and of his stern dictum that psychoanalysis 'as a specialist science, a branch of psychology – a depth psychology or psychology of the unconscious – . . . is quite unfit to construct a *Weltanschauung* of its own: it must accept the scientific one' (p. 158).

7 The concept of the *Weltanschauung* has been studied extensively, from the psychoanalytic point of view, by Reyna Hernández-Tubert (Hernández Hernández, 2010; Hernández de Tubert, 2000); it is further discussed in Chapter 5 and in Appendix II.

8 The only mention of Dilthey in one of Freud's publications is in *The Sigmund Freud-Ludwig Binswanger Correspondence 1908–1938* (Fichtner, 2003), in which Ludwig Binswanger (1925) argues, in his letter to Freud of February 15, 1925, that 'psychoanalytic interpretation and understanding are, in principle and historically, highly significant extensions and reinforcements of the so-called hermeneutic interpretation and exegesis as practised and investigated at length, especially by Schleiermacher and Dilthey' (p. 176). But Freud did not consider the hermeneutic aspect of interpretation in his reply.

9 Charles Rycroft (1966) offers another possible interpretation of the biological nature of psychoanalysis, when he says that

> The statement that psychoanalysis is a theory of meaning is incomplete and misleading unless one qualifies it by saying that it is a biological theory of meaning. By this I mean that psychoanalysis interprets human behaviour in terms of the self that experiences it and not in terms of entities external to it, such as other-worldly deities or political parties and leaders, and that it regards the self as a psychobiological entity which is always striving for self-realization and self-fulfilment. In

other words, it regards mankind as sharing with the animal and plant world the intrinsic drive to create and recreate its own nature.

(p. 20)

Consequently, it is a theory that looks for the meaning of symbols in the vital experience of bodily existence, but still a semantic theory of meaning, and not a natural science (see Chapter 14).

10 In 1892, Gottlob Frege posed that *meaning* (and, hence, interpretation) resulted of two factors: *reference* and *sense*. The reference of any given term or statement is the non-semiotic or non-textual reality it refers to. Its *sense*, on the other hand, is determined by the syntactic structure of the whole text or expression and the nature, properties, and tradition of the symbolic system or language in which it is formulated. Hence, every experience, perception, thought, or statement about reality is necessarily an interpretation, but not an arbitrary one. Consequently, not all interpretations are equivalent: some of them are better, others not-so-good, poor, or even bad, and this depends on the reference (denotation) and the richness and depth of their sense (connotation). More about this in Appendix I on Analogical Hermeneutics.

11 This very same idea is repeated and expanded thirty-eight years later in 'Lecture XXXI – Dissection of the psychical personality', of his *New Introductory Lectures on Psycho-Analysis* (Freud, 1933a, pp. 57–80), in which he writes,

> we are familiar with the notion that pathology, by making things larger and coarser, can draw our attention to normal conditions which would otherwise have escaped us. Where it points to a breach or a rent, there may normally be an articulation present. If we throw a crystal to the floor, it breaks; but not into haphazard pieces. It comes apart along its lines of cleavage into fragments whose boundaries, though they were invisible, were predetermined by the crystal's structure. Mental patients are split and broken structures of this same kind.

(pp. 58–59)

12 Of course, Freud postulated an inherent superiority of the secondary process over the primary process, this being a consequence of his rationalistic position. My own view, more akin to Ignacio Matte-Blanco's (1988) conception of a 'bi-logic', is that verbal and iconic thinking (secondary and primary processes) are complementary and mutually regulating, and that multi-dimensional thought requires both. This is also Beuchot's (1997) conception of analogy, which we developed in the book we wrote together (Tubert-Oklander & Beuchot Puente, 2008; see also Appendix I).

13 I say that I think I was helped by Rudnytsky's use of this idiom because I was not aware, at the time of choosing the translation, that I had recently read it in a new book I had just finished reading. This sort of cryptomnesia is frequent in writers, and it is also a testimony of the social nature of thinking and writing.

Chapter 2

Inclusion and exclusion in psychoanalysis (2013)

From splitting to integration in our theory and practice

Reyna Hernández-Tubert

*This chapter is a revised version of a paper I read at the conference of the International Association for Relational Psychoanalysis and Psychotherapy, held in Santiago, Chile, in November 2013 (Hernández-Tubert, 2015). It was part of a panel called 'Body, self, and society: From the isolated individual to collective life, by means of relationship', which was chaired by Charles Levin (2015a, 2015b) and included the participations of Haim Weinberg (2015), Juan Tubert-Oklander (2015) [Chapter 14]), and myself, all of which were published in 2015 in the **Canadian Journal of Psychoanalysis**. These ideas I had put forward in a previous paper in Spanish, called 'The principle of exclusion in the development of the psychoanalytic movement', read in July 2000 at the 7th International Meeting of the International Association for the History of Psychoanalysis, held in Versailles, France (Hernández de Tubert, 2000).*

However, the basic underlying assumption – that our understanding of the psychoanalytic theories, techniques, and practice, and indeed of any other discipline, depends on a series of previous assumptions that constitute our Conception of the World – had already been the focus of my attention since 1992. In my very first psychoanalytic paper, called 'The myth of mestization' (Hernández Hernández, 1994), read during the 2nd International Congress on Myths, held in Oaxaca, Mexico, in 1992, I recounted that, when the Spanish arrived to Tenochtitlan, in present-day Mexico, the Aztecs were quite willing to include this new God of the Cross in their pantheon, since it was a common practice for them to do so with the gods of all the peoples that were incorporated to their Confederation. Hence, they were astounded and horrified when they discovered that these foreign newcomers intended that this new god should replace all others (Soustelle, 1955). This was a fatal misunderstanding between a culture of inclusion and a culture of exclusion.

*When I met Juan Tubert-Oklander in 1992, the very same year in which I had read this paper, we started discussing and developing together these ideas, which were the basis for my later studies on the **Weltanschauung** (Hernández Hernández, 2010; Hernández de Tubert, 2009a), as well as for the present book.*

Psychoanalysis has been split, throughout its history, in its theory, practice, and membership, in oppositional conceptual and ideological pairs, such as

DOI: 10.4324/9780429055287-4

intrapsychic-interpersonal, instinctual drives-relationships, individual-society, or constitution-environment. I have referred in the past to this *either/or* thinking as the 'principle of exclusion', as opposed to the 'principle of inclusion', framed in terms of *both/and* (Hernández de Tubert, 2000; Hernández Hernández, 2010).[1]

I believe the principle of exclusion to be a defence, aimed at avoiding the intense anxiety generated by the hyper-complex and ambiguous processes of reality that cannot be comprehended by conscious thought, nor submitted to or controlled by formal rationality. This occurs simultaneously at the individual, interpersonal, and collective levels.

At the societal level, it produces the emergence of warring groups, parties, religions, or schools (Pines, 1998). At the beginning, this natural tendency of psychoanalysis to expansion and differentiation was curbed through dogmatism and a strict adherence and loyalty towards the Founding Father and idealised leader, and by expelling those who failed to comply. This fostered the irrational belief in the existence of a single theoretical system, which would account for all phenomena, problems, and doubts of our profession, thus neutralising our feelings of uncertainty, doubt, confusion, impotence, and ignorance. Such system was supposed to exist in the mind of the Grand Master and, especially after his death, in his writings, turned into a foundational text. This is the phenomenon that Jacques Lacan (1973) named *le sujet supposé savoir* (the 'supposed subject of knowledge' or the 'subject which is supposed to know').

This attempt to build a monolithic unity for the psychoanalytic movement, by taming the subversive potential of psychoanalysis and harnessing it to the yoke of logical thinking and standardised technique, was bound to fail, since Mind and the major instrument for its enquiry – psychoanalysis – are just not amenable to such gelding. Freud himself was contradictory about this. On the one hand, he intended to develop psychoanalysis as a strictly scientific-technological enterprise, and on the other, he acknowledged the never-ending and polymorphic character of the psychoanalytic enquiry (Tubert-Oklander, 2008a [Chapter 1]).

It is worthwhile to observe that, although the psychoanalytic institution was created in order to guarantee such unity by means of keeping the theoretical, technical, and training standards, this has not prevented psychoanalysis from flourishing into a most fruitful diversity.

As Greenberg and Mitchell (1983) have pointed out, the major dichotomy is that of two polar conceptions of the human being. One of them, stemming from the work of Plato and continuing with the English Empiricists that were so dear to Freud, depicts him as a primarily and perennially isolated being, which is only forced to relate to others and participate in groups by the sheer pressure of his bodily demands – the instinctual drives – and by the merciless need of survival. People are essentially antisocial, self-centred, and egotistical, and all morality is imposed from outside, as an unwanted and deeply resented restraint. Hence, all experience and behaviour are determined solely by the inner organisation and functioning of the individual, particularly the drives, and the coercive pressure of dire need and society (Freud, 1927c, 1930a; Hernández de Tubert, 2008 [Chapter 5]).

The other – introduced by Aristotle and later developed by Rousseau, Hegel, and Marx – conceives human beings as primarily social and in need to relate with others. Empathy, sympathy, and compassion are primary, and are only lost and replaced by the selfish, voracious, and cannibalistic urges that Freud called 'drives', as a result of traumatic experiences, both with others and with an unfair society (Hernández de Tubert, 1997, 2006b). Social groups, trends, rules, and traditions are real and have a momentous influence on individuals and relationships. The individual is shaped by her social, cultural, political, and family environment.

But we need not choose one of them, since these two approaches exist, side by side. Some situations are better thought in Freudian terms, and others in relational and social terms. A balanced synthesis would preserve the various points of view and maintain a dialectical tension between them, integrating them, but without losing their specificity or blurring their differences. This is what Mauricio Beuchot (1997) calls 'analogy'.[2]

Nonetheless, this only refers to the theoretical level, since every theory is necessarily partial, thus allowing the integration of contrasting but complementary approaches. There is, however, a deeper level, which includes the whole set of assumptions, beliefs, and values characteristic of each person, group, or society. This is what we call the *Conception of the World* (*Weltanschauung*) and the *Conception of Life* (*Lebensanschauung*); these are not negotiable, since they represent the essence of our position vis-à-vis ourselves, existence, the others, and the world (Hernández de Tubert, 2004a, 2009a).[3] Such differences between us can only be identified, made explicit, acknowledged, and accepted, but never eliminated or ignored. This generates a dialectic tension in our community, which cannot be solved, but with which we can live, as long as we acknowledge and accept it.

This is not merely a question of theoretical interest, but has a major influence on our therapeutic practice and on the experience we provide to our patients. The analyst's neutrality means that he or she makes a systematic effort in order not to take sides in the patient's conflicts (Hernández Hernández, 1994 [1999–2000]; Tubert-Oklander, 2013a). Thus, for instance, when a patient is torn between his love for his wife and the dissatisfaction he experiences in his marriage, we avoid identifying with any of these two feelings and rejecting or disqualifying the other, since both are a part of the patient's emotional life, and they cannot be omitted or ignored, even though the patient often tries to do so, in order to prevent the emergence of the suffering generated by the conflict. On the contrary, we strive to help him to get back in touch with and acknowledge as his own all these feelings, and then seek a way of negotiating the conflict that may help him to find a solution for it.

But this does not imply that the psychoanalytic treatment may ever be conducted in an axiological vacuum. Values are an essential part of human existence and should be taken into account in the analysis, just as we do with perceptions, thoughts, feelings, and actions, since all of them are part and parcel of reality, understood as the sum of all that exists beyond and independently from our wishes (Hernández Hernández, 2010; Tubert-Oklander & Hernández de Tubert, 2004; Tubert-Oklander, 2016 [Chapter 7]).

On the one hand, there are certain ethical values that are necessarily an unavoidable aspect of every analysis. Thus, for example, all situations of abuse, cruelty, and maltreatment should be acknowledged and named as such. In this, we cannot hide behind the concept of 'neutrality', since this is tantamount to a denial of our own commitment and responsibility towards our patient and society, and to endorse abuse. This was clearly stated by Archbishop Desmond Tutu, one of our great contemporary ethical thinkers:

> If you are neutral in situations of injustice, you have chosen the side of the oppressor. If an elephant has its foot on the tail of a mouse and you say that you are neutral, the mouse will not appreciate your neutrality.
>
> (Tutu, Quoted by Younge, 2009)

This is just as valid in the case of those situations in which the patient abuses or is abused by others, and especially in those in which the patient abuses the analyst or the analyst abuses the patient (Hernández de Tubert, 2004b). All these should become a subject for the psychoanalytic enquiry and dialogue.

This is where values come to play, both the patient's values and the analyst's, in relation to their shared task. It is not only the content of the analyst's thoughts and interpretations that matter; the main issue is whether the analysis develops in a climate of an open or a closed mind. If the analyst poses each and every interpretation as a revealed and unquestionable truth, the result is that the patient incorporates the conviction that thinking is always something for others to do, and that truth is something to be revealed, not sought for, and certainly never questioned.

But if the analyst engages in an open dialogue with the patient, in which she communicates (interprets) whatever she has come to understand of what is being said and happens in the session, and then listens carefully and with an open mind and heart to what the patient has to say on the matter, the latter will incorporate a new conception of relations, thinking, and truth. Nonetheless, one should not expect every patient to feel comfortable with such a proposal, or to immediately accept it. Although some patients feel liberated and enthusiastic when they discover that the analyst does not claim to have the monopoly of knowledge, there are others for whom this generates intense unbearable feelings of uncertainty and anxiety, and this requires a protracted analytic work, based on interpretation and an empathic holding relationship, until they are able to dare not to know beforehand what is going to happen, and even enjoy the process of discovering it.

Besides, we should take into account that many patients have internalised a bond with an omnipotent and omniscient authority figure (what is usually called an authoritarian and rigid Superego), which equally forbids uncertainty, having one's own thoughts, the spontaneous gesture, and a happy and creative life. If the analysis is carried out in a climate of openness, understanding of the individual's unique experience, respect for differences, and appreciation of the creative thinking that is shared through dialogue, this makes it possible to re-structure and re-signify the internalised bonds. This represents a healing of a Superego that fell sick as a consequence of repetitive traumatic experiences, lived during the constitutive years of the personality, as well as in later life.

But this opposition between the various ways of conceiving knowledge, the treatment, and relations in general is also to be found in the collective dimension of our institutions and the psychoanalytic community as a whole. Throughout the history of psychoanalysis, we find three different basic positions (Beuchot, 1997; Hernández Hernández, 2010; Tubert-Oklander, 2013b, 2014; Tubert-Oklander & Beuchot Puente, 2008).[4] The first is the *univocal* view that characterises what has been called 'orthodox psychoanalysis', which emphasises the universality of psychoanalytic knowledge and theories, as well as their being strictly true. Inasmuch as this point of view considers that there is one, and only one, true interpretation for any event that takes place in an analysis, it tends to favour a dogmatic and authoritarian attitude, which disqualifies as 'anti-analytic' any other way of seeing things.

The second is the *equivocal* view, held by some Post-Modern versions of psychoanalysis, which affirms the never-ending multiplicity of alternative interpretations and that it is only possible to choose one among them on the basis of personal taste or practical convenience. The result is an extreme relativism that discards the very possibility of a search for truth. Surprisingly enough, those who uphold this position are simultaneously univocal, dogmatic, and authoritarian in imposing this view and absolutely rejecting any other. Hence, they end up by being as excluding as the previous one.

Finally, we have an *analogical* conception that, although denying the possibility of attaining any absolute and definitive truth, considers that it is possible to achieve approximations to truth, from diverse interpretative perspectives, which may nonetheless be critically evaluated, by means of testing them with the only unquestionable aspect of psychoanalysis, which is the *analytic experience* shared by the analyst and the analysand, and worked conjointly through the analytic dialogue (Ferenczi & Rank, 1924). This inclusive form of conceiving our practice, in terms of 'both/and', corresponds to the relational perspective of psychoanalysis (Hernández Hernández, 2010; Tubert-Oklander, 2013b, 2014). This may help to heal the split between the opposing pairs that have torn asunder our profession.

Nonetheless, the defenders of classical psychoanalysis tend to impose – on patients, students, and colleagues alike – their view, which they deem to be the sole truth. On the other hand, those of us who take a relational perspective usually show a greater respect for differences and allow ourselves to learn from patients, students, and colleagues. This is why we cannot always conciliate but must rather actively defend this set of positive values that rule over our living experience, as well as on our professional thought and action.

Notes

1 Authors who identify with relational psychoanalysis usually refer to 'either/or' and 'both/and' modes of thinking (Aron, 1996). I prefer to use the terms 'principle of exclusion' and 'principle of inclusion', which I introduced in my paper 'The principle of

exclusion in the development of the psychoanalytic movement' (Hernández de Tubert, 2000), because it emphasised my criticism of the traditional 'principle of the excluded middle'.

2 See Appendix I.
3 The psychoanalytic concept of the *Weltanschaung*, which is treated in several chapters of the book, is summarised in Appendix II.
4 This paragraph and the following two are a direct application of Mauricio Beuchot's Analogical Hermeneutics, which is another theme that runs through this book. It is summarised in Appendix I.

Chapter 3

Donald Winnicott

A revolutionary *malgré lui* (2017)

Juan Tubert-Oklander

This chapter is a revised version of a paper I read at the 26th Latin-American Meeting on Winnicott's Thought that took place in Mexico City in November 2017 (Tubert-Oklander, 2017d). We devised a Panel for that conference, called 'The revolutionary impact of Winnicott on contemporary psychoanalysis'. The other members of the panel were Reyna Hernández-Tubert (2017b, [Chapter 4]), who spoke on Winnicott's ideas on the fundamental role of aggression and hate in the psychoanalytic treatment, and Marcela Sánchez-Darvasi (2017), a Chilean-Mexican colleague, who addressed the effect of an analysis in enabling the patient's capacity for creative reading, on the basis of Winnicott's conception of creativity. I introduced the panel with this paper, in which I suggested that Winnicott's contributions were far more revolutionary than what he was willing to admit, and that this was based on his need to preserve a positive transference with Freud.

The chairperson who conducted the meeting was visibly appalled at this picture of a Winnicott that differed so much from the Freudian-Kleinian tradition, particularly in Reyna's paper and mine, but she nonetheless managed to fulfil her role satisfactorily. The audience was clearly interested, and this generated a stimulating discussion.

Donald Woods Winnicott (1958c, 1965, 1971b) did not consider himself a revolutionary. He adhered in principle to the generally accepted Freudian theory, albeit he always affirmed his right to formulate his own ideas in his own language.[1] He thus managed to develop an utterly novel clinical and theoretical thought, without realising its inherent incompatibility with some of the fundamental concepts of Freudian theory. I think that he attained this improbable feat by means of splitting, which allowed him to keep two parallel mutually incompatible lines of thought, without ever letting them enter contact, much as in Freud's (1940b) concept of *Spaltung*. I believe that his unconscious motivation for this was his need to preserve his positive transference bond with Freud as a benign paternal figure.

How did this paradoxical admixture of innovation and traditionalism come about? Winnicott had a compelling need to think and speak with his own words,

DOI: 10.4324/9780429055287-5

and not with those of any other. He considered this to be a personal symptom and acknowledged how irritating it could be for those colleagues who wished to count with a common language in order to understand each other and found it in Freud's metapsychology, which Laplanche and Pontalis (1967) called 'the language of psychoanalysis'. Nonetheless, he demanded that everyone's right to follow his or her own path in exploring the universe of enquiry opened by the founder of our discipline be respected, since the vitality and continuity of the development of psychoanalysis was fully dependent on this (Rodman, 1987).

But side by side with this ideological and existential position also lay his complex and ambivalent transference bond with Freud. On the one hand, there was his love and gratitude towards this great intellectual parent and his acknowledgement that all his work and thought derived from Freud's legacy and belonged to the horizons revealed by him. On the other, his rebelliousness led him to reject reading metapsychology. He identified with Freud in the practice of psychoanalysis, but he strongly felt that he should always formulate his reflections and conclusions, derived from his clinical experience, in his own language, and not in that of the Master.[2]

However, his feeling vis-à-vis this attitude was also ambivalent. It was obvious that he prided himself on this search for his personal originality, but he also felt guilty about his rejection of the study and his limited mastery of the orthodox theory and language. This led him more than once to apologise in his letters. For instance, he wrote to Clifford Scott, during his first period as President of the British Psychoanalytical Society, in 1956, 'I feel odd when in the president's chair because I don't know *my Freud* in the way a president should do; yet I do find I have Freud in my bones' (Winnicott, 1956, quoted in Kahr, 1996, p. 70).

The use of the expression 'my Freud', with its elementary school connotations, clearly refers to a master-pupil relationship, while the idea of 'Freud in my bones' is a colourful metaphor for an identification. This seems to be an acid comment of the schoolboy-to-teacher nature of the psychoanalytic community's relation with Freud (Tubert-Oklander, 2009–2014), since his metapsychology has been taken as an established knowledge as unquestionable as the 'Three Rs'.

It is worth noting that his rejection of reading is not restricted to his rebelliousness towards a father figure, but also extended to the contributions of an intellectual sibling who might have reached before him similar conclusions to those he was elaborating. On this matter, F. Robert Rodman (personal communication to Dodi Goldman, 1993) tells that 'Winnicott was reluctant to read the works of Ferenczi, lest he discover that he had actually stolen ideas from him' (p. 5). However, he did acknowledge having perused his writings, when he wrote, 'I never know what I've got out of glancing at Ferenczi, for instance, or glancing at a footnote to Freud' (Winnicott, 1967, p. 579).

But his rejection of reading covered an even wider field. Masud Khan (1975) recounts an occasion in which he was trying to convince Winnicott to read Lionel Trilling's *Freud and the Crisis of Our Culture*, and his friend replied with a dramatic gesture:

He hid his face in his hands, paused, convulsed himself into visibility and said: 'It is no use, Masud, asking me to read anything! If it bores me I shall fall asleep in the middle of the first page, and if it interests me, I will start re-writing it by the end of that page. Of course he was pulling his own leg, and both of mine, and he had a puckish knack for that indeed. But he was also telling the truth.

(p. xvi)

Obviously, it is not a question of Winnicott not reading at all, but rather that he only read something if and when it interested him, and never because he must. There is no doubt that his thinking emerged from an inner and outer dialogue with others, particularly those colleagues with whom he had a personal relationship, as can be seen in his published letters (Rodman, 1987). Nonetheless, his writings include very few references and there is no effort to compare and contrast the personal ideas he is putting forward with those of other authors, nor to organise and systematise them into a formal theory. When one reads his writings, there is a feeling of having a chat with a good friend and colleague, who lets his thoughts flow freely and plays with them, in the fascination, which he shares with us, of contemplating the emergence and interaction of ideas, which have a life of their own.

This particular style of thought and writing, akin to a table talk, results easy, friendly, and fascinating for some readers, and confusing, irritating, and even incomprehensible for others. This depends, of course, on the organisation of the reader's personality and cognitive processes, and his capacity for play. It is possible that those psychoanalysts and psychotherapists who work with children might tend to feel at home with a discourse such as Winnicott's, while those who work only with adults, particularly if they do it in terms of a medical conception, would feel lost and miss the order and clarity, and the theoretical and technical precision. It is likely that Freud, whose thinking tended to the meticulosity and order of an obsessive structure, would not have felt comfortable in reading it.

This characteristic of Winnicott's thought and writing may be considered a personality trait of his that, when facing the ever-present dialectic of imagination and rigour, led him to opt regularly for the former. This way of being allowed him to develop an exceptional clinical sensitivity, a freely creative therapeutic practice, and an excellent and intimate contact with and understanding of children of all ages, including the inner child who dwells in the deep of every adult. But it also obstructed the transmission, understanding, and acceptance of his ideas and suggestions in professional and academic circles.

To this, I would like to add the already mentioned hypothesis that there was also at play an emotional and relational factor that led him to avoid any confrontation with Freud as an idealised paternal figure. This he managed to attain by means of not extracting the theoretical consequences of the unorthodox ideas he was putting forward.[3]

For instance, in his revolutionary article on 'The capacity to be alone' (Winnicott, 1958a), he introduces the concept of 'ego-relatedness' to refer to a non-instinctual bond between the baby and its mother, or between the patient and the analyst, which he deems to be most significant,

> It will be seen that I attach a great importance to this relationship, as I consider that it is the stuff out of which friendship is made. It may turn out to be the *matrix of transference*
>
> (p. 33).

Then, he specifies more clearly the essential difference between this relational experience and an instinctual one,

> In my opinion, if we compare the happy play of a child or the experience of an adult at a concert with a sexual experience, the difference is so great that we should do no harm in allowing a different term for the description of the two experiences. Whatever the unconscious symbolism, the quantity of actual physical excitement is minimal in the one type of experience and maximal in the other
>
> (p. 35)

He is obviously putting forward a novel concept of unconscious motivation, quite at odds with the theory of instinctual drives, but all along this paper he is striving to affirm both the essential difference between these two types of motivation and the coexistence between them. His stand in this is conciliatory a priori, and he thus arrives at the surprising conclusion that 'We may pay tribute to the importance of ego-relatedness *per se* without giving up the ideas that underlie the concept of sublimation' (p. 35). But the concept of sublimation implies that all the apparently non-instinctual activities, such as children's play and the concert in his example, are nothing but an expression of aim-inhibited instinctual wishes – that is, a discharge of de-sexualised and de-aggressivised instinctual wishes. In other words, he is erasing with the elbow what he has just written with his hand.

But he had already introduced, a few years before, in his paper called 'Metapsychological and clinical aspects of regression within the psycho-analytical set-up' (Winnicott, 1954), the distinction between *wishes* and *needs*, in the following terms:

> It is proper to speak of the patient's *wishes*, the wish (for instance) to be quiet. With the regressed patient the word wish is incorrect; instead we use the word *need*. If a regressed patient *needs* quiet, then without it nothing can be done at all. If the need is not met the result is not anger, only a reproduction of the environmental failure situation which stopped the process of self growth. The individual's capacity to 'wish' had become interfered with, and we witness the reappearance of the original sense of futility.
>
> (p. 288)

It can readily be seen that our author was exploring, already in 1954, the concept of a motivational system that differed from the discharge of organic tension postulated by drive theory (Freud, 1915c), although he restricted its application to the case of primitive mental states, characteristic of early infancy and regression during the treatment of severe personality disorders. This is a frequent manoeuvre in the writings of those psychoanalytic authors that are striving to soften their new ideas so that they do not conflict with Freudian theory (Mitchell, 1984). Their rationale is more or less as follows: Freud was right, but his theory of instinctual drives and the conflicts derived from them is valid only after the establishment of the Oedipal organisation of the personality and in the treatment of neurotic patients, but when dealing with more primitive organisations, such as those of infancy and the treatment of non-neurotic patients, suffering from a developmental arrest, one should apply a relational theory. It thus covers up the conflict with Freudian theory and upholds the illusion that one can 'eat the cake and have it'.[4]

In 1960, Winnicott comes back to the subject in 'Ego distortion in terms of true and false self'. There, he postulates a difference between 'id-needs' and 'ego-needs'. *Id-needs* are the instinctual wishes, either sexual or aggressive, of drive theory. They are organic tensions aiming at a discharge, which brings about pleasure; this is what we call 'gratification'. When this does not happen, there is an experience of displeasure, called 'frustration', which implies irritation and anger. *Ego-needs*, on the other hand, require a personal, loving, understanding, and empathic response from another human being. Hence, they are relational needs. Ego-needs are neither gratified, nor frustrated, since they have nothing to do with the pleasure-displeasure dyad, but they rather find a human response or not. If there is an adequate response, what the subject experiences is not pleasure, but a feeling of harmony and wellbeing, that everything is just as it should. If there is no response at all, or if it is discordant, the experience is not that of frustration, but a feeling of futility, hopelessness, and meaninglessness. We have seen that Winnicott had suggested to reserve the term 'wishes' for what he is now calling id-needs, and 'needs' for the ego-needs. I feel that perhaps a more adequate term for the latter would be 'yearnings' or 'longings'.

A baby's ego-needs are the need to be loved, cuddled, seen, touched, spoken to, understood, acknowledged, cared for, and valued – that is, what Heinz Kohut (1984) would call 'narcissistic needs', understanding narcissism as a healthy development of the self. When such needs are not responded to, even though his or her physical necessities had been attended, the baby is forced to prematurely take charge of them. The result is the development of a false self (Winnicott, 1960b), a false personality, built on an exploitation of his innate ego resources, in order to construct a pseudo adult that might care for her when the primary caretakers fail.

From this point of view, instinctual wishes appear as a disturbance, which may only be integrated into the core of the personality and strengthen it if a true self has been previously established, on the basis of good-enough maternal care. The primary need is that of having an adequate relation with another human being. If this is not met, the child does not develop a personal capacity for wishing, and experiences instead a pressure of ego-alien impersonal drives, which are felt to be 'as much external as a clap of thunder or a hit' (Winnicott, 1960b, p. 141), just as in Freud's (1915c) description. But here they are conceived as a secondary phenomenon, the result of a thwarted development.[5]

In this series of articles, in which Winnicott picks up, further develops, and states explicitly a set of theoretical preoccupations he has had ever since the beginning of his career, twenty years before, we see him formulating the starting point of a clearly relational theory of human mental life and experience. But, in his usual way, he does it while attempting to preserve the previous theory. Consequently, he closes his article with the astonishing conclusion that the new concept that he had just introduced of a False Self, derived from the experience of not-good-enough mothering, hiding the True Self, 'is able to have an important effect on psychoanalytic work [but,] as far as I can see, *it involves no important change in basic theory*' (Winnicott, 1960b, p. 162, my italics).

In sum, what Winnicott was actually doing was to introduce a major revision of the psychoanalytical theory of motivation, which would have had to replace drive theory, but was unwilling or unable to acknowledge this necessary consequence of his novel ideas. Hence, he would rather circumvent the otherwise unavoidable conclusion that an acceptance of his revolutionary theoretical propositions would require discarding, or at least substantially reframing, the theory of instinctual drives.

One of his contemporaries whose theoretical approach was very similar to Winnicott's, but who had no qualms about openly expressing his utter disagreement with this aspect of Freudian theory, was Ronald Fairbairn (1952). He clearly stated that the human being's main motivation for his experience, thought, feeling, and behaviour is the search of an object – that is, of a relation – and not that of pleasure. This he stated in the following terms:

> [L]ibido is primarily object-seeking (rather than pleasure-seeking, as in the classic theory), and that it is to disturbances in the object-relationships of the developing ego that we must look for the ultimate origin of all psychopathological conditions.
>
> (p. 82)

Although most psychoanalysts acknowledged at that time the high theoretical level of Fairbairn's ideas, there also were stern criticisms of them, on account of the enormity of his revision of the theory, which amounted to an explicit introduction of a new paradigm. Winnicott, in particular, co-authored with Masud Khan a review of Fairbairn's (1952) book, *Psychoanalytic Studies of the Personality*, in which, in spite of posing an overall highly positive evaluation of it, they severely called into question the fact that the author openly rejected and proposed a theoretical alternative to some of the basic assumptions of Freud's theory. The language of their criticism betrays a certain irritation, shown, for instance, when they write that Fairbairn's good work is tarnished by his claim that his own theory substitute Freud's, and add, in a rather scandalised tone, 'If Fairbairn is right, then we teach Fairbairn and not Freud to our students' (Winnicott & Khan, 1953, p. 329).

This argument is, of course, a fallacy, which can only be understood as an expression of the dogmatic and authoritarian way in which psychoanalysis was taught at the time (and still is, in many quarters). If there are two contrasting and possibly incompatible views of a fundamental theoretical problem, the only rational option for dealing with this is to study them both and to discuss them extensively, but this is obstructed when there is a cult of personality of the founder of a school (Tubert-Oklander, 2009–2014). It must be said, however, that both of them later recanted from what they then wrote and confessed that they had not really understood Fairbairn's ideas at the time (Clarke, 2014, p. 303).[6]

In conclusion, Winnicott identified, just like Fairbairn, the non-instinctual nature of the primary need for relationship, but he did not openly reject the theory of instinctual drives, although he did utterly reject the concept of the death drive (Winnicott, 1962, p. 177).[7] His contributions opened the path towards the current relational perspective, which had been initiated by Ferenczi, without acknowledging the necessary need for a radical theoretical change. However, his novel theoretical and clinical conceptions were fundamental, together with Fairbairn's, for the emergence and development of the implicit new psychoanalytic paradigm that underlay the thinking and practice of the British Independents, and paved the way for some of the major developments of contemporary psychoanalysis, such as self-psychology, intersubjective theory, and relational psychoanalysis, all of them based on the recognition of the primacy of personal relations as the primary motor of human experience, thinking, and behaviour (Clarke & Scharff, 2014).

In the light of the previous considerations, Winnicott appears to us as a bold and daring explorer of new territories, an enormously sensitive, intuitive, and creative clinician and thinker, who nonetheless halted on the very threshold of acknowledging the truly revolutionary character of his contributions. And the deep motivation that lay behind this last-minute indecisiveness was to be found precisely in a relational need, such as those he rightly described: the need to preserve a loving bond with the master and spiritual father of all of us who have the profession of psychoanalysis, and the unconscious wish to agree with him (Tubert-Oklander, 2009–2014). Because true adulthood, both personal and professional, can only be attained when we dare to differentiate ourselves from our forefathers. It is a most solitary state, in which we must take full responsibility for our thoughts, words, actions, values, and convictions, this being a very heavy burden. Hence, we all have to deal with the same dilemma that hindered Winnicott. But breaking away from tradition is not innocuous. As an old Arab proverb says, 'No one attains sanctity until one hundred men declare him, in good faith, to be a heretic'.

Notes

1 In a letter to Anna Freud of March 18, 1954, he wrote

> I have an irritating way of saying things in my own language instead of learn-
> ing how to use the terms of psycho-analytic metapsychology. I am trying to find
> out why it is that I am so deeply suspicious of these terms. Is it because they can
> give the appearance of a common understanding when such understanding does not
> exist? Or is it because of something in myself? It can, of course, be both.
>
> (Rodman, 1987, p. 58)

And, in a letter to Melanie Klein of November 17, 1952, he said

> I can see how annoying it is that when something develops in me out of my own
> growth and out of my analytic experience I want to put it in my own language. This
> is annoying because I suppose everyone wants to do the same thing, and in a sci-
> entific society one of our aims is to find a common language. This language must,
> however, be kept alive as there is nothing worse than a dead language.
>
> (p. 34)

2 Thus, he wrote, in a letter to David Rapaport of October 9, 1953,

> I am one of those people who feel compelled to work in my own way and to express
> myself in my own language first; by a struggle I sometimes come around to rewor-
> ing what I am saying to bring it in line with other work, in which case I usually find
> that my own 'original' ideas were not so original as I had to think they were when
> they were emerging. I suppose other people are like this too.
>
> (Rodman, 1987, pp. 53–54)

3 Indeed, the only subject on which he openly disagreed with Freud was that of the death
drive, on which he wrote, 'I have never been able to follow anyone else, not even Freud.
But Freud was easy to criticise because he was always critical of himself. For instance,
I simply cannot find value in his idea of a Death Instinct' (Winnicott, 1962, p. 177, my
italics; see also Hernández-Tubert, 2017b [Chapter 5]).

4 I must confess that I also used this strategic resource, which I now consider untenable,
in some of my psychopathological writings of the 1980s. Of course, I was at the time
following the steps of such admired writers as Winnicott and Kohut.

5 This idea – that Freud's instinctual drives are really a psychopathological phenomenon, corresponding to a splitting or fragmentation of the self, derived from the noxious
impact of traumatic experiences – is also found in the work of Fairbairn (1952) and
Kohut (1982). See also Chapter 14.

6 Winnicott wrote, in one of his last writings, called 'D.W.W. on D.W.W.' (Winnicott,
1967), the following lines: 'At that time [when Fairbairn came to talk to Klein and her
disciples] I couldn't see anything in Fairbairn. I saw later that he'd got an extremely
important thing to say which had to do with going beyond instinctual satisfactions and
frustrations to the idea of object-seeking (p. 579) . . . I now became aware that Fairbairn
had made a tremendous contribution, even if we only take two things. One is object-
seeking, which comes into the area of transitional phenomena and so on, and the other is
this thing of feeling real instead of feeling unreal' (p. 582).

7 Of course, it may well be argued that the tendency towards relationship is instinctive,
in the ethological meaning of the term 'instinct', but when I talk about the 'non-instinctual nature of the primary need for relationship', I am referring to the Freudian concept
of *Triebe*, which is best translated as 'instinctual drives' – i.e., internal tensions that
necessarily seek a discharge. Throughout this book, we have systematically used the
term 'instinct' and 'instinctive' for the ethological concept, and 'instinctual drive' and
'instinctual' for the Freudian *Trieb*.

Chapter 4

The fundamental role of aggression and hate in the psychoanalytic treatment (2017)

Reyna Hernández-Tubert

This chapter is a revised version of the paper I read at the Latin-American Meeting on Winnicott's Thought that took place in Mexico City in November 2017, in the panel called 'The revolutionary impact of Winnicott on contemporary psychoanalysis'. Here I deal with the central place he assigned to aggression, as a vital expression, while flatly rejecting the concept of a 'Death Instinct'. This is a subject Juan Tubert-Oklander and I had explored extensively in a series of papers written in the 1990s (Hernández-Hernández & Tubert-Oklander, 1995, 1996; Tubert-Oklander & Hernández de Tubert, 1996), in my paper on Freud's social writings (Hernández de Tubert, 2008 [Chapter 5]), and in my doctoral dissertation on 'The unconscious and the Weltanschauung' (Hernández Hernández, 2010). In all these, we had contested the concept of the Death Drive and argued that aggression is an expression of Life and not a primarily destructive or self-destructive tendency. Of course, Winnicott was present in all these discussions, but the present chapter focuses specifically on his theoretical and clinical concept of aggression and the consequences this had for him.

From my point of view, Donald Winnicott is the author who has assigned the greatest importance to aggression and hate, both in life and in the psychoanalytic treatment. This may sound surprising, since many orthodox psychoanalysts, particularly those of a Kleinian orientation, have criticised him for not taking these traits into account, and offering a sentimental and idealised version, both of the early mother-child relationship and the analytic relation.

What actually happens is that Winnicott assigns a particular importance to hate and aggression, but not as an expression of an alleged death drive, but as a manifestation of a vital and potentially creative tendency, which is indispensable for relating with other human beings and dealing with reality. Thus, he affirms, in 'Hate in the countertransference' (Winnicott, 1949), that both analyst and patient should acknowledge, accept, and express their mutual hatred, as well as their mutual love.[1] The same principle applies to the mother-child relationship. A mother should allow herself to experience hate towards her child, and not only love. We may well say that she teaches her child how to love, by loving him, and how to hate, by hating him.

DOI: 10.4324/9780429055287-6

This also applies to the relation with the father, the family, teachers, doctors, the community, and the analyst or therapist. A real relationship, one that can foster development, requires both care, which is an expression of love, and setting limits, which is an expression of hate. Quite unlike what his critics claim, Winnicott did not have a sentimental view of human relations, as he clearly states in the following quotation:

> This is not a sentimental rhyme. Sentimentality is useless for parents, as it contains a denial of hate, and sentimentality in a mother is no good at all from the infant's point of view.
>
> (Winnicott, 1949, p. 202)

What he did reject, categorically, was the concept of the death drive. On this, he wrote in the following terms, when he explained why he had never been part of the Kleinian group:

> I have never been able to follow anyone else, not even Freud. But Freud was easy to criticise because he was always critical of himself. For instance, I simply cannot find any value in his idea of a Death Instinct.
>
> (Winnicott, 1962, p. 177)

For Winnicott, who was a physician and paediatrician, the concept of a death drive, which aims at one's own destruction, is biological nonsense. Aggression is a vital expression and it is necessary for the establishment of human relations and reality itself (Winnicott, 1950–55, 1959–64). Already in 1950, in his contribution to a symposium on aggression, he had clearly stated this, in the following terms,

> The main idea behind this study of aggression is that if society is in danger, it is not because of man's aggressiveness but because of the repression of personal aggressiveness in individuals.
>
> (Winnicott, 1950–55, p. 204)

Thus, he later arrives to the conclusion that, 'The concept of the death instinct seems to disappear simply through being unnecessary. Aggression is seen more as an evidence of life' (Winnicott, 1959–64, p. 127).

In his 1950 paper, the author suggests that the most primitive form of love has an intrinsically destructive component, without there being still an intention to destroy.[2] Here, aggression is a part of love. He then adds the hypothesis that when aggression, which is intimately linked with muscular motility when facing oppositions, differentiates from love, which tends to fusion, this establishes the subject-object discrimination and, consequently, the sense of reality of both self and object.

This hypothesis attains its final and mature form in his paper 'The use of an object and relating through identifications' (Winnicott, 1969), read to the New

York Psychoanalytic Society in late 1968. In this, which was his last major theoretical writing and one of his most important ones, Winnicott tells us about what he conceived as 'the positive value of destructiveness' (p. 94). Here he affirms that for the object – that is, the mother – to become real for the child, it is indispensable that he destroy it in fantasy, and then discover that Mother has survived. This generates the idea that she exists beyond and without the baby's sphere of omnipotence. Up to this point, the mother had been for the baby a 'subjective object', felt to have been omnipotently created by his wish, an *object of relation*. Now, when she becomes real and external, the child can use her and profit from what she has to offer, that is, she becomes an *object of use*.

For Winnicott, this process is fundamental for the sense of reality and continues during our whole life. Perception itself is based on a continuous process of reality-testing, by which reality is constantly destroyed and re-created, in order to place it beyond the subject's omnipotent control (Goldman, 1993, p. 203).

Winnicott's presentation in New York was responded by Edith Jacobson, Samuel Ritvo, and Bernard Fine, who sternly criticised it, rejecting his positive evaluation of destructiveness and his use of a personal language, instead of abiding by the mandatory use of the language of Freudian metapsychology. Apparently, they did not understand the conceptual difference drawn by the author between 'object-relating' and 'object-use'. Their commentaries used up all the available time, so there was no discussion with the audience. Winnicott felt clearly frustrated by not having been able to convey an idea that was obviously most important to him. He had arrived at the meeting with the beginning of a bout of influenza, which later worsened with a cardiac complication that required hospitalisation. A few weeks afterwards, he returned to London, but he never fully recovered and died a year after that.

Many believe that this illness was precipitated by the hostile treatment he received from his American colleagues. Dodi Goldman (1993), who investigated extensively this episode, tells us that a revision of the transcription of the commentaries and the summary of the meeting, which are kept in the archive of the New York Psychoanalytic Society, 'point at a spirited intellectual exchange without signs of personal animosity or rancour' (p. 210). However, the testimonies of some witnesses who were there give us a different image,

> Still, some participants at the meeting clearly recall an atmosphere of profound intolerance towards Winnicott's originality (Annie Bergman, personal communication, June 16, 1992). In the aftermath of the formal presentation, one participant noticed Winnicott to be visibly shaken and overheard him commenting that he now understood better why America was in Vietnam (Steve Ellman, personal communication, May 15, 1992). Winnicott obviously felt that he was the target of aggression. The least one could say is that there was an absence of openness in respect to the ingenuity of Winnicott's formulations. Both Winnicott's exceptional need to find a personal route from clinical experience to theory building and his desire to make theory

feel real to himself by being splendidly original had apparently engendered suspicion among the more doctrinaire and close-minded elements within the New York Psychoanalytic Society.

(pp. 210–211)

What was there in Winnicott's propositions that could generate such hostility and rejection? In the first place, there is his positive evaluation of aggression and destructivity. A commonplace assumption in psychoanalytic thinking is that aggression is inherently 'bad', and this finds its utmost expression in those theoreticians, like Freud and Klein, who explain it in terms of genetic inheritance. Winnicott's (1971a) curt comment on this is that 'The concept of the death instinct could be described as a reassertion of the principle of original sin' (p. 96).

In this, we can see the echo of the Judaeo-Christian thought, but also a powerful socio-political factor, related to an aspect Winnicott did not consider, which is the use of aggression in order to change reality. Although the author always emphasised the importance of the environment for the individual's life and development, he did it in terms of its beneficial or noxious impact on the latter. But aggression is a vital expression that allows us to confront, modify, reject, or destroy, in reality and not only in the internal world, those aspects of our environment that we cannot or should not accept. This is what Enrique Pichon-Rivière (1971a) calls 'active adaptation to reality' (Tubert-Oklander & Hernández de Tubert, 2004). But this makes it potentially subversive for a society based on the maintenance of the established order and the ablation of those active tendencies of individuals or groups that might oppose it. Consequently, society, through parents, teachers, doctors, the police, judges, therapists, or other figures of authority, strives to inhibit aggressive or simply active expressions, which are considered to be 'bad', because they can unhinge a social system based on the passive acceptance of existing norms. But this suppression affects not only aggression, but also sexuality, joy, pleasure, happiness, creativity, originality, and independent and critical thought.[3]

We can now better understand the meaning of the hostile rejection suffered by Winnicott, not only in that meeting in New York, but also during a significant part of his career, which had him vetoed as a teacher, for many years, at the Institute of Psychoanalysis.[4]

This rejection is quite similar to the one suffered by Freud, when he put forward his so-called 'seduction theory' – a most inadequate name, since it was really a theory of the traumatic pathogenic effect of the sexual abuse of children by their adult caretakers. As this theory implied a denunciation of social authority, as represented by parents and other caretaking adults, it became threatening and subversive for the social order, since, if it were accepted that parents and other adults frequently abuse their authority over those children who are their charges, the same would apply to others who are in charge of taking care of people who depend on them, such as doctors, teachers, priests, therapists, psychoanalysts, or government authorities (Hernández-Tubert, 2011a [Chapter 12], 2017a). All this must have weighed heavily on the young Freud, who finally abandoned his theory in 1897 and replaced it by another one, centred on the child's antisocial tendencies and the study of the intrapsychic, with total exclusion of all environmental factors (Tubert-Oklander, 2016 [Chapter 7]). The result was that, when Sándor Ferenczi recouped and revamped, thirty-five years later, the traumatic theory of neuroses, he was the object of a similar hostile and malignant rejection by Freud and his circle of disciples and followers (Tubert-Oklander, 1999).

This kind of hostile rejection and abuse by colleagues is not innocuous: Winnicott fell severely ill after that meeting in New York and so did Ferenczi after the 1932 Wiesbaden Congress, in which he read his last paper (Ferenczi, 1933), which led Freud to break with him, and both died soon afterwards (Roustang, 1976). Freud, on his part, managed to go on, after his 1897 crisis, but paying the heavy price of reformulating his theory in terms that excluded a large part of his initial concerns. This allowed him to develop a deep and fruitful investigation of many previously unknown aspects of human existence, but obstructed the enquiry of others, which nonetheless kept emerging periodically throughout the history of psychoanalysis.

The psychoanalytic treatment aims at restoring the integrity and developing the potential capacities of the human being, which have been mutilated by the splitting off and repudiation of vast areas of his or her being, at the service of the instruments of social control, initially implanted by the family and later reinforced and compounded by groups, institutions, the media, and society-as-a-whole. The therapist's analytic frame and attitude favour the emergence of the disavowed and forgotten aspects of the patient's being, which, on finding in the analyst acceptance, respect, willingness to understand, and openness to dialogue, are thus validated and re-integrated into the patient's self and life.

This allows patients to attain a greater fullness, develop their potentialities, and transform their lives in order to achieve a greater happiness. But these previously rejected aspects of the personality are precisely those that are subversive to the existing social order, especially sexuality, aggression, independent thinking, and the demand for justice. Consequently, it is not infrequent for patients and their treatment to be questioned and disqualified by their immediate environment and their closest and nominally dearest, who try to induce them to end their analyses, 'because it's utterly useless', 'it's a fraud', and 'you're worse every day' (i.e., acting in discordance to the other person's expectations). Society and its institutions, on their part, also attack psychoanalysis and group analysis, which they perceive – and rightly so! – as a threat to their usual way of functioning.[5]

Facing the threat of social repudiation and ostracism, many psychoanalysts and group analysts have responded by trying to turn analysis, sometimes unconsciously, into something more acceptable to the social system. One of them has been the attempt to submit it to the demands of the scientific method and the so-called 'evidence-based therapies'. If we turn analytic treatment into a merely technical procedure, purposive, controlled, and aimed at the attainment of pre-ordained concrete therapeutic goals, we are thus eschewing the risk of the emergence of thoughts, feelings, or actions that might scandalise conventional well-meaning citizens.

Another way of neutralising the subversive and deeply troubling potential of analysis consists in reducing the depth and intensity of the emotional experience that ensues between the participants in the treatment – whether bi-personal or group-analytic – and especially avoiding the intense negative feelings of anger, hate, and violence that emerge in both parties and which, according to Winnicott, are the only ones that may give a feeling of realness to the relation.

This strategy is particularly damaging for the treatment and the patient, since it tends to generate an apparently good analytic relation, intellectualised and conflict-free, that reinforces and validates the socially induced repression of the patient's aggressive potential. And, if we agree with Winnicott in his positive valuation of destructiveness, this keeps the patient maimed, docile, easy to manipulate, and incapable of facing, thinking through, and solving external conflicts. In other words, this reinforces that kind of pathology of the personality that we call 'normalcy', which represents a passive adaptation to the established order. All this acts against the possibility of leading a free and joyful life, and to use one's aggressive potential in order to develop an independent thought and to act towards changing the world, thus attaining an active adaptation to reality.

Another reason why many analysts avoid experiencing and analysing aggression in the transference-countertransference with their patients, or disqualify such feelings by interpreting them away as an expression of the patient's innate destructiveness, is that this implies a most difficult and painful process for both parties, and the risk of having to face, acknowledge, and honestly respond to their patients' questioning, when all their training, including their own analyses, has conditioned them to defensively avoid this kind of confrontations. But avoiding this intense emotional commitment requires not doing any character analysis, but only an intellectualised symptom analysis that turns into a mere explanation of the symptom, without a real understanding, based on shared emotional experience. Character analysis, which calls into question the patient's very way of being, generates strong feelings of hatred and/or the terrifying experience of nonexistence, and none of this can be truly navigated and solved if the analyst remains aloof and 'objective'.

Winnicott (1960b) describes this in his ground-breaking paper 'Ego distortion in terms of true and false self'. In it, he proposed the concept of a false self, an inauthentic and non-existent personality based on an exploitation of the various ego skills to construct a fictional character that acts as a 'caretaking self', which takes care of the more sensitive, vital, and fragile part of the personality, which remains hidden. This is constructed as an attempt to deal with and compensate a deficiency of parental care during infancy. The result is that the patient who comes to treatment is not a real person, but a fictional character, able to perform cognitive and conative functions properly, but incapable of developing an affective connection. In such a situation, real analysis is not possible, and the patient only learns to think and speak in terms of psychoanalytic theory. This is what Winnicott says about the matter,

A principle might be enunciated, that in the False Self area of our analytic practice, we find we make more headway by recognition of the patient's non-existence than by a long-continued working with the patient on the basis of ego-defence mechanisms. The patient's False Self can collaborate indefinitely with the analyst in the analysis of defences, being so to speak on the analyst's side in the game. This unrewarding work is only cut short profitably when the analyst can point to and specify an absence of some essential feature.

(p. 152)

But when this is done and turns out to be effective, the patient's response is the emergence of pent-up feelings, in a relational process usually referred to – perhaps inaccurately – as 'regression'. This only can make the relation and the analysis real. And, for Winnicott (1949, 1969), hate is the essential factor in this process.

But, if an analyst has not been able to experience and validate his own capacity for hate and aggression in his own personal analysis, he will be ill equipped to deal with it with his patients. But, if she decides to attempt it, there are two great teachers who can provide the necessary orientation for this momentous trip. They are Sándor Ferenczi (1933), who stressed the unavoidable need for the analyst to acknowledge and analyse explicitly with the patient his or her negative counter-transference, and Donald Woods Winnicott (1949), for whom the analyst must accept, analyse, and inform the patient of her feeling of hatred towards him. This is the most difficult path that Winnicott used to call 'research analysis' – that is, the analysis of patients who had been previously deemed to be 'unanalysable' – which brings about a new stage in the analyst's own analysis,

Psycho-analytic research is perhaps always to some extent an attempt on part of an analyst to carry the work of his own analysis further than the point to which his own analyst could take him.

(Winnicott, 1949, p. 196)

This is, perhaps, the greatest legacy of Winnicott's work, and a major learning, for both analysts and therapists, on the one hand, and society at large, on the other.

Our present society has demonised aggression, violence, anger, and hate, considering them to be intrinsically destructive and 'bad'. But this judgement usually only applies to those expressions of rejection, protest, or criticism of authority and the attempts to modify the established order, while many even more destructive actions by the powers that be are regularly justified. In the international arena, we see how hegemonic countries, the media, and public opinion violently attack all expressions of protest, criticism, opposition, independence, or sovereignty by Third World countries, while they ignore, promote, or uncritically accept all truly criminal acts of imposition by the First World (Hernández-Tubert, 2017a).

This same value judgement permeates, as we have seen, a large part of psycho-analytical theory and practice. This implicit endorsement of authority has served as a justification for those who exercise a vertical or autocratic power. It is a sorry fact that many psychoanalytic institutions have organised the training of new generations of psychoanalysts in similar vertical, authoritarian, and dogmatic terms. This surprising phenomenon may be interpreted as yet another form of reaction of the social system to neutralise the radical revolutionary potential of analysis.

An analytic treatment ought to call into question and revise this value judgement, in order that the patient may recover a whole area of her being that has been split off and disavowed, with the cost of great suffering and distortions for individuals, groups, and the whole contemporary society. Those psychoanalysts who consider ourselves to be heirs to the tradition of Freud, Ferenczi, and Winnicott are bound to apply this perspective in our treatment and also share, as much as possible, this knowledge with the wider community.[6]

Notes

1 This idea was, of course, first introduced by Ferenczi (1933), in his last paper called 'Confusion of the tongues between the adults and the child – (The language of tenderness and of passion)', in which he stresses the need for the analyst to analyse his or her negative countertransference and openly discuss it with the patient.

2 The same idea had been suggested by Sabina Spielrein (1912 [1994], 1912 [1995], 2019), who called it 'the destructive component of the sexual instinct' (Spielrein, 1912 [1994], p. 169), and Michael Balint (1952, 1968), in his concept of 'primary love'.

3 This was poignantly depicted in George Orwell's (1949) novel *1984*.

4 Winnicott did not explicitly refer to this source of societal rejection, which he probably would have considered not to be a part of the psychoanalytic enquiry, but the fact that he connected the hostile rejection he received in New York with the American presence in Viet Nam shows that he was aware of it.

The rejection he suffered in the Institute of the British Society was less violent, and consistent with the English tradition of good manners, but highly efficient in preventing him from teaching his unorthodox views, as he explains in his letter to Adam Limentani of September 27, 1968:

> For a long time, as you know, I was not asked to do any teaching of psycho-analysis because neither Miss Freud nor Mrs. Klein would use me or allow their students to come to me for regular teaching even in child analysis. I therefore missed at a critical time in my life the stimulus which would have made me work up a lecture series definitely orientated to the teaching of technique. When later on I became acceptable and was invited to do some teaching, I had already had some original ideas and naturally these came to mind when I was planning to talk to the students.
> (Rodman, 1987, p. 179)

5 Even though Winnicott was never involved in group analysis, the following paragraphs will refer to psychoanalysis and group analysis as a single field of 'analysis', since I believe that this interpretation of society's rejection applies similarly to both of them. The reason for identifying these two disciplines is clearly explained throughout the book.

6 This, of course, also applies to group analysts who identify with the traditions of Radical Foulkes (Dalal, 1998) and Enrique Pichon-Rivière.

Chapter 5

Freudian anthropology and metasociology (2008)

Reyna Hernández-Tubert

This chapter is based on a paper I read at a continuous education seminar on Metapsychology for training analysts of the Institute of Psychoanalysis of the Mexican Psychoanalytic Association in 2007. Each of us wrote and presented a paper on some aspect of metapsychology, and I chose to enquire the theoretical underpinnings of Freud's social writings. This is a revised version of the text that was later published in **Revista de Psicoanálisis** *(Hernández de Tubert, 2008). It was also included as a chapter in my doctoral dissertation on 'Psychoanalysis and the* **Weltanschauung'** *(Hernández Hernández, 2010). Here, I review Freud's main social writings, in order to identify in them the ontological, epistemological, and axiological assumptions that underlie his manifest theoretical constructions, which were a part of his Conception of the World or* **Weltanschauung** *and his Conception of Life or* **Lebensanschauung** *– what I call the 'Freudian anthropology' – as well as the basis of the theory of individual and collective mental processes that underlies his arguments – a metapsychology of social life, which I have called 'metasociology'.*

Usually, the term 'metapsychology' is used to refer to Freud's more abstract theory, but this is not quite correct, since there may be other metapsychologies. As we have seen in Chapter 1, Freud introduced this term to refer to a psychology that goes beyond consciousness and believed this to be of a biological nature and the truly scientific causal theory of psychoanalysis. This scientist version of psychoanalytic theory has been the target of many criticisms, but if we reserve this term for the general theory of Mind that underlies our clinical theories, it is quite obvious that we need 'something like a metapsychology – i.e., a general theory of Mind, compatible with our clinical experiences, theories, and practices' (Tubert-Oklander, 2014, p. 40). In this we have to thank Freud for explicitly spelling out for us quite a few of his epistemological and axiomatic assumptions, since this makes it easier for us to make a critical reading of his theories. But this demands that those of us who do not share his assumptions explicitly acknowledge those that underlie our theories. The present book is an attempt to develop 'a new metapsychology, to be shared by psychoanalysis and group analysis' (Tubert-Oklander, 2014, p. 33). But this requires, of course, a prior critical revision of Freud's metapsychology, and this is what I intend to do in my revision of Freud's social writings.

DOI: 10.4324/9780429055287-7

Introduction

Freud's works do not only present a set of psychological theories, but also contain a general conception of the human being, that is, an anthropology (Beuchot, 2004). This is most evident in what have been called his 'social writings'. In these texts, he tackles a double task: to expound his conception of life, the human being, and society – what we may well call 'Freudian anthropology' – and to construct a theory of the unconscious aspect of social phenomena, from the psychoanalytic vantage point. This metapsychology of social life we may call 'metasociology'. Although these two tasks are complementary and appear simultaneously in his work, they are by no means equal and should be analysed separately, each one in its own context.

In a series of previous writings (Hernández Hernández, 2010; Hernández de Tubert, 2000, 2004a, 2004c, 2009a), I have argued for the need to study psychoanalytic theories and practice in terms of the *Weltanschauung* or *Conception of the World*.[1] This is a real mental structure, which is mainly unconscious, that consists in a highly complex set of assumptions about the nature of what exists and what does not exist, the possibility and forms of knowing it, human nature, values, and the ways of representing, thinking, communicating, and acting on all this. In other word, the conception of the world includes a spontaneous and unconscious ontology, epistemology, axiology, ethics, aesthetics, logic, and semiotics. All these derive from the very first introjections of primary object relations and from the later experiences of participation in various collective entities, from the family to formal institutions and the wider communities.

Consequently, all these assumptions are established long before any formal study and the subject is unconscious of them, and particularly of the fact that they *are* assumptions, since he uncritically considers them to be just 'the way things are'. And this is reinforced, over and over again, by the so-called 'common sense', which is nothing but the set of assumptions, values, prejudices, and procedures shared by the community of which the subject is a member, and which requires them in order to uphold its particular construction of reality (Berger & Luckmann, 1966). Marx and Engels's (1932) enquiry of *The German Ideology*, written in 1845, and the more recent studies by the members of the Frankfurt School, such as Horkheimer and Adorno (Horkheimer, 1937; Hernández de Tubert, 2006a), have clearly stated the social, political, and economic determinants of this common sense view.

Freud could not escape this universal determination of human thought, so that his writings inevitably reveal his prejudices – in the logical sense of judgement made before any enquiry or evidence – on human affairs. But, as Hans-Georg Gadamer (1960), the great theoretician of hermeneutics, showed in his writings, prejudices are necessarily the starting point of any interpretative endeavour. Hence, interpretive activity is bound to take the form of a dialogue between the interpreter and the material to be interpreted, be it a written text, living discourse, dialogue, non-verbal behaviour, social relations, or another human being.

We all have these prejudices as the basis of our conception of the world, and the only thing we can do about it is to identify them, examine them, and submit them to a conscious critique, before deciding to maintain, revise, or discard them. Hence, in the study and interpretation of any given text – in the hermeneutical technical sense of any form of human expression capable of bearing and transmitting a meaning – it is essential to identify the author's and the interpreter's underlying assumptions, values, and perspective, in order to attain a better understanding of how his arguments and conclusions, on the one hand, and the reader's interpretations of them, on the other, are constructed.

Consequently, when studying Freud's works – as well as any other author's – it is necessary to distinguish in them three different kinds of elements. The first one are his *discoveries*, acquired from experience and reflection, such as child sexuality, transference, and the latent meaning of dreams, parapraxes, and neurotic symptoms. Second are the *theories* he created in order to account for these discoveries, such as the concepts of the unconscious, instinctual drives, and the psychic apparatus. And third are the *assumptions, beliefs, and values* that are the starting point for carrying out his observations and the construction of his theories. These are necessarily previous to the beginning of his enquiry, although the development of his arguments frequently makes it appear as if they were conclusions derived from its results.

Obviously, any discussion of human nature and personal and social relations invokes all the common-sense assumptions that were incorporated during the formative years and later reinforced by all social interactions. This is clearly illustrated, for instance, by Freud's (1930a) discussion of the Christian concept of universal love, in *Civilization and Its Discontents*.

His analysis starts with the observation that there is a small number of human beings who find joy through love, albeit in a particular way, by substituting the main value of being loved by the act of loving. In other words, their main joy is derived from the experience of loving unconditionally, without expecting any response. This he considers to be a transformation of an instinctual drive into an 'aim-inhibited drive'.

Here, he points out, quite accurately, the connection of this technique for striving for happiness, with religion, in the following terms:

> Perhaps St. Francis of Assisi went furthest in thus exploiting love for the benefit of an inner feeling of happiness. Moreover, what we have recognized as one of the techniques for fulfilling the pleasure principle has often been brought into connection with religion; this connection may lie in the remote regions where the distinction between the ego and objects or between objects themselves is neglected.
>
> (p. 102)

The Christian conception of life conceives this to be the highest attainment of the human spirit. However, Freud immediately poses two objections: '[Firstly] a love that does not discriminate seems to me to forfeit a part of its own value, by doing an injustice to its object; and secondly, not all men are worthy of love' (p. 102).

Later, he further clarifies the bases of his argument, when discussing 'one of the ideal demands . . . of civilized society. It runs: "Thou shalt love thy neighbour as thyself"' (p. 109), as it can be appreciated in the following quotation:

> Let us adopt a naive attitude towards it, as though we were hearing it for the first time; we shall be unable then to suppress a feeling of surprise and bewilderment. Why should we do it? What good will it do us? But, above all, how shall we achieve it? How can it be possible? *My love is something valuable to me which I ought not to throw away without reflection. It imposes duties on me for whose fulfilment I must be ready to make sacrifices. If I love someone, he must deserve it in some way. . . .* He deserves it if he is so like me in important ways that I can love myself in him; and he deserves it if he is so much more perfect than myself that I can love my ideal of my own self in him. Again, I have to love him if he is my friend's son, since the pain my friend would feel if any harm came to him would be my pain too – I should have to share it. But if he is a stranger to me and if he cannot attract me by any worth of his own or any significance that he may already have acquired for my emotional life, it will be hard for me to love him. *Indeed, I should be wrong to do so, for my love is valued by all my own people as a sign of my preferring them, and it is an injustice to them if I put a stranger on a par with them.*
>
> (pp. 109–110, my italics)

Here we can see Freud's assumption about human relations: love cannot be for free, it must be deserved – that is, earned – and it should be distributed according to a rule of justice. The Frankfurt critical philosophers would probably interpret this as an expression of the ethos of an ascending bourgeoisie,[2] for whom everything has a price, according to its market value. Nonetheless, even if we do not accept this typically Marxist interpretation, it is quite clear that Freud's thought stemmed from some unquestioned cultural common-sense assumptions, which certainly would not have been shared by the Saint of Assisi.

But apart from this value judgement, there is another assumption, of a theoretical nature, that is worth mentioning. This is that there is a limited amount of love available to any person, a valuable possession that ought to be administered fairly and prudently, so as not to waste it:

> But if I am to love him (with this universal love) merely because he, too, is an inhabitant of this earth, like an insect, an earth-worm or a grass-snake, then *I fear that only a small modicum of my love will fall to his share – not by any possibility as much as, by the judgement of my reason, I am entitled to retain for myself.* What is the point of a precept enunciated with so much solemnity if its fulfilment cannot be recommended as reasonable?
>
> (pp. 110, my italics)

Once more, we are faced with an idea of love as a possession, a limited good that we should carefully hoard, like capital, and used according to convenience. This, however, is at odds with the Christian conception of love as a human capacity that improves with practice, so that the more you love, the more love you have to give.

Quite apart from the possibility and the need to enquire the theoretical and clinical value of these two conceptions of love, there is still the fact that there are quite a few ideological statements in the foundations of the group of texts we are dealing with. What Freud seems to be saying is, 'I do not find the Christian proposal to be attractive. I do not live in this way and I do not deem it to be either possible or desirable'. This is, of course, his right. But we cannot ignore that such divergences of conceptions about human nature and the life projects that are adequate for individuals and communities lie behind all political and ideological conflicts. And, to this day, we have not been able to solve such conflicts by means of argumentation or research, but only through the acknowledgement and acceptance of differences, and a search for viable transactions that make coexistence possible.

Freud himself seems to have been partially aware of the fact that many of his arguments could not be considered an outcome of psychoanalytic research but stemmed from other sources in his own intellectual formation. Thus, on several occasions, in both *The Future of an Illusion* (1927) and *Civilization and Its Discontents* (1930a), he affirms that there is nothing new in the arguments he is putting forward – particularly in those against religion – and then goes on to expound what he actually has to say – that is, the discoveries and theories of psychoanalysis. But he does not seem to be aware that the old assumptions are infiltrated into his new ideas.

I am not saying here that Freud's conception of life is wrong and that another one is right, but that there is an ideological underpinning to every theory or discourse, and that this determines the meaning one assigns to that particular argument. Freud's presentation of psychoanalysis is suffused by a meaning derived from his particular conception of the world and conception of life, but his theories and technique, and the practice he initiated acquire new meanings when interpreted by readers and practitioners who have a different *Weltanschauung* and *Lebensanschauung*. If being a psychoanalyst requires being Freudian, in the sense of abiding by his pre-psychoanalytic set of assumptions, values, and beliefs, then this is not psychoanalysis. But the psychoanalytic community and its thinkers include many people with different persuasions: Freud was a militant atheist – 'an infidel Jew', as he once said – Karl Menninger was a devout believer, and the members of the British Independent Group had all been raised in Protestantism.

Hence, in this brief exposition and analysis of Freud's social writings, I shall differentiate between his new discoveries, the theoretical developments he puts forward in order to account for them, and the ideological assumptions that act as the foundations of his thought. This is particularly important, since it is indeed possible for a psychoanalyst to fully accept his discoveries and operate with the theories he posed, without necessarily sharing his conception of the world and values. Indeed, as we have seen in Chapter 2, many of the insoluble controversies in the psychoanalytical world seem to derive from the fact that the real discussion is not about theories, but about the underlying conceptions of the world held by the opposing factions (Hernández Hernández, 2010; Hernández de Tubert, 2000, 2004a, 2004c, 2009a; Hernández-Tubert, 2015 [Chapter 2]).

This difficulty cannot be side-tracked by the formal resort of splitting Freud's writings into two large groups, theoretical and philosophical, since, on the one hand, all of them somehow reflect his conception of the world and, on the other, even his most philosophical texts – such as his social writings – cannot be considered 'applied psychoanalysis' – that is, an application of well-established psychoanalytic theories to social issues. These were also an integral part of the psychoanalytic enquiry and theorisation (Esman, 1998). Hence, their analysis is truly important for the study of the Freudian metapsychology.

Paul-Laurent Assoun (2000) has identified three meanings for the term 'metapsychology' in Freud's work. First, it is *a psychology of the unconscious* or, better still, a psychology that includes the development of the consequences of accepting the hypothesis of unconscious mental processes. As such, metapsychology is identical to psychoanalytic theory.

Second, it is *a method for the description and theorisation* of those phenomena that occupy psychoanalysis. This provides us with a set of analogical models and a language for formulating and discussing ideas within the psychoanalytic community. Nonetheless, it should be pointed out that, even if accepting the need for such a method, there are presently controversies in our professional community about which would be the most adequate method and language for fulfilling this function, and this has brought about the development of metapsychological models that differ from Freud's. French psychoanalysts such as Assoun, however, tend to consider Freudian metapsychology as the mandatory method and language of psychoanalysis (Laplanche & Pontalis, 1967).

Thirdly, metapsychology would be *a path for the generation of new ideas*, what Freud called 'fantasising'.[3] This was a kind of thinking that resembled daydreaming, quite distant from his ideal of scientific objectivity; hence, he compared metapsychology with 'the Witch' that Faust must invoke in order to regain his youth, once all usual common-sense recipes have failed:

> If we are asked by what methods and means this result is achieved, it is not easy to find an answer. We can only say: '*So muss denn doch die Hexe dran!*'['We must call the Witch to our help after all', Goethe, *Faust*, Part I, Scene 6] – the Witch Meta-psychology. Without metapsychological speculation and theorizing – I had almost said 'phantasying' – we shall not get another step forward. Unfortunately, here as elsewhere, what our Witch reveals is neither very clear nor very detailed.
>
> (Freud, 1937a, p. 225)

Quite apart from the definition of metapsychology posed in the introduction to this chapter, it seems that we cannot limit our understanding of Freudian metapsychology to a single one of these three senses of the word, but that it is essential to maintain the polysemy and ambiguity of the author's original formulation. Having this in mind, I shall now examine Freud's main social writings.

Totem and Taboo (1912–1913)

This book, whose subtitle is 'Some Points of Agreement between the Mental Lives of Savages and Neurotics', comprises four essays, in which the author first painstakingly reviews the anthropological literature of his time, then establishes a comparison between these primitive religious phenomena and neuroses, and finally proposes a daring speculative theory of the origins of society, its institutions, and myths.

This study has been the target of many criticisms, based on the discordance between its historical reconstruction and present-day anthropological and ethological studies. This argument stems from a literal reading of the Freudian narrative, which was constructed from the then-available information, but it is readily dispelled if we opt to take it as a metaphorical portrayal that describes, analogically, certain universal human fantasies about collective living.[4] This is the interpretative path I intend to follow, focusing on the strictly psychoanalytic aspects of this enquiry and its contribution to metapsychology.

Let us remember that the first published mention of the term 'metapsychology' – in *The Psychopathology of Everyday Life* (1901b) – was posed in direct opposition to the mythological conception of the world, in the following terms:

> In point of fact I believe that a large part of the mythological view of the world, which extends a long way into the most modern religions, *is nothing but psychology projected into the external world.* The obscure recognition (the endopsychic perception, as it were) of psychical factors and relations in the unconscious is mirrored . . . in the construction of a *supernatural reality,* which is destined to be changed back once more by science into the *psychology of the unconscious.* One could venture to explain in this way the myths of paradise and the fall of man, of God, of good and evil, of immortality, and so on, and to transform *metaphysics* into *metapsychology.*
>
> (pp. 258–259)

In other words, for Freud, the development of metapsychology, as a psychology of the unconscious, was indissolubly linked to the liquidation of religious beliefs. In this, he conflates two things that do not necessarily come together: the exploration of the consequences of the introduction of the hypothesis of the unconscious and the philosophical and ideological project of an atheist, a true child of the Illustration, who was firmly convinced that the illusions of religion should be finally dispelled and replaced by the certainties of science.

Although this is essential to his conception of the world and of the human being, we can still discuss whether it is pertinent to the construction of the theory of psychoanalysis, or not. No psychoanalyst would question the compelling need to develop an integral psychological theory that included as a central element the concept of the unconscious, but many of them, whose thinking was based on a set of assumptions that differed from Freud's, would take exception to a proposal that subordinated psychoanalysis to a philosophical view not shared by all psychoanalysts.

These differences in their respective conceptions of the world, which are necessarily previous to their first contact with psychoanalysis, also determine major consequences for the conception and understanding of the psychoanalytic theory, technique, and clinic. One clear instance of this are the striking differences in thought and practice between Freud – who called himself 'an infidel Jew' (Freud, 1928a, p. 170) – and the members of the British Independent Group of Object Relations Theory – like Winnicott, who was a Methodist, and Fairbairn, a member of the Church of Scotland – who were all reared in the Christian tradition.

Consequently, leaving aside the project of demolishing mythology and religion, what actual contributions to psychoanalysis can we find in this text? In the first three essays – 'The horror of incest', 'Taboo and emotional ambivalence', and 'Animism, magic and the omnipotence of thought' – the author presents a painstaking review of the anthropological and historical literature on these subjects, available at the time. Nonetheless, psychoanalysis is already entering the stage when he compares the beliefs and practices of 'primitive' – that is, non-European – peoples with the unconsciously determined attitudes and feelings that emerge in everyday life. For instance, when he compares the traditionally conflictive relation that ensues between a married man and his mother-in-law, with the incest taboo, by applying the theory of the Oedipus complex, conceived as 'the nuclear complex of neurosis' (Freud, 1912–1913, pp. 14–17).

Always within the scope of the already known psychoanalytic concepts, he applies the concept of projection to the understanding of animism and the taboo of the dead (pp. 62–63). He thus starts a comparison between the phenomena of magic, myth, and religion, on the one hand, and those of psychopathology, on the other, which can be observed in the clinic. Thus, taboo can be connected with the mental processes of phobias and paranoia, and magical thinking with obsessional neurosis. Indeed, the very concept of the 'omnipotence of thoughts' was suggested to Freud by his obsessional patient, whom we usually call the 'Rat Man' (pp. 85–88).

However, the author's enquiry goes far beyond the mere unmodified application of pre-existing psychoanalytic knowledge and theories to a non-clinical field, since it uses the comparison between the two sets of phenomena to further develop the theory.[5] For instance, the analogy between taboos and the mental processes of the obsessional neurosis leads him to clarify the origins of moral conscience, relating it to ambivalence,

> Thus it seems probable that conscience too arose, on a basis of emotional ambivalence, from quite specific human relations to which this ambivalence

was attached; and that it arose under the conditions which we have shown to apply in the case of taboo and of obsessional neurosis – namely, that one of the opposing feelings involved shall be unconscious and kept under repression by the compulsive domination of the other one.

(p. 68)

But the real theoretical innovation comes in the fourth essay, called 'The return of totemism in childhood'. Here, he compares the primitive's relation with the totem with that between a child and animals. He bases this argument on his own case history of 'Little Hans' (Freud, 1909b), with his phobia of horses, and on Ferenczi's (1913b) case of five-year-old Arpad, with his ambivalent identification with the cock that had bit his penis, when he was two and a half years old (Freud, 1912–1913, pp. 126–132).

Starting from these observations, coming from the two quite different fields of anthropology and the clinic, Freud develops a striking historical fantasy, in which he postulates the existence of a primeval horde, ruled by a primitive and tyrannical father, who monopolised all the women in the clan and relegated his sons to an imposed homosexuality. The band of brothers would have rebelled against their father, killing him and devouring his corpse. This put an end to the *patriarchal horde*, to be replaced by the *fraternal clan*, in which the brothers relinquish having sex with women of their own group, in order to avoid the repetition of that tragic conflict. This original story, which would have ever since survived in the unconscious of the peoples, is the origin of social structure, the incest taboo, and the practice of exogamy. It is recalled, in a disguised form, through totemism and the totem feast, in which the sacred animal that represents the murdered father is sacrificed to the god, which corresponds to the preserved spirit of the Father, and is incorporated by eating it, the most recent derivative of this ritual being the Christian Eucharist.

This is a paradigmatic example of that theory-building strategy he called 'fantasising' (*Phantasieren*), which we have already discussed in Chapter 1 and is clearly described as follows in his letter to Wilhelm Fliess of May 25, 1895:

During the past weeks I have devoted every free minute to such work; have spent the hours of the night from eleven to two with such *fantasizing, interpreting, and guessing*, and invariably stopped only when somewhere I came up against an absurdity or when I actually and seriously overworked, so that I had no interest left in my daily medical activities. It will still be a long time before you can ask me about results.

(Freud, 1895, p. 129, my italics)

This heuristic procedure begets daring speculations, framed as a dramatic narrative that enlightens, analogically, various aspects of the problematic that is being clarified. Interestingly enough, myths seem to have fulfilled the same function in the development of collective thought. Bion (1962) says, 'In the group the myth has some claim to be regarded as filling the same role in the society as the model has in scientific work of the individual' (p. 69). Hence, myth may be considered as a highly complex holistic theory, stated in a narrative form, in order to preserve the interrelation and mutual determination of the various elements, which is destroyed by the linearity of conventional thought,

> The myth by virtue of its narrative form binds the various components in the story in a manner analogous to the fixation of the elements of a scientific deductive system by their inclusion in the system: it is similar to the fixation of the elements in the corresponding algebraic calculus where that exists. No element, such as the sexual element, can be comprehended save in its relationship with other elements.
>
> (Bion, 1963, p. 45)

Hence, he points out that, in Freud's use of the Oedipus myth, the sexual component should not be extracted from its relation with the other elements in the narrative, such as

> the determination with which Oedipus pursues his inquiry into the crime despite the warnings of Tiresias. It is consequently not possible to isolate the sexual component, or any other, without distortion. Sex, in the Oedipal situation, has a quality that can only be described by the implications conferred on it by its inclusion in the story. If it is removed from the story it loses its quality unless its meaning is preserved by an express reservation that 'sex' is a term used to represent sex as it is experienced in the context of the myth. The same is true of all other elements that lend themselves to abstraction from the myth.
>
> (pp. 45–46)

It is certainly ironical that Freud, who wanted to do away with myths, should be forced by his material to create a new scientific myth in order to clarify social and cultural phenomena.

Beyond the problem of the veracity of its alleged historical truth, Freud's myth of the original parricide clarifies and allows us to comprehend some universal fantasies that underlie collective living, which have been clearly observed and analysed by those of us who work analytically with groups (Tubert-Oklander & Hernández de Tubert, 2004).

In the final pages of this essay, anticipating a possible objection to his analysis, Freud introduces the following methodological reflection:

> No one can have failed to observe, in the first place, that *I have taken as the basis of my whole position the existence of a collective mind, in which mental processes occur just as they do in the mind of an individual.* In particular, I have supposed that the sense of guilt for an action has persisted for many thousands of years and has remained operative in generations which can have

had no knowledge of that action. I have supposed that an emotional process, such as might have developed in generations of sons who were ill-treated by their father, has extended to new generations which were exempt from such treatment for the very reason that their father had been eliminated. It must be admitted that these are grave difficulties; and any explanation that could avoid presumptions of such a kind would seem to be preferable.

(Freud, 1912–1913, pp. 157–158, my italics)

However, he immediately affirms that it is not possible to dispense with such conjecture, based on the following argument:

Without the assumption of a collective mind, which makes it possible to neglect the interruptions of mental acts caused by the extinction of the individual, social psychology in general cannot exist. Unless psychical processes were continued from one generation to another, if each generation were obliged to acquire its attitude to life anew, there would be no progress in this field and next to no development.

(p. 158)

As to the mechanism for transmission of this knowledge, Freud considers two possibilities. On the one hand, sticking to the Lamarckian hypothesis (which he never abandoned) of the inheritance of acquired characters, he does not discard the possibility of 'the inheritance of psychical dispositions which, however, need to be given some sort of impetus in the life of the individual before they can be roused into actual operation' (p. 158), but he then turns to a much more convincing psychological hypothesis,

The problem would seem even more difficult if we had to admit that mental impulses could be so completely suppressed as to leave no trace whatever behind them. But that is not the case. Even the most ruthless suppression must leave room for distorted surrogate impulses and for reactions resulting from them. If so, however, we may safely assume that no generation is able to conceal any of its more important mental processes from its successor. For psycho-analysis has shown us that everyone possesses in his unconscious mental activity an apparatus which enables him to interpret other people's reactions, that is, to undo the distortions which other people have imposed on the expression of their feelings. An unconscious understanding such as this of all the customs, ceremonies and dogmas left behind by the original relation to the father may have made it possible for later generations to take over their heritage of emotion.

(pp. 158–159)

With these observations, Freud anticipates the current development of the theory of transgenerational transmission of trauma (Kaës et al., 1993; Hernández de

Tubert, 1996, 1999a). But he also suggests, without further developing its implications, a new theoretical problem, that of collective mental processes.

In the beginning, the concept of the unconscious had a distinctive functionalist character, which presented it as a sort of internal organ, a part of the individual's psychic apparatus (Tubert-Oklander, 2004c). But in the preceding quotations the unconscious appears as a hidden and unknown dimension of that set of collective mental process that Freud calls the 'collective mind' (*Massenpsyche*). This forces us to abandon, in the study of the unconscious, any reference to the nervous system or an imaginary 'mental apparatus' and transcend the limits of the individual, in order to tackle the study of collective mental processes.[6] Such task would require a thorough revision of metapsychology, originally framed in terms of the individual paradigm, which has not yet been carried out (Hernández de Tubert & Tubert-Oklander, 2005; Tubert-Oklander, 2019c [Chapter 15]).

Group Psychology and the Analysis of the Ego (1921c)

Even if this is usually considered Freud's main writing about social psychology, paradoxically there is very little to be found in it about the investigation of collective mental processes. This is due to the fact that here he studies collective phenomena mainly from the standpoint of the individual. In this, the author identifies with one of the two great traditions in social psychology. The first one consists in studying the transformations induced in the individual psyche whenever a person is placed in a collective situation. In this conception, individuality is the primary form of human existence, and groups and other collective entities somehow distort it. The second, on the other hand, corresponds to the study of collective processes – inter- and trans-personal – that become apparent when people get together and relate (Olmsted, 1959). This view is usually focused on the primary social nature of the human being, so that collective processes are seen as prior to the emergence of the individual. Freud's enquiry in this text is clearly placed in the first of these two stances, as can be seen in the following quote:

> The contrast between individual psychology and social or group psychology, which at a first glance may seem to be full of significance, loses a great deal of its sharpness when it is examined more closely. It is true that individual psychology is concerned with the individual man and explores the paths by which he seeks to find satisfaction for his instinctual impulses; but only rarely and under certain exceptional conditions is individual psychology in a position to disregard the relations of this individual to others. In the individual's mental life someone else is invariably involved, as a model, as an object, as a helper, as an opponent; and so from the very first individual psychology, in this extended but entirely justifiable sense of the words, is at the same time social psychology as well.
>
> (Freud, 1921c, p. 69)

What Freud is saying here is that psychology – and, consequently, psychoanalysis – is always necessarily *relational*, and this he calls 'social'. A subject's relations with her parents and siblings, with her love object, and with her doctor are, for Freud, social phenomena, which are opposed to narcissistic phenomena. Hence,

> Group psychology is therefore concerned with the individual man as a member of a race, of a nation, of a caste, of a profession, of an institution, or as a component part of a crowd of people who have been organized into a group at some particular time for some definite purpose.
>
> (p. 70)

Given such a starting point, it is not surprising that this piece of work has contributed much more to individual psychology than to collective and social psychology. Nevertheless, its contributions to the study of object relations and identification make it one of the major theoretical texts of psychoanalysis.

This particular orientation may be due to two reasons. The first one is that Freud never worked clinically with groups, so that he did not have the opportunity to enquire directly the unconscious aspect of collective processes. His main sources, in this field, were everyday experiences and the study of the literature that was available at the time. The second is that the point of departure of his analysis in this text is Gustave Le Bon's (1895) *Psychologie des foules*, unfortunately translated into English as *The Crowd: A Study of the Popular Mind*. This author was fundamentally interested in the loss of the higher psychological functions suffered by individuals when they are part of a crowd. Here some issues of translation are worth mentioning. The word used in the original title, *foule*, may certainly be translated as 'crowd', but it also means 'mob', with all its derogatory connotations, and even 'the mob', referring to ordinary people. In French *la foule* (the mob), used to refer to the uncouth lower classes, is opposed to *l'élite* (the elite), that is, a select, refined, and allegedly superior stratum of society.

Freud translated this term with the more neutral German word *Massenpsychologie*, which is equivalent to 'collective psychology', but he retained the conservative ideological underpinning of Le Bon's work, which was very similar to his own prejudices.[7] For those of us who have to read Freud in English, James Strachey further confused the issue when he systematically translated *Masse* as 'group', and substituting 'group' for 'crowd' even in the extracts from the English translation of Le Bon.

Be it as it may, the first problem Freud deals with in this text is that of the loss of intellectual and cognitive functions, and the predominance of affectivity in a crowd. His answer is that this is due to regression. On the other hand, even though he also studies the ideas of other authors, such as William McDougall (1920), who, in his book *The Group Mind*, speaks of 'organised groups' that no longer show the characteristics of an unorganised crowd, he interprets this as an attempt 'to procure for the group precisely those features which were characteristic of the individual and which are extinguished in him by the formation of the group'

(Freud, 1921c, p. 86) Hence, he maintains his assumption that all the higher mental functions necessarily belong to the individual and that the 'group mind' is primitive and irrational.

However, he does provide a valuable interpretation of the nature of institutions (McDougall's 'organised groups'), which he calls 'artificial masses', taking as his paradigmatic examples the church and the army. His hypothesis is that these crowds are organised by means of the identification with a leader (Christ in the case of the church and a general or commander in that of the army), on which all the members of the group project their ego ideal. This is indeed the first description of that mechanism that would be later called 'projective identification' (Klein, 1946).

This description of leadership, conceived from the perspective of the individual's internal processes, may be complemented by a collective vision, if we assume, like Bion (1961), that these institutions express, contain, and profit from the driving force of certain universal fantasies of human groups, which he calls 'basic assumptions' (abbreviated 'ba'). These are the fantasy that the group members have joined in order to depend from an all-mighty leader who will fulfil all their needs (the 'ba dependence', which is predominant in the church), or to follow a daring leader in fight or flight when facing an external menace (the 'ba fight-flight', which shapes the army). To these two, he adds a third basic assumption, called 'ba pairing', by which the group shares the fantasy that they have come together to witness the mating of a subgroup, or couple, that will give birth to a Messiah, who will respond to all their needs. The corresponding institution is aristocracy.

Although Bion derived these ideas from his analytic clinical work with groups, their origin can be traced to this work by Freud.

In the rest of the text, Freud masterfully articulates a series of observations about suggestion, hypnosis, falling in love, and the establishment of the ego ideal. He clearly affirms that the formation of human groups is based on the libidinal bond among its members and resumes his narrative of the original parricide, pointing out that human institutions are derived from the measures taken by the brotherly horde, in order to avoid a repetition of the tragedy: 'Thus the group [*Masse*, in the original German text] appears to us as a revival of the primal horde' (Freud, 1921c, p. 123). In sum, the key moment in the psychic development of Humankind was the passage from collective life to individual existence, and any move towards collectivisation can only be understood as a regression and a degradation of psychic life. Obviously, it is possible to interpret this particular conception as being, at least in part, an expression of the author's conservative ideology, which was much similar to Le Bon's. But, be it as it may, there is no doubt that this was an assumption of his prior to any psychoanalytic study of the problem.

The Future of an Illusion (1927c)

This is, perhaps, among Freud's social writings, the one that has contributed less to the development of metapsychology. This is due to two reasons. First, as the author himself points out, a large part of his argument is nothing new, since it reproduces most of the criticisms of religion that have become commonplace since the Enlightenment. Second, because, even when he adds the particular point of view provided by psychoanalysis, he only uses a series of already known concepts as a basis for his main argument, instead of formulating new ones. Hence, this is only a work of applied psychoanalysis, rather than a piece of psychoanalytic research.

The image of human beings he puts forward is quite disheartening: 'men are not spontaneously fond of work and . . . arguments are of no avail against their passions' (p. 8), so that institutions and cultural norms can only be imposed by coercive measures, since 'every civilization rests on a compulsion to work and a renunciation of instinct' (p. 9).

This is, of course, the moral contained in the myth of the Garden of Eden. But, in a non-religious context, Freud fully adheres to Thomas Hobbes's (1651) moral and political philosophy, which affirmed, in his *Leviathan*, that man, in his natural state, is 'solitary, poore, nasty, brutish, and short' (p. 186), so that he requires a strong sovereign to impose order and avoid a deadly war among human beings.

But we must bear in mind that these philosophical assumptions represent only one of the possible conceptions of the human condition – in other words, they constitute Hobbes's and Freud's *Lebensanschauung*. Side by side with this belief that there is an essential irreconcilable antagonism between the individual, always selfish and moved by primitive passions, and society, which demands his submission in order to ensure survival, there is a radically different and contrasting view, which is that of Jean Jacques Rousseau (1762). This philosopher believed that 'Man is born free, and everywhere he is in chains', and that this antagonism is generated by an inadequate and unjust society, since the human being has an essential need to relate and belong to a community, in order to attain and fully develop the human condition.[8]

Once again, we see how Freud's conception of the world and of the human being determines the way in which he approaches and understands the problems of existence and social life. Particularly, his unquestioned assumption that the happiness every human being strives for is the unrestricted gratification of his or her instinctual sexual and aggressive wishes, so that such happiness is impossible in practice and incompatible with social life, which is the requisite for survival. In his own words,

> We have spoken of the hostility to civilization which is produced by the pressure that civilization exercises, the renunciations of instinct which it demands. If one imagines its prohibitions lifted – if, then, one may take any woman one pleases as a sexual object, if one may without hesitation kill one's rival for her love or anyone else who stands in one's way, if, too, one can carry off any of the other man's belongings without asking leave – how splendid, what a string of satisfactions one's life would be! True, one soon comes across the first difficulty: everyone else has exactly the same wishes as I have and will treat me with no more consideration than I treat him. And

so in reality only one person could be made unrestrictedly happy by such a removal of the restrictions of civilization, and he would be a tyrant, a dictator, who had seized all the means to power. And even he would have every reason to wish that the others would observe at least one cultural commandment: 'thou shalt not kill'.

(Freud, 1927, p. 15)

We know, of course, that many thinkers and ordinary citizens share this point of view, but also that many others have an opposing view. One result of these differences are the political and ideological conflicts among groups that hold different projects for a same community and for Humankind. In this, Freud's position is quite clear, and he expresses it brilliantly and in a most powerful language.

Nonetheless, apart from the exposition of his philosophy, the author introduces some very interesting arguments, from the strictly psychoanalytic point of view. The unavoidable helplessness (*Hilflosigkeit*) that characterises the human condition vis-à-vis the dangers of a hostile world is very similar to that of a small child, so that adults, when facing the multiple threatening circumstances beyond their control, tend to seek an omnipotent father figure, as they did in their childhood, that may offer them protection and consolation, and tell them what to do. This is the origin of the idea of God.[9]

Religious ideas are, to Freud, mere *illusions*, that is, distortions of our perception of reality, that aim to fulfil our deepest and most intense wishes. The function of science is to do away with these illusions and replace them with a real knowledge. Only science can really comfort us, since it allows a greater dominion on reality and provides rational courses of action, which are to be preferred under any circumstance. In this, Freud appears as a staunch defender of the ideals of Modernity.

However, this argument may be called into question in terms of two possible counterarguments. First, even if be true that the idea of God is derived from the child's feeling of helplessness and the experience of being cared for by the parents, this does not solve the metaphysical problem of the existence or non-existence of God, since it may be argued that motherly love gives the child its first inkling of what she will later acknowledge as the concept of God. Second, although there is no doubt that the psychopathological phenomena involved in religious beliefs, described by Freud, indeed do occur, should we consider them to be the very essence of religion (as he does), or only as its pathology, a distortion similar to that which can affect all human activities and projects, including science and psychoanalysis?

Being an unwavering atheist, Freud does not even consider the first objection, but he deals with the second question at the beginning of his next book on the subject, in which he expounds his belief that religion is indeed a form of psychopathology that must be transcended.

Civilization and Its Discontents (1930a)

This is a much more complex book since, even though it picks up again his criticism of religious thinking, it also develops a deep examination of the philosophy of human existence and provides new essential elements for the construction of psychoanalytic theory. Here his analysis starts where he had left it at the end of his previous book, by discussing a comment on it made by his friend Romain Rolland, who felt that Freud had omitted to consider what he deemed to be the real source of religious feeling. This was Freud's account of Rolland's letter:

> One of these exceptional few [great men] calls himself my friend in his letters to me. I had sent him my small book that treats religion as an illusion, and he answered that he entirely agreed with my judgement upon religion, but that he was sorry I had not properly appreciated *the true source of religious sentiments*. This, he says, consists in a peculiar feeling, which he himself is never without, which he finds confirmed by many others, and which he may suppose is present in millions of people. *It is a feeling which he would like to call a sensation of 'eternity', a feeling as of something limitless, unbounded – as it were, 'oceanic'*. This feeling, he adds, is a purely subjective fact, not an article of faith; it brings with it no assurance of personal immortality, but it is the source of the religious energy which is seized upon by the various Churches and religious systems, directed by them into particular channels, and doubtless also exhausted by them. One may, he thinks, rightly call one-self religious on the ground of this oceanic feeling alone, even if one rejects every belief and every illusion.
>
> (p. 64, my italics)

Even though Freud cannot find in himself the slightest trace of such a feeling, he embarks on a deep study of its possible meaning, and describes it as 'a feeling of an indissoluble bond, of being one with the external world as a whole' (p. 65). Not having had this emotional experience himself, he tends to view as 'something rather in the nature of an intellectual perception, which is not, it is true, without an accompanying feeling-tone, but only such as would be present with any other act of thought of equal range'. However, he acknowledges that 'It is not easy to deal scientifically with feelings', and adds,

> From my own experience I could not convince myself of the primary nature of such a feeling. But this gives me no right to deny that it does in fact occur in other people. The only question is whether it is being correctly interpreted and whether it ought to be regarded as the *fons et origo* of the whole need for religion.
>
> (ibid.)

His approach to the problem consists in 'attempting to discover a psycho-analytic – that is, a genetic – explanation of such a feeling'.[10] His conclusion is that it represents the survival of a primitive organisation of experience, char-acteristic of 'an infant at the breast [who] does not as yet distinguish his ego from the external world as the source of the sensations flowing in upon him' (pp. 66–67).

The development of the subject-object differentiation, between self and the surrounding world, follows a long and complex process, which generates a new organisation of experience that will coexist with that other primary organisation during the whole lifespan. This is how he describes it:

> In this way, then, the ego detaches itself from the external world. Or, to put it more correctly, originally the ego includes everything, later it separates off an external world from itself. Our present ego-feeling is, therefore, only a shrunken residue of a much more inclusive – indeed, an all-embracing – feeling which corresponded to a more intimate bond between the ego and the world about it. If we may assume that there are many people in whose mental life this primary ego-feeling has persisted to a greater or less degree, it would exist in them side by side with the narrower and more sharply demarcated ego-feeling of maturity, like a kind of counterpart to it. In that case, the ideational contents appropriate to it would be precisely those of limitlessness and of a bond with the universe – the same ideas with which my friend elucidated the 'oceanic' feeling.
>
> (p. 68)

This penetrating analysis paves the way for a series of new perspectives in psychoanalytic theory, which were explored by authors such as Hans Loewald (1951), José Bleger (1967), Margaret Mahler (1968), Blanca Montevechio (1999, 2002), and Juan Tubert-Oklander (2004a, 2004b, 2014). All of them developed further Freud's idea that 'only in the mind is such a preservation of all the earlier stages alongside of the final form possible' (p. 71). However, the founder of psychoanalysis chose to restrict this conclusion in the case of the 'oceanic feeling', since it may pave the way to mysticism (or, as he frequently said, 'occultism'), which he rejected, even though, unsurprisingly, he felt a lifelong fascination with it. Consequently, he cautiously wrote that 'perhaps we ought to content ourselves with asserting that what is past in mental life may be preserved and is not necessarily destroyed' (ibid.), albeit he could not avoid acknowledging the fact that 'it is rather the rule than the exception for the past to be preserved in mental life' (p. 72)

Coming back to the subject of religion, he reaffirms his conviction that this feeling of unity with everything that is cannot have the necessary motivational force to be the basis for religion. In this, he follows his belief that only instinctual needs motivate human behaviour and experience,

> After all, a feeling can only be a source of energy if it is itself the expression of a strong need. The derivation of religious needs from the infant's helplessness and the longing for the father aroused by it seems to me incontrovertible, especially since the feeling is not simply prolonged from childhood days, but is permanently sustained by fear of the superior power of Fate. I cannot think of any need in childhood as strong as the need for a father's protection. Thus the part played by the oceanic feeling, which might seek something like the

restoration of limitless narcissism, is ousted from a place in the foreground. The origin of the religious attitude can be traced back in clear outlines as far as the feeling of infantile helplessness. [But then he adds] There may be something further behind that, but for the present it is wrapped in obscurity.

(p. 72)

Nonetheless, he later acknowledges that, in *The Future of an Illusion* (1927), he 'was concerned much less with the deepest sources of the religious feeling than with what the common man understands by his religion' and that this is 'the only religion which ought to bear that name' (Freud, 1930a, p. 74). (Here, he was summarily discarding the ideas of those philosophers 'who think they can rescue the God of religion by replacing him by an impersonal, shadowy and abstract principle' [ibid.].) We can, however, question this policy of studying only the more infantile, primitive, and even pathological versions of religion, in order to reach the conclusion that this demonstrates the unavoidable infantile, primitive, and pathological nature of all religion, this being an instance of the fallacy known as the 'straw man argument'. Theories and social practices can only be refuted by taking issue with their best examples, and not with their worst. Freud himself had to deal with this sort of fallacious attacks on psychoanalysis in his article 'The question of lay analysis' (1926e). Be it as it may, this corresponds to the discussion of Freud's philosophical position and social criticism, rather than to the contributions to psychoanalytic theory that may be found in this text.

Here, his basic theoretical assumption, which is the point of departure of his whole discussion, is that 'we assume quite generally that the motive force of all human activities is a striving towards the two confluent goals of utility and a yield of pleasure' (Freud, 1930a, p. 94). Hence, culture (*Kultur*, a term that Strachey mistranslated as 'civilisation')[11] should be at the service of both, even if it demands a partial renunciation of unrestricted pleasure, in order to attain survival and the necessary practical benefits.

The author then turns to discuss the consequences of his having introduced the concept of the duality of the primary drives – the Life and Death Drives. This work is indeed a further development of the ideas he introduced in *Beyond the Pleasure Principle* (Freud, 1920g).

The central element in this veritable theoretical revolution was the concept of the Death Drive, which generated much opposition from the psychoanalytic community, but Freud emphatically affirms it, when he writes,

To begin with it was only tentatively that I put forward the views I have developed here, but in the course of time they have gained such a hold upon me that I can no longer think in any other way.

(Freud, 1930a, p. 119)

The endless struggle between Eros and the Death Drive propels and shapes the cultural process, as well as the ontogenetic development and organic life in general.

In the social field, the Death Drive is expressed as 'a portion of the instinct [that] is diverted towards the external world and comes to light as an instinct of aggressiveness and destructiveness' (p. 119). This primary aggressiveness is the source of the essential opposition and threat towards social organisation and culture, since these are born from the erotic bond between the individuals and the pressure exerted by dire need,

> Eros and Ananke [Love and Necessity] have become the parents of human civilisation [*Kultur*] too. The first result of civilization was that even a fairly large number of people were now able to live together in a community. And since these two great powers were co-operating in this, one might expect that the further development of civilization would proceed smoothly towards an even better control over the external world and towards a further extension of the number of people included in the community.
>
> (p. 101)

But as society was unavoidably threatened by the instinctual aggression of its members, it had to develop a series of cultural means, such as religion, that aim to control it.[12]

From here he goes on to an ample discussion on the establishment of the super-ego and guilt feelings, which he interprets as a turning of these aggressive drives on oneself. This would justify his previous assertion that 'What is now holding sway in the super-ego is, as it were, a pure culture of the death instinct, and in fact it often enough succeeds in driving the ego into death' (Freud, 1923b, p. 53).

Freud's final conclusion reaffirms his Hobbesian point of departure that assumes the existence of an intrinsic opposition between the interests of the individual and those of the collectivity. This determines hostility towards civilisation (*Kultur*) and an insoluble conflict that generates that particular form of chronic malaise which he calls 'discontent in civilization'.

All this leads him to a novel question, which he cannot solve at the time. If we accept that there is an ample analogy between the development of culture and that of the individual, would it be valid to think that there is such thing as a pathology of cultures? In other words, would it be possible that a whole community, a nation, or even Humankind itself might lose their way and fall prey to solutions, beliefs, and practices that we might deem to be 'neurotic', 'perverse', or 'psychotic'? Freud does not take a position on this, but he reminds us that these are only analogies, and not full identities, between two fields of human existence, so that not all the properties of one of them would necessarily have an equivalent in the other. Besides, in the case of the individual, pathology can be identified by contrast with the situation of most people in the environment, which is assumed to be 'normal', and we have no such element of comparison in the case of social pathology, so that this standard should be sought elsewhere – that is, in an ideological critique of culture and society, which he clearly feels to be beyond the scope of an objective science as psychoanalysis.[13] Nonetheless, he opens the possibility that someone else might do it in the future, a task he himself would later initiate in *Moses and Monotheism* (Freud, 1939a).

The Question of a *Weltanschauung* (1933a)[14]

This is not one of Freud's major social writings, since it does not add much to what he has already said, but it is worth mentioning because it deals with a concept we have frequently referred to, which is that of the Conception of the World (*Weltanschauung*).[15] Here, he defines it in the following terms:

> '*Weltanschauung*' is . . . a specifically German concept, the translation of which into foreign languages might well raise difficulties. . . . In my opinion, . . . a *Weltanschauung* is an intellectual construction which solves all the problems of our existence uniformly on the basis of one overriding hypothesis, which, accordingly, leaves no question unanswered and in which everything that interests us finds its fixed place. It will easily be understood that the possession of a *Weltanschauung* of this kind is among the ideal wishes of human beings. Believing in it one can feel secure in life, one can know what to strive for, and how one can deal most expediently with one's emotions and interests.
>
> (p. 158)

Obviously, this extensive explanation of the world, as a comprehensive, rational, and conscious system, strikingly differs from that real, concrete, and mostly unconscious psychological structure, to be found in every human being, which we have been using in this and the previous chapters. But it is on the basis of this definition, which could be applied to Hegel's system of philosophy or a religious theology, that Freud emphatically affirms that psychoanalysis '[being] a specialist science, a branch of psychology – a depth-psychology or psychology of the unconscious – . . . is quite unfit to construct a *Weltanschauung* of its own: it must accept the scientific one' (p. 158). For him, the latter is the only acceptable conception of the world and 'of the three powers which may dispute the basic position of science [as the only valid source of knowledge – art, philosophy, and religion], religion alone is to be taken seriously as an enemy' (p. 160).

The rest of this lecture intends to systematically refute religion, in terms akin to those of *The Future of an Illusion* (1927). Religion is an intermediate phase in the evolution of Humankind, between animism and real knowledge, which must be fully overcome by science, which is necessarily at war with it.

In the final part of this text, he contrasts the scientific conception of the world with two others: one that denies the existence of a single truth – which he calls 'anarchism' and we would nowadays call 'Postmodernism' – and that of Marxism, which he had started to question in *Civilization and Its Discontents* (Freud, 1930a). Here, he acknowledges that the latter has made a contribution by taking into account the influence of the economy on social processes but criticises it for ignoring both the psychological dimension and the cultural process. He then adds the suggestion of a possible integration of the various factors and writes,

> If anyone were in a position to show in detail the way in which these different factors – the general inherited human disposition, its racial variations and its cultural transformations – inhibit and promote one another under the conditions of social rank, profession and earning capacity – if anyone were able to do this, he would have supplemented Marxism so that it was made into a genuine social science.
>
> (p. 179)

But then he adds an astonishing conclusion,

> For sociology too, dealing as it does with the behaviour of people in society, cannot be anything but applied psychology. Strictly speaking there are only two sciences: psychology, pure and applied, and natural science.
>
> (ibid.)

Such a statement would indeed be true if we used the term 'psychology' to refer to that ample set of enquires and theories that Wilhelm Dilthey (1883) called the 'Sciences of the Spirit' (*Geisteswissenschaften*) – that is, the Human Sciences – but it is more likely that, in the context of Freud's thought, it referred to his unwavering conviction that there are only two ontological realities: the material world and subjective experience. Nonetheless, in his last social writing, *Moses and Monotheism* (1939a), he would explore a much wider dimension of this problem.

Moses and Monotheism: Three Essays (1939a)

This is, perhaps, the most important of Freud's social writings and the culmination of that momentous enquiry that began in 1912 with *Totem and Taboo*. Here, he carries out with a perceptive and profound study of *cultural evolution* (*Kulturentwicklung* – 'cultural development', which Strachey translated as 'evolution of civilisation'), understood as a collective mental process, which is so analogous to the psychological evolution of the individual that they can be conceived as just two aspects of one and the same reality.[16]

Written between 1934 and 1938, this book has an irregular and repetitive structure, which reflects the many misgivings and doubts the author had about publishing it, for fear of suffering repudiation and persecution in his native Austria. Only on his arrival in Britain he finally decided to do it.

The first two essays, called 'Moses an Egyptian' and 'If Moses was an Egyptian', which he had already published separately, constitute a masterful exercise in the interpretation of texts, and a powerful argument in favour of the contention that psychoanalysis is a hermeneutic science (Tubert-Oklander & Beuchot Puente, 2008). Even though there are not many references to psychoanalysis, his whole enquiry of the history of Moses and the inception of the monotheistic religion is truly a paradigmatic example of psychoanalytic thinking. Here, Freud tackles the analysis of the history of the Jewish people in the very same way in which he questions, interprets, and reconstructs a patient's personal history, transcending all his omissions, suppressions, and distortions.

In sum, his argument is as follows. The first recorded monotheistic religion was born in Egypt. It was the cult of Aton, the sun god of the young pharaoh Akhenaton, who carried out a veritable cultural revolution in his empire. When he died, the reaction of the priests and the faithful of the previous polytheistic religion restored the old gods and erased any reference to or record of the existence of this new religion. Moses was really an educated Egyptian – a priest and/or a nobleman – who joined the Jewish people, took them out of Egypt, and imposed on them a religion, an ethics, and the practice of circumcision. The primitive and uneducated Hebrews finally rebelled against and killed him, but a group his followers, which constituted the tribe of the Levites, preserved his tradition.

Two or three generations later, having the Jewish tribes incorporated the cult of Yahweh, a cruel volcanic god, there was a meeting, in an oasis called Meribah-Kadesh, between the followers of Moses and the priests of Yahweh, in which it was decided that the people would accept this new religion, but fusing it with the previous tradition of Moses. To that end, the new cult was projected onto the past and attributed to the patriarchs of Israel; Moses was defined as Yahweh's emissary and this new god was transformed by assigning to Him the unique and abstract characteristic of the deity proposed by Moses. And all the memories of the magnicide were erased.

Even though the validity of this historical reconstruction will ultimately depend on the confirmatory or falsifying elements provided by expert historians, one can only be impressed by the way in which Freud interprets his material and the power of conviction of the conclusions he builds from its psychological verisimilitude.

The third essay, called 'Moses, his people and monotheistic religion', was the main source of his doubts about publishing the book, since it openly engaged in an analysis of the Christian religion, in terms that could not fail to antagonise both the Church and many believers. The argument he here develops is extremely complex and would deserve a study on its own. Now I shall only highlight those aspects that represent developments in the psychoanalytic enquiry and theory.

The first point to be mentioned is methodological: *this whole enquiry is based on analogy*. Freud compares here the historical and cultural process of the Jewish people and their religion with the ontogenetic development of the individual. The key concept is that of the *latency period*. In the case of history, this is represented by the generation during which the Mosaic religion was forgotten, before its resurgence at the Kadesh meeting; in that of child development, it is the latency of sexuality, until it flourishes again in puberty. From this comparison emerges a new theory of the processes of human mental development.

In the child, the memory of the previous sexual experiences, which has been forgotten (repressed) during latency, persists in the unconscious. In the case of peoples, the suppressed fragments of history are preserved in a *tradition*, which is in sharp contrast with the official version of that story, whether written or oral. The myths of religion contain, just like the delusions of an individual, a kernel of truth, and they are an expression of the general principle of the *return of the repressed*. The Christian myth of the death of the Son, who is also God the Father, re-signifies the historical truth of the primeval parricide, which was later reissued in the murder of Moses.

Here, Freud introduces, once again, the psychoanalytic myth of the original parricide from *Totem and Taboo* (1912–1913), but in a more detailed version and clarifying some of its more obscure aspects. He acknowledges that the story he tells has been distorted by the unavoidable major condensation, into a single episode, of a lengthy process that really took thousands of years and required a great many iterations before being internalised. Then, he questions again how could the knowledge of this historical truth be transmitted. Unlike what he had suggested in *Totem and Taboo*, he now turns to the Lamarckian hypothesis of the inheritance of acquired characters. His rationale for this is his belief that an information acquired through communication could ill have such a deep and powerful effect on human beings, since they could always either accept it or criticise it and reject it.

But this argument is based only on conscious communication and ignores the possibility of an unconscious transmission. Besides, in his first formulation of 1913, he had suggested that all cultural products and practices have latent meanings – that is, unconscious – that spoke directly to the individual unconscious. Perhaps in this his thought was restricted by his firm belief that the only ontological realities were the material and the individual subjective realities, which led him to deny the reality of social processes and the symbolic systems that constitute culture, which he saw as a by-product of psychological, and ultimately biological, processes, in spite of the fact that all his analysis in this book may be seen as an implicit affirmation of their existence.[17]

Finally, although Freud does not explicitly return here to the question of social pathologies, his evolutive conception of the social process clearly implies that, for him, not all social organisations are equally valid. Some of them can only be accepted as an intermediate phase in the evolution towards a particular development which he deems to be superior and desirable. Some critics have attributed this view to a Eurocentric prejudice, but, whether one shares or not his conception of what would be a better society and culture, the idea remains that perhaps not all social systems may be equally valid, in terms of ensuring human survival, development, and happiness. But disagreements in such evaluations are the basis of political and ideological struggles, so that there is no way in which social research may ever be value-free. Of course, Freud would not have accepted this statement, which conflicts with his epistemological persuasion.

Conclusions

In all the texts I have just discussed, Freud carries out simultaneously several tasks, which should nonetheless be conceptually discriminated. These are:

1   An exposition of his own conception of the human being and the world, in a series of brilliant essays that constitute a major contribution to the discussion of the most significant controversies about philosophy, social life, and politics
2   The application of the discoveries and theories of psychoanalysis, derived from his clinical research, to the particular case of social problems, in an attempt to attain a different and wider understanding of them
3   The comparative study, through analogy, of the mental processes and functioning of the individual, and those of the historic and cultural evolution of the peoples, which leads him to novel conclusions that enrich and widen the previous discoveries in both fields
4   The formulation of new metapsychological concepts and the revision and updating of the old ones, in order to attain a higher level of abstraction that incorporates and accounts for these new findings

Hence, Freud's social writings, minimised by some as mere exercises in the application of the findings of 'true' (clinical) psychoanalysis, are truly a most important chapter in the development of the Freudian enquiry and the evolution of psychoanalytic theory. Hence, they require a serious and painstaking critical study, in order to identify their underlying assumptions and extract their theoretical and practical consequences, in the light of later and contemporary research, experiences, and concepts.

Notes

1 This concept is further discussed in Appendix II.
2 The term 'ethos' refers to 'The characteristic spirit of a culture, era, or community as manifested in its attitudes and aspirations' (OED), so that it would be a part of what I prefer to call its *Weltanschauung*.
3 See Chapter 1.
4 As we have seen in Chapter 1, Mauricio Beuchot (1985), in his meticulous study of Freud's 1895 (1950a) *Project*, posed that this long unpublished text, which was the template for his later metapsychology, could (and should) be read in two quite different ways: one of them *literal* (metonymic), as a quasi-neurophysiological theory of mind, and the other *allegorical* (metaphorical), as a mythical description of some most abstract mental processes.
5 Aaron H. Esman (1998) has argued, in his paper 'What is "applied" in "applied" psychoanalysis?', against the alleged opposition between 'true' (clinical) and 'applied' psychoanalysis, which is based on the assumption that new psychoanalytic knowledge can only come from the clinic, and that the analysis of social and cultural phenomena is a mere unmodified 'application' of pre-existing theories. On the contrary, he claims that

> such 'applications' were integral to the early development of the field and that, indeed, many of Freud's basic ideas were derived from non-clinical (i.e., cultural) sources. The continuing impact of cultural forces on clinical concepts can be seen in the recent reformulations of our views on the psychology of women. Psychoanalysis is to be seen, therefore, as a constantly evolving system of propositions and hypotheses that are capable of 'application' and study in both clinical and extra-clinical settings.
>
> (p. 741)

6 Of course, this argument would not be accepted by many colleagues. French analysts, for instance, who tend to think that no argument is truly psychoanalytic unless it is formulated in the language of Freudian metapsychology, would certainly take exception to it. René Kaës (1976), for instance, has proposed the concept of a 'group mental apparatus' in order to explain group mental processes. But we do not consider this approach to be fruitful, but rather an attempt to 'put new wine into old wineskins' (Mark 2:22).

7 Freud's disparaging view of the lower classes, which was already explicit, is his letter to his fiancée Marta Barnays, of August 29, 1883 (Freud, 1883), when he was only twenty-seven years old, reappeared, basically unmodified, in the ideological position exposed in *Civilization and Its Discontents* (Freud, 1930a), forty-seven years after. This is extensively discussed in Chapter 6.

8 A similar view can be found, of course, in other thinkers, such as Aristotle and Carl Marx, and in the writings of group analysts and relational psychoanalysts.

9 But this helplessness of the newborn baby is clearly compensated by a food-enough maternal care. And, since this is the physiologic average expected environment, one can rightly say that, whenever a baby experiences a dire feeling of helplessness, this is already a traumatic – i.e., pathological – situation, on account of a deficiency in maternal care. Freud (1911b) seems to have been aware of this, as he wrote, in 'Formulations on the Two Principles of Mental Functioning', that

> It will rightly be objected that an organization which was a slave to the pleasure principle and neglected the reality of the external world could not maintain itself alive for the shortest time, so that it could not have come into existence at all. The employment of a fiction like this is, however, justified when one considers that *the infant – provided one includes with it the care it receives from its mother – does almost realize a psychical system of this kind.*
>
> (p. 219, note 4)

Winnicott's famous phrase 'There is no such thing as an infant' obviously referred to this problem. This he uttered spontaneously during a discussion in 1940, and only much later connected this with this observation made, in passing, by Freud:

> I once said: 'There is no such thing as an infant', meaning, of course, that whenever one finds an infant one finds maternal care, and without maternal care there would be no infant. (Discussion at a Scientific Meeting of the British Psycho-Analytical Society, circa 1940.) Was I influenced, without knowing it, by this footnote of Freud's?
>
> (Winnicott, 1960a, p. 39, note 1)

Hence, if we were to reframe Freud's argument in contemporary psychoanalytical terms, we should say that the idea of God is derived from a maternal, not a paternal, image.

10 Here we are faced once again with Freud's epistemological assumption that scientific knowledge must necessarily be framed in terms of causal explanations. This probably accounts for his difficulty in studying feelings, which can only be understood in phenomenological – i.e., experiential – terms. Hence his misunderstanding of Romain Rolland's argument.

11 For a thorough discussion about the conceptual differences between the German and English terms, see Norbert Elias's (1939) *The Civilizing Process*.

12 William Golding's (1954) novel, *Lord of the Flies*, which describes how a group of English boys cast away on a desert island revert into savagery, violence, and homicide, illustrates his philosophy, which is very similar to Freud's. But the Dutch historian Rutger C. Bregman (2020b) has found and studied the real-life case of six boys who

survived for fifteen months on a desert island and cooperated, avoided quarrels, and took care of each other. This illustrates and upholds his more benign view of human nature (Bregman, 2020a) – Aristotle or Rousseau, not Hobbes – which is quite opposite to Golding's or Freud's.

13 The full quotation is as follows:

> Moreover, the diagnosis of communal neuroses is faced with a special difficulty. In an individual neurosis we take as our starting point the contrast that distinguishes the patient from his environment, which is assumed to be 'normal'. For a group all of whose members are affected by one and the same disorder no such background could exist; it would have to be found elsewhere.
>
> (Freud, 1930a, p. 144)

Of course, the diagnostic criterion based on identifying 'healthy' with normal is open to criticism. If we believe that the individual illness is somehow related to social pathology, we cannot dispense with a value-laden criticism of society and culture. This is a task I attempted in a paper called 'The politics of the despair' (Hernández-Tubert, 2011a [Chapter 12]).

14 This text is actually a chapter of a book, Conference XXXV of *New Introductory Lectures to Psycho-Analysis* (pp. 158–182), but the reference in the Freud Bibliography of the *Standard Edition* refers only to the whole book.

15 See Appendix II.

16 We should bear in mind that, from his reductionistic point of view, Freud actually believed that the cultural process (*Kulturprozeß* – 'process of civilisation' in the *Standard Edition*), was an organic process, indistinguishable from that of Darwinian evolution. See the Editor's Introduction to *Civilization and Its Discontents* (Strachey, 1961).

17 The Austrian-born British philosopher Karl Raimund Popper (1972) considered human knowledge to be objective, both in that it is objectively true and in having an existence of its own, as an object, independently from the thinking subject that generated it. For him, the human mind secretes the symbolic systems of knowledge, just as the spider weaves its web, which persists long after it has left or died. Hence, he postulates, in his 1972 book *Objective Knowledge: An Evolutionary Approach*, the existence of three worlds – i.e., three ontological categories. *World One* is the material world of physical states, which is studied by the natural sciences. *World Two* is the world of mind, or mental states, ideas, and perceptions, studied by psychology. And *World Three* being the body of human knowledge, in its many expressions, such as books, papers, paintings, music pieces, and all the products of the human mind. This Third World has an existence and evolution in itself, quite independent of the knowing subjects. Now, Popper only considered the products of cognitive functions and their material registers, but if we add other mental functions, such as emotions, actions, communications, and relations, we can include in the Third World culture, tradition, language, and values, which exist and evolve independently, not only of subjects, but also of any material substratum. These are the unacknowledged implications of Freud's concept of cultural evolution.

Chapter 6

The work of culture (*Kulturarbeit*) in Freud (2012)

Reyna Hernández-Tubert

*On December 2011, I was asked to write a commentary for a presentation to be made in February 2012 of a paper by Erik Smadja (2012), a French psychoanalyst, in a scientific meeting of the Mexican Psychoanalytic Association. The paper was called 'The notion of **Kulturarbeit** (the work of culture) in Freud's writings', of which a previous shorter version had been published in English, in **Psychoanalysis, Culture & Society** (Smadja, 2008). The contrast between his paper and mine and the subsequent discussion, in which both authors of this book participated, clearly showed both our agreements and our differences. Smadja is both a psychoanalyst and an anthropologist, so we basically agreed on the importance of the socio-cultural dimension, but he interpreted this, as most French analysts regularly do, in terms of Freudian metapsychology, while we are stern critics of this theoretical approach and language. Nonetheless, this encounter gave us an opportunity to clarify our own understanding of this problematics. I am here reproducing this paper as it was read, with a few minor annotations (Hernández-Tubert, 2012).*

The author's purpose

First of all, I would like to congratulate Dr Eric Smadja for a most interesting and thought-provoking piece of writing, whose reading has nurtured my own thinking, in a fruitful dialogue with the author, which I sincerely hope may continue in the future.

I shall start by analysing the nature of the text he has now shared with us, before turning to its contents.

Smadja's explicit intention in writing this paper is to identify and interpret a conceptual line in Freud's thought on the relations between individuals and society, as it emerges from his social writings. This is provided by Freud's concept of *Kulturarbeit*, which has been translated into English as 'the work of civilization' or 'cultural activities' – terms that do not adequately convey the full meaning of the original German term, as we shall see. I have therefore chosen to refer to it as 'the work of culture'.

DOI: 10.4324/9780429055287-8

The author frames his basic hypothesis in the following terms:

> We suggest the hypothesis of a latent presence, as an ever-present filigree, of the *work of culture*, both in Freud's writings and in his mind. This notion is also to be discovered through its multiple contents, processes, functions, and meanings, scattered along the various texts.
>
> (Smadja, 2012)

This is therefore a hermeneutic and almost philological study of Freud's writings. Its main purpose is to establish what Freud really thought about the matter, rather than discussing the issues he was writing about. Such task demands that we define how are the texts going to be read, interpreted, and discussed.[1]

Hermeneutics is defined as the discipline that studies the theory and practice of the interpretation of texts. There are several parties of the interpretative act: the *author*, the *text*, the *reader*, the *reference*, and the *context*. Each of them should be given its due – what Umberto Eco (1990, 1992) would call their 'rights' – and the final interpretation emerges from the negotiation between them all (Ricoeur, 1965; Beuchot, 1997, 1998; Tubert-Oklander, 2009, 2011a; Tubert-Oklander & Beuchot Puente, 2008; Hernández Hernández, 2010).

Here we meet several oppositions that have steered the course of hermeneutical controversies for centuries. First is that between the *author's intentions* and *what the text actually says*. The former are rather difficult to establish, so that some thinkers like Eco (1990, 1992) would rather focus on the text's meaning, which appears to be more objective. But, as psychoanalysts, we are necessarily interested in the discrepancies between what the author consciously wanted to say and what he actually wrote or said, and we are bound to include some interpretation of the author's unconscious motivations.

Another opposition is between the *author's rights* and the *reader's rights*. Should we, as readers, submit passively to what the author meant to say and what the text says, or do we have the freedom to generate new meanings, in terms of our present context, interests, and assumptions? In other words, is the interpretation of texts an act of discovery or one of creation? You will notice that this is the very issue of an ongoing controversy in our profession about the nature of the psychoanalytic interpretation.

Finally, there is the opposition between inquiring about the *meaning* of the text or discussing its *reference*. The meaning is derived from the inner structure of the text, its relation to other texts, and the linguistic and semiotic codes it uses to attain its goals. Hence, it does not take into account non-textual reality; we could therefore analyse and interpret an ancient Greek text on unicorns, without having to deal with the problem of whether unicorns actually exist or not. On the other hand, if we take into account the reference as an essential element in the interpretation of a text, then we have to consider the dialectics between textual and non-textual realities as a part of our interpretative work.

For example, those philosophers who attempt to analyse Freud's writings without knowing anything about psychoanalysis run the risk of misunderstanding the author, since Freud was always writing in terms of the psychoanalytic experience. Hence, I consider that any serious reading of Freud's social writings should take into consideration not only the meaning of what he wrote, but also the very pressing questions about society he was dealing with. In other words, we should not only read Freud, but enter into a dialogue, and even a controversy, with him.[2]

This is, for me, the true meaning of 'going back to Freud', not a submission to or a repetition of what he believed, thought, said, and wrote, but a psychoanalytic interpretation and recreation of the inner dialogue he shared with us, now turned into an outer dialogue, much as we do in our everyday practice (Tubert-Oklander, 2009–2014).

This requires a psychoanalytic reading of Freud's writings, rediscovering Freud, not only in his monumental achievements, but also in his unconscious prejudices and conflicts, which also determined his theoretical choices.

Why are we now going back to Freud's social writings? Because the evolution of our contemporary world, an evolution he could not possibly have envisaged, has originated new social, relational, individual, and psychopathological phenomena that challenge our established theories and practices, which are no longer able to deal with many of our patients' needs and demands.

Rediscovering Freud's social thinking is an urgent task because the mainstream version of psychoanalysis has expunged much of what was revolutionary and valuable in them, and we need to salvage it. Such recovery should not be a submissive repetition of his conclusions, but rather a revival of his incessant questioning and his dialectic method of enquiry. This is what Dr Smadja brings us for our consideration today.

Definition of the term

The translation of the Freudian concept of *Kulturarbeit*, as Smadja tells us, poses quite a few problems. The German language has the option of creating highly complex words, by the articulation of others, and the result is often quite difficult to translate to other languages, on account of its multiple connotations. *Arbeit* is clearly 'work' and it refers to an expenditure of energy in order to effect some transformation in a previous state of affairs. In Freud, this always implies the economic point of view. But *Zivilisation* is not 'civilisation' and *Kultur* is not equal to 'culture'. In English and French, 'civilisation' refers to all the achievements of Humankind, or some particular human group, in the process of advancing from the purely animal level to 'an ideal state of human culture characterised by complete absence of barbarism and non-rational behaviour, optimum utilization of physical, cultural, spiritual, and human resources, and perfect adjustment of the individual within the social framework' (Merriam-Webster, 2002, entry 'civilization'). Hence, it includes the whole 'progressive development of arts, sciences, statecraft, and human aspirations and spirituality' (op. cit.). For the Germans, according to Smadja (2012) 'this refers over all to the exterior aspect of man, the surface of human existence'. But the term *Kultur* is used whenever the speaker wants to define social identity and express pride about his or her own prowess or that of his or her group, community, or nation. Hence, it refers mainly to intellectual, artistic, religious, philosophical, or scientific achievements, leaving out those political, economic, and social facts that define national differences, which are essential to the English concept of 'culture'. Since Germany arrived lately to a state of national unity, the search for national identity and self-esteem became a pivot of German thought.

Consequently, *Kulturarbeit* is a far cry from being 'the work of civilization' or 'cultural activities'. It is a collective effort to overcome the most primitive trends in human nature – those that Freud identified as sexual and aggressive instinctual drives, and which he believed were characteristic of neurotics, children, women, the lower classes, and the 'primitive' (i.e., non-European) peoples – and transmute them into the more refined features of a civilised society, such as Law and Order, Literacy, Cleanliness, Rationality, Philosophy, Religion, Art, and, over all, Science. This is, of course, the Modern ideal of Progress that evolved in Western Europe since the rise of the mercantile bourgeoisie in the Renaissance (Sabato, 1941).

In Freud's metasociology, socialisation implied a transmutation of the original instinct-driven human animal into a full human being, in terms of rationality and restraint. This he defined, both for the individual in psychoanalytic treatment and for the cultural evolution of society, as follows: 'Where id was, there ego shall be. It is a work of culture – not unlike the draining of the Zwider Zee' (Freud, 1933a, p. 80). In the context of his metapsychology, conceived as a general psychoanalytic theory of the structure and function of the human mind, this required to introduce the concept of 'sublimation'.

Now, it is easy to understand how this may happen in the case of individual human beings, such as the child, during her or his education, or the patient undergoing a psychoanalytic treatment, but how does this process come about in the case of communities, societies, and Humankind in general? Freud's answer to this question, in *Totem and Taboo* (1912–1913), consisted in inventing a myth of the origins of human society, which we all know.[3]

But how is it that the impact of this ancient drama has been transmitted over the generations up to the present? Freud believed that the aftermath of this traumatic experience of the pre-history has been transmitted along the generations for thousands of years, since 'without the assumption of a collective mind, which makes it possible to neglect the interruptions of mental acts caused by the extinction of the individual, social psychology in general cannot exist' (p. 158).

Such transgenerational transmission implies either that this information is borne by the genes, which would require an inheritance of acquired characteristics, or that it is conveyed through the unconscious interpersonal communication from one generation to the next. Freud initially favoured the psychological hypothesis, although later (Freud, 1939a) he turned to the biological one.

This poses a new theoretical problem: that of the existence of collective mental processes, which he calls a 'collective mind' (*Massenpsyche*). In the beginning, the concept of the *unconscious* was strictly functional and appeared as some sort of internal organ, a piece of the individual's 'psychic apparatus'. Nonetheless, in this new development, the unconscious appears as a hidden and unknown dimension of that set of collective mental processes that Freud calls the 'collective mind'. This forces us to leave behind, in the study of the social unconscious, any relation to the nervous system, and to go beyond the boundaries of the individual. Such a move would require a revision in depth of metapsychology, which has not yet been tackled (Hernández de Tubert, 2008 [Chapter 5]; Hernández de Tubert & Tubert-Oklander, 2005). However, Malcolm Pines's (1998) and Earl Hopper's (2003a, 2003b; Hopper & Weinberg, 2011a) work – and, among us, Juan Tubert-Oklander's and my own (Tubert-Oklander & Hernández-Tubert, 2014a [Chapter 9], 2014b [Chapter 10], 2014c [Chapter 11]) – on the social unconscious is the beginning of such revision of our theory and technique.

The study of such collective mental processes can only be attained through the inclusion in our psychoanalytic theory of many of the findings of the social sciences, such as anthropology, sociology, social psychology, history, linguistics, semiotics, and political science. And the concrete investigation of these processes requires the extension of the analytic enquiry to a group setting, such as it is done in group analysis (Foulkes, 1948, 1964a, 1975a, 1990; Pichon-Rivière, 1971a, 1979; Hernández-Tubert, 2011a [Chapter 12]; Tubert-Oklander, 2006a, 2010a, 2011b; Tubert-Oklander & Hernández de Tubert, 2004). This would also allow us to re-integrate into the psychoanalytic theory and practice the political dimension that has been excluded from psychoanalysis for so long.

Freud's thoughts on society

As I have noted earlier, I believe that our present re-reading of Freud should imply an interpretation of the texts and of their author, in both psychoanalytic and socio-dynamic terms. This is what I shall now attempt to do.

As we have seen in the previous chapters, a thinker and author cannot start cogitating from scratch, but rather begins from a whole set of assumptions about reality, knowledge, values, procedures, and human nature, which are part of the lore of the society in which she or he has been conceived and reared. Such assumptions, which are largely unconscious, have been internalised with the very first identifications, so that they are hardly ever questioned, or even perceived, but taken uncritically as 'the way things are' (Hernández Hernández, 2010; Hernández de Tubert, 2004a, 2009a). In philosophical writings, this mental structure is named by the German terms *Weltanschauung* (Conception of the World) and *Lebensanschauung* (Conception of Life), to refer to its cosmological and anthropological aspects, respectively.[4] The German word *Anschauung* means both 'conception' and 'intuition'; hence, it conveys the idea of a non-rational knowledge and certainty.[5]

Every person who arrives to psychoanalysis, as a patient, student, practitioner, or theoretician, does so with this set of deeply engrained convictions, and Freud was no exception. His ideological conception of life, based on a latent philosophical anthropology, was already present in him long before he invented psychoanalysis. This is evident in his letter to his fiancée, Martha Barnays, of August 29, 1883, when he was only twenty-seven years old,

> I remember something that occurred to me while watching a performance of *Carmen*: the mob gives vent to its appetites, and we deprive ourselves. We deprive ourselves in order to maintain our integrity, we economize in our health, our capacity for enjoyment, our emotions; we save ourselves for something, not knowing for what. And this habit of constant suppression of natural instincts gives us the quality of refinement. We also feel more deeply and so dare not demand much of ourselves . . . We strive more toward avoiding pain than seeking pleasure . . . Our whole conduct of life presupposes that we are protected from the direst poverty and that the possibility exists of being able to free ourselves increasingly from social ills. The poor people, the masses, could not survive without their thick skins and their easy-going ways . . . The poor are too helpless, too exposed, to behave like us . . . It would be easy to demonstrate how 'the people' judge, think, hope, and work in a manner utterly different from ourselves. There is a psychology of the common man which differs considerably from ours. They also have more community spirit than we have; only for them is it natural that one man continues the life of the other, whereas for each of us the world comes to an end with our death.
>
> (Freud, 1883, pp. 50–51, my italics)

So, what he was expressing was his bourgeois conception of life: the inherent superiority of the elite vis-à-vis the 'mob' (the lower classes), the duty to economise resources – economic, physical, and emotional – for more serious business, refinement as the suppression of natural instincts, a view of life based on the security of being 'protected from the direst poverty', and the attribution of a community spirit to the poor, as different from 'us' who are naturally individualistic. Are not all these assumptions of Freud built into the psychoanalytic theory later developed by him? For instance, his ideological position exposed in *Civilization and Its Discontents* (Freud, 1930a) is basically the same as the one he delivered to Martha, forty-seven years before.

This letter also includes Freud's theory of motivation, which only recognises two basic human motives: pleasure and practical utility, as he also expresses in the aforementioned book.

Freud's social thought is therefore based on an ideal image of the cultured human being, which coincides with that of Western European middle and higher classes, to which both Freud and most of his patients belonged. It must be borne in mind that Freud was politically conservative, and hence committed to the maintenance of the status quo, although intellectually he recognised the inequalities of society and the suffering of the lower classes, but he seemed to feel that this was the unavoidable nature of things.

Freud had aspired, during his adolescence, to be a lawyer and follow a political career, but he later abandoned these plans and turned to seek a scientific career through his medical studies (Pines, 1989). His views, which were quite radical in his youth, changed, and he developed a harsh rejection of politics in his thinking. This was clearly shown by his words of advice to Hans Herzl, the son of Theodore Herzl, the founder of Zionism, in 1913, nine years after the latter's death,

> Your father is one of those people who have turned dreams into reality. This is a very rare and dangerous breed. It includes the Garibaldis, the Edisons, the Herzls, the Lenins . . . I would simply call them the sharpest opponents of my scientific work. It is my modest profession to simplify dreams, to make them clear and ordinary. They, on the contrary, confuse the issue, turn it upside down, command the world while they themselves remain on the other side of the psychic mirror. It is a group specializing in the realization of dreams. I deal in psychoanalysis, they deal in psychosynthesis . . . They are robbers in the underground of unconscious world. . . . Stay away from them, young man . . . Stay away, even though one of them was your father . . . perhaps because of that.
>
> (Freud, quoted by Herzl, in Falk, 1978, pp. 380–381)[6]

This wholesale rejection of politics and social action (it is interesting to see that Freud also included Edison, an inventor, together with three politicians) was compounded by an acceptance of the social status quo, considered to be unchangeable, the 'reality' to which the child should adjust during development and the patient during treatment.[7] Such ideological choice was bound to shape his theory of the human being, especially in the direction of a denial of environmental factors in the development and functioning of the mind. His well-doctored account of the Oedipus myth, for instance, omitted any reference to Laius's crimes, which were the cause of the curse that was imposed on him by the Gods, or of his filicidal acts; in Freud's narrative, all the violence was attributed to the son, and none to the father. If those in authority – parents, teachers, doctors, priests, rulers – were in no way responsible for human unhappiness in the community, then there would be no point in trying to change the social order, and social reformers could be interpreted away as dream-mongers.

The historians William J. McGrath (1986) and Carl E. Schorske (1974, 1980), and the British psychoanalyst and group analyst Malcolm Pines (1989, 1998) have studied Freud's utter denial of politics, from both the psycho-biographic and the social-political points of view. They all focused on his 'Revolutionary Dream', also known as the 'Count Thun dream' (Freud, 1900a, pp. 207–219), which had a clearly political stimulus – his chance meeting with this character, who was the Prime Minister of Austria and the most powerful man in the Empire, an arrogant aristocrat who trampled over any commoner who stood in his way, including Freud – and an overtly revolutionary meaning, both in its manifest content and in his associations to it. However, Freud's final interpretation was restricted to his childhood conflict with his father. Schorske (1974) comments that the central principle of Freud's 'mature political theory . . . is that all politics is reducible to the primal conflict between father and son . . . *Patricide replaces regicide; psychoanalysis overcomes history. Politics is neutralized by a counterpolitical psychology*' (p. 54, my italics).

Malcolm Pines (1989) turns this statement of fact into a psychoanalytical interpretation:

> Through psychoanalysis, Freud was able to reduce all environmental conflicts, all situations of helplessness and rage, to the terms of a universal, infantile, oedipal phase. Aspects of current reality could be pushed aside and the past put in the place of the present. Thus politics was replaced by Freud's invention of psychoanalysis, where he himself was the triumphant leader.
>
> (p. 179)

In this dream, there is a condensation of various factors. There was, of course, the traumatic effect of the inequalities of society, but also the scourge of anti-Semitism, which the dreamer had suffered and was suffering at the time, when being discriminated against in his desire to be a University Professor, and his conflict with a father who had not only oppressed and humiliated him, but also disappointed him by being mild and submissive vis-à-vis anti-Semitic attacks (Freud, 1900a).

But any emotional tendency or mental content that has been repressed, denied, or even foreclosed is bound to return, as Freud taught us, so that the political aspect that he had banished from his theory and from his whole conception of the human being came back uninvited. Becoming the undisputed leader of a burgeoning movement was a political feat, and the inner functioning of the psychoanalytic institution he founded reproduced some of the worst features of the aristocracy he was unconsciously criticising in his Revolutionary Dream.

Freud identified, as a child, with Hannibal Barca, the great Semitic general who defeated the Aryan Roman legions and occupied most of Italy for fifteen years but was finally defeated and betrayed. During his youth, this was replaced by Ferdinand Lasalle, the Jewish founder of the international socialist movement. Later, Freud the man identified with the Biblical Joseph, interpreter of dreams, the assimilated Jew who became the most powerful man in Egypt, the favourite of both his father and the Pharaoh, who finally rescued the very brothers who had tried to kill him, out of jealousy and envy. Finally, Freud the elder leader identified with Moses, the founding father of a new religion, a leader who ordered the Levites to kill three thousand men who had worshiped the Golden Calf, in order to keep his community free of idolatry. Such an evolution seems to be an illustration of the traditional cynical comment that 'A man who is not a communist at the age of twenty has no heart, but if he is not a conservative at forty, he has no brains'.

But politics is the recognition that there are always different views, in any community, about what society should be, that these have to be negotiated somehow, and that the result is always unpredictable. The same is true in the case of the internal negotiation that the ego has to carry out in order to integrate the self's various motivations, feelings, goals, values, abilities, and knowledge. But when both the individual and society's evolution are conceived in terms of an epigenetic sequence of pre-ordained phases, as a result of having defined it as a universal – hence, a-historic and non-contextual – feature of human nature, the outcome becomes ideologically laden.

The result of this universalising tendency was an epigenetic conception of the human being, both in the individual's ontogenetic development and in that phylogenetic development of society and Humankind that Freud (1933a, p. 147) called 'cultural evolution'. Such evolution is predetermined, as a series of stages that lead to a final goal. In the case of the individual, one such formulation is that of libido theory, originally posed by Freud (1905d), and later schematised by Karl Abraham (1924). Another one is the line of development of the ego, also initially introduced by Freud (1911b) and Ferenczi (1913a). Erik Erikson (1950) attempted to integrate in a single schema the development of libido, the ego, object relations, and psycho-social identity all along the life cycle.

In the case of the evolution of society, the same principle applies: growth and development follow a path that moves away from the direct satisfaction of instinctual drives, by means of repression and other defence mechanisms, towards an ideal of the supremacy of intellect and science, the suppression of crass instinctual satisfaction, and an ever-increasing tendency to abstraction (Freud, 1939a). This is supposed to be a necessary organic process, whose end result is as predictable as that of the development of a fertilised egg; of course, it is not guaranteed, as something may always go wrong, but yet there is only one possible result, when the process goes as it should. This concept was clearly stated in 'Why war?' (Freud, 1933b) – his open letter to Albert Einstein – where he wrote that 'we are still unfamiliar with *the notion that the evolution of civilization is an organic process . . . There are organic grounds for the changes in our ethical and aesthetic ideals*' (pp. 214–215, my italics).

One main consequence of this point of view is that it completely eschews the political dimension, in both the individual and the collective arenas: if the end result of human development is predetermined, there is no point in discussing or negotiating alternative paths or goals, and the only thing worth considering is whether a person, a group, or a community is advancing in the right direction or not. If it is not, that is pathology. Hence, any form of life or behaviour that differs from the generally accepted blueprint can easily be described as a 'disease' (Szasz, 1960, 1961, 2003).

The very same line of questioning is valid for a criticism of Freud's structuralist view. He clearly saw that the development of the child required setting boundaries that acted as organising principles for experience, relations, and thought. But he restricted his inquiry to those oppositional pairs that could be seen as universal, a-historic, non-contextual, and non-controversial, as they are derived from biological facts: the difference between sexes (not genders, please note)[8] and between generations. But he left out other oppositions that also organise individual, interpersonal, and social life: rich-poor, empowered-disempowered, individualistic-compassionate, conservative-liberal, among others. Since such oppositions are bound to generate all sorts of conflicts, most of them unconscious, there is a clinical need to enquire and interpret them in our analyses.

In Mexico, José Remus Araico (1988) described the unconscious construction of ideology, built upon identifications, that determines what he called the 'conservative-liberal polarity'. Since all of us have both conservative and liberal nuclei in our personalities, albeit there usually is a clear predominance of one of them, we are bound to be involved in ideological conflicts both at the individual and at the interpersonal and transpersonal levels.

All of this was significantly left out of Freud's epoch-making enquiry of human existence.

The author's contribution

Although Smadja's major contribution is the clarification of the full meaning of Freud's concept of *Kulturarbeit*, there are in the paper some very important statements of his own view of the problematic opened by Freud's psychoanalytic enquiry of culture and society. I have identified six of them.

The ubiquitous work of culture

As I have already noted, the author's main hypothesis is that there is

> a latent presence, as an ever-present filigree, of the *work of culture*, both in Freud's writings and in his mind. This notion is also to be discovered through its multiple contents, processes, functions, and meanings, scattered along the various texts.
>
> (Smadja, 2012)

In other words, the concept of *Kulturarbeit* is not a minor one, relevant only to Freud's social and cultural speculations, but one of the cornerstones of his conception of the human being. Freudian anthropology is unthinkable without this assumption that individuals, groups, and communities are necessarily part of an ongoing collective effort to overcome the more primitive and animalistic traits of human beings, turning them into elaborate cultural achievements, by means of symbolisation, sublimation, and abstraction.

I believe that one of Smadja's major achievements in his investigation of Freud's work has been the demonstration of this thesis, on the basis of his painstaking examination of Freudian texts.

The underlying anthropology

For Freud, the original natural human being is a creature of instinctual drives and passionate action that tends to discharge the tensions they generate, thus gratifying the instinctual wishes that are their psychic corollary. The work of culture strives to modify such primeval state and turn human individuals and groups into active participants in their culture. This is the way Smadja puts it,

> Being inspired by Freud, who tried to define the concept of the instinctual drive [*Trieb* in German and *pulsion* in French], we would say that the work of culture would also be the psychic work demanded from each individual by the culture, relayed and sustained by the Superego, as a result of its connection with the social dimension, that is, of its social incorporation and hence its cultural participation.

This statement is also solidly based on the author's thorough reading of Freud's writings.

The basis of sublimation

How are the suppression of instinctual wishes and their symbolisation articulated with sublimations? This is a highly complex issue, which has not yet been adequately investigated. But Smadja conceives it in terms of complex interrelations between the subject and his or her psychic, bodily, and socio-cultural realities, both internal and external.

The problem, as Paul Ricoeur (1965) showed almost half a century ago, is how to articulate the energetics and the hermeneutics of psychoanalysis. It is quite clear that Freudian theory is always both, at one and the same time, but it has never been able to explain how the quantitative aspect of drives turns into the qualitative one of meaning. The author suggests that the answer may be found in the concepts of de-sexualised and de-aggressivised energies, and that of the binding of excitement, but he leaves this task open for future research.

Religion and identity

The text in which Freud (1939a) gives us a major example of the accomplishment of a work of culture is *Moses and Monotheism*. There he shows how Moses, the Founding Father of a new religion, shapes the ideology and identity of a community, through the religion he introduced, thus creating the Jewish people. Smadja asserts that the founder of a religion 'constructs' the identity of a people through the religious ideology that organises both the individual and the community. Therefore, religion, as part of the culture, plays a role in the structuring of its members.

Psychoanalysis and anthropology

Smadja, who is both an anthropologist and a psychoanalyst, believes that, as a consequence of the fact that they have a same primary object of study in common – human beings – the two disciplines must necessarily share two of the major traits of its humanity: the *unconscious* and *culture*. Consequently, they constitute together a new epistemology that favours the development of a fruitful collaboration between psychoanalysts and anthropologists.

The dialectic dimension

After reviewing the work of various anthropologists who think their work and theory in psychoanalytic terms, trying to articulate the individual and the collective dimensions, the author observes that 'each of them questions one of the aspects that are viewed in terms of the notion under study, without tackling its dialectic dimension, which is so rich and complex'. In other words, it is not a question of splitting the complexity of human existence and experience into two allegedly separate realms – the individual and the collective – and then try to articulate them meaningfully, but of considering, from the very beginning, their essential unity, which stems from their having a single object of study, which is undistinguishable from the subject who is studying it. The only possible way to do it is a dialectic approach.

Conclusions

Eric Smadja has carried us along a fascinating trip through those of Freud's writings that deal with or touch the problematic of society and culture, and their relationship with individual dynamics and development. He has shown us that a psychoanalytic concept that had previously been considered rather lateral, an auxiliary notion introduced in the service of applied psychoanalysis – that of the work of culture – is really one of the pillars of Freudian theory. This I deem to be a major theoretical achievement.

However, the whole theoretical structure thus presented is based on the acceptance of a series of assumptions about human nature that are essential to the Freudian *Lebensanschauung*, but which are far from being shared by all analysts. Hence, having arrived, thanks to Smadja's meticulous reading of Freud, at a better and deeper understanding of his conception of culture and social life, we are now left with the major task of discussing and thinking through those most complex problems that Freud was trying to cogitate, contrasting his ideas with those that stem from other assumptions and perspectives, with our living experience of being, as individuals, a part of society, and with the analysis of these questions in our treatments.

This points at one of the major tasks of contemporary psychoanalytic research: that of the study of the hyper-complex relations between individual and collective mental processes. This has been carried out by a group of clinicians and thinkers, identified with group analysis, ever since S. H. Foulkes and Enrique Pichon-Rivière began their theoretical and clinical research in the early forties. From a rather different perspective, one that attempts to conceive and theorise the mental processes in the group in terms of Freudian metapsychology, René Kaës

(1976, 2007) has developed his own approach to what he calls the 'group psychic apparatus'. Such an approach, which is shared by various other schools that strive to understand group processes from the vantage point of a theory of the individual mind, preserves, from my point of view, the old paradigm of human nature that Freud inherited from his teachers and his tradition. However, there is in Freud's work the beginning of a new paradigm, that of the individual in relation and as a part of collective processes, as we have seen when discussing his social writings.[9] Both paradigms coexist in his work, but different psychoanalysts have chosen to emphasise one or the other. Perhaps we do not have to choose between them, but maintain the dialectic tension generated by their difference, as Smadja suggests.

The construction of a sorely needed new dialectic paradigm of the human being will probably give us what we need in order to better understand this tension. This work is being carried out by a number of psychoanalysts, group analysts, and social scientists, in an attempt to think through and give adequate responses to the predicament of our Postmodern world, which is a source of great suffering for the majority of the world's population and a menace for the very survival of Humankind.[10]

Notes

1 See also Appendix I on Analogical Hermeneutics.
2 This is what we have done in Chapters 1 and 5.
3 See Chapter 5.
4 See Appendix II on the Conception of the World.
5 From the perspective of contemporary neuroscience, Antonio Damasio (1994) has proposed that emotion and intuition precede and orient rational thought and other cognitive processes and have a direct bearing on decision-making in general and social cognition and behaviour in particular, as well as in ethical and esthetical judgements.
6 This most interesting paper came to my attention when I found it quoted by Pines (1989, p. 172). Indeed, Freud (1900a) had explained away the content of dreams and declared them to be worthless, from a cognitive point of view. On the contrary, Erich Fromm (1951), in *The Forgotten Language*, and Charles Rycroft (1979), in *The Innocence of Dreams*, have proposed a contrasting point of view, which emphasises the function of dreams as an alternative form of thought that complements conscious rational thinking. This is clearly in line with Damasio's (1994) neuro-psychological 'somatic-marker hypothesis' in which 'emotion [is] in the loop of reason, and that emotion [can] assist the reasoning process rather than necessarily disturb it, as it was commonly assumed' (p. x).
7 Compare this, for instance, with Ferenczi's assertion that the family should adapt to the child (1928a) and the analytic technique to the patient (1928b).
8 As feminist theory has shown, sex is a biological given, while gender is a social construction.
9 See Chapter 5.
10 See Chapters 8 and 12. The question of the new paradigm is further discussed in Chapter 15.

Chapter 7

The quest for the real (2016)

Juan Tubert-Oklander

> *In 2015, I was invited by Gabriela Legorreta to contribute a chapter for a book she was editing, with Lawrence J. Brown, to be called **On Freud's 'Formulations on the Two Principles of Mental Functioning'**. I immediately accepted, since I felt that this was an excellent opportunity to reflect on a couple of subjects that had occupied my thought for a long time: Freud's abandonment of his traumatic theory of neurosis and the concept of truth in psychoanalysis. Freud's abrupt theoretical turn, in 1897, has been considered, in the official history of psychoanalysis, to be its true beginning, since it provided a new focus on the intrapsychic that replaced the previous environmental theory. There is no doubt that this new perspective paved the path for a most fruitful enquiry of the inner dimension of human experience, but it also left out, and even forbade, any enquiry of the interpersonal and the transpersonal. Indeed, the unswerving belief in the absolute primacy of the intrapsychic became a shibboleth to distinguish between 'true psychoanalysis' and 'what is not psychoanalysis'. Consequently, most schisms in the psychoanalytic movement have derived from the attempts to reintroduce the enquiry of interpersonal and transpersonal processes into the psychoanalytic field. However, since many of the more recent developments in the analytic theory and practice have been in that direction, we believe it is high time to re-evaluate that theoretical turn.*
>
> *This is, of course, related to the problem of truth. The search for truth, understood as reliable knowledge, has been held as the aim of several disciplines, such as science, philosophy, religion, and art, but each of them has its own definition of it. Freud (1933a) believed the scientific conception of truth to be the only one worthy of that name, but this is far from obvious. Hence, we strongly feel that the very concept of truth needs to be enquired. I had done so in a previous writing (Tubert-Oklander, 2008b), in which I proposed the concept of a psychoanalytic truth, and I came back to it in the present chapter (Tubert-Oklander, 2016).*

Two principles of minding[1]

In his seminal paper called 'Formulations on the Two Principles of Mental Functioning', Freud (1911b) gave shape to some of his basic concepts of his theory of Mind, which he had been ruminating on ever since his unpublished *Project* (1950a). Ernest Jones (1953, p. 349) tells us that when, on October 26, 1910, he

DOI: 10.4324/9780429055287-9

gave a preliminary presentation of the theme before the Vienna Society, the audience found it too difficult to understand and was so unresponsive that even he felt displeased with the ideas he had presented. We can now see that the problem was that they were too abstract and condensed, so that they became practically unintelligible for a group of disciples who knew nothing about their early development in the *Project*, and could not yet grasp their relation with the equally abstract concepts he had put forward in Chapter 7 of *The Interpretation of Dreams* (1900a).

Freud began writing this essay in December and the paper was finished by the end of January 1911. Ever since its publication in the *Jahrbuch*, late that spring, this brief piece has become one of the basic texts on the fundamentals of Freudian theory. It is so clear in its formulation that it has been a keen stimulus, both for those thinkers who adhere to the basic tenets of Freudian thought and for those who criticise and revise them.

The basic concepts of the theory that he put forward are the *pleasure principle* and the *reality principle*, which are, of course, related to those of the *primary process* and the *secondary process* that had been introduced in his dream book. They are related to his theoretical strategy of comparing the organisation of the mind, 'the instrument which carries out our mental functions [. . . with] a compound microscope or a photographic apparatus, or something of the kind' (1900a, p. 536). This implies viewing Mind as a functional entity, a structure akin to that of the nervous system, intended to process the excitation induced by stimuli stemming from the body and the sense organs, and conduce it to its final discharge through action. Such a process must somehow be regulated, and this is where the two principles intervene.

The pleasure principle is supposed to be the primary mode of mental functioning. In such a situation, motor discharge of excess stimuli occurs without any previous deliberation and is not corrected by its consequences, fantasied mental images are not distinguished from perceptions, since the mind only represents what is pleasurable, and this precludes any learning from experience, which requires knowledge of the real.[2] The obvious insufficiency of this kind of minding sooner or later brings about the instauration of the reality principle, so that now 'what was presented in the mind was no longer what was agreeable but what was real, even if it happened to be disagreeable' (1911b, p. 219).

This very simple and thought-provoking schema of the early development of Mind has been taken as an essential element of a Freudian credo by some – usually referred to as 'orthodox Freudians' – and firmly criticised by others – such as object-relations theorists, interpersonalists, and relational psychoanalysts – who take exception at some of its underlying assumptions. Such criticism has been basically aimed at two questions: what do we mean by 'reality'? and who is to decide what is and what is not real?[3] I shall discuss them accordingly.

Fantasy or fact?

Psychoanalysis has been, from its very beginning, a dialectic of fantasy and reality. This came about as a consequence of the radical theoretical turn taken by

Freud in 1897, when he discarded his so-called 'seduction theory'. This was a rather unfortunate term, since it referred to an aetiological theory of neuroses that explained them as resulting from the traumatic effect of the sexual abuse of children by their parents, relatives, or caregivers. Hence, the use of the word 'seduction' was surely a euphemism, intended to bowdlerise the subversive impact of a theory that denounced that those people who were in charge of the welfare of others could, and often did, abuse their authority and damage their charges. For, if parents and relatives could not be fully trusted, this would surely also apply to nurses, teachers, doctors, priests, policemen, and government officers, thus undermining the very basis of authority in society. No wonder that such ideas generated widespread animosity and outrage among the young doctor's colleagues!

Besides, Freud himself had quite a few doubts and misgivings about his theory. If it were true that neurotic disturbances were caused by the perverse acts of parents and other trusted adults, vis-à-vis their children, how was he to account for the presence of neurotic symptoms in his sisters and himself? The only logical explanation was that his own father had been guilty of such transgressions. In his letter of September 21, 1897, to Fliess, he voiced his surprise at finding out that 'in all cases, the *father*, not excluding my own, had to be accused of being perverse' (Freud, 1897, p. 264).

This, together with the unsettling discoveries from his self-analysis and the violently hostile reactions of the medical community towards his ideas, must have induced in him a distress that compounded his doubts. These were generated by the confluence of what he felt to be an essential unlikelihood of finding such a widespread prevalence of perversion in parents, particularly in fathers, inconsistencies in his patients' narratives of their childhood traumas, and the discovery of his own incestuous and parricidal wishes in his self-analysis (Jones, 1953, p. 358). All this led him to his final abandonment of his traumatic theory of neuroses.

Strangely enough, although this implied the demise of the theory from which he had hoped to attain fame and recognition, his feelings at the time were not of hopelessness or depression, but of liberation and elation. As he wrote in the same letter of September 21, 1897, 'I have more the feeling of a victory than a defeat', and also,

> If I were depressed, confused, exhausted, such doubts would surely have to be interpreted as signs of weakness. Since I am in an opposite state, I must recognize them as the result of honest and vigorous intellectual work and must be proud that after going so deep I am still capable of such criticism. Can it be that this doubt merely represents an episode in the advance toward further insight?
>
> (Freud, 1897, p. 265)

This was surely a most unsettling situation for any researcher, since his whole aetiological theory had collapsed under his newfound certainty that the traumatic events he had so laboriously unearthed had not happened at all. But he emerged from this predicament through the formulation of a brilliant and audacious hypothesis: that it was not necessary for these childhood events to have happened *in reality* for them to have a traumatic effect, but that it sufficed that the subject believed in them, that is, that they existed *in fantasy*. This was the origin of the concept of *psychic reality*.

From that moment on, the dialectic between fantasy and reality, or between *psychic reality* ('internal') and *material reality* ('external'), came to the fore in psychoanalytical theorising and practice. There also emerged a generalised prejudice that rejected as worthless and 'non-analytic' any interpretation framed in terms of real external events, whether interpersonal or social. Indeed, the main conflicts and splits in the psychoanalytic movement have been related to the discussion of the impact of 'external reality', as opposed to the exclusive emphasis on 'internal' processes that defines what is usually called 'orthodox psychoanalysis' (Tubert-Oklander, 2006a).

It must be said, however, that Freud's stance on the matter was rather ambivalent. On the one hand, he firmly maintained that psychoanalysis dealt exclusively with psychic reality and rejected any attempt to explain mental dynamics and psychopathology in environmental terms. This clear-cut position, which was enthusiastically shared by the initial group of analysts that followed him, was the essential disagreement that determined his rupture with Ferenczi.

But, on the other hand, he uneasily sought a material basis for early experiences in actual occurrences that could be validated by evidence, as in the case of his efforts to prove that the Wolf Man (Freud, 1918b) had *actually* witnessed parental intercourse at the age of one and a half years. This led him to publish a brief note in the *Zentralblatt für Psychoanalyse*, in early autumn of 1912, in which he wrote,

> I should be glad if those of my colleagues who are practising analysts would collect and analyse carefully any of their patients' dreams whose interpretation justifies the conclusion that *the dreamers had been witnesses of sexual intercourse in their early years.*
>
> (Freud, quoted by Strachey, 1955, p. 4)

Even though he appeared to recant his original seduction theory, which proposed an environmental causation of neuroses, and affirmed that this turn had been based on unquestionable clinical evidence, he still recorded a number of clinical observations that attributed the child's responses to actual parental behaviour. One such instance appeared in the *Three Essays on the Theory of Sexuality* (1905d), where he wrote,

> If there are quarrels between the parents or if their marriage is unhappy, the ground will be prepared in their children for the severest predisposition to a disturbance of sexual development or to a neurotic illness.
>
> (p. 228)

A more forceful exposition of this idea is to be found in the *Introductory Lectures on Psycho-Analysis* (1916–1917), which says as follows:

> Incidentally, *children often react in their Oedipus attitude to a stimulus coming from their parents*, who are frequently led in their preferences by

difference of sex, so that the father will choose his daughter and the mother her son as a favourite, or, in case of a cooling-off in the marriage, as a substitute for a love-object that has lost its value.

(p. 207, my italics)

Later in the book, in a more extensive discussion of the Oedipus complex, he repeats his observation, but now with a caveat,

We must not omit to add that *the parents themselves often exercise a determining influence on the awakening of a child's Oedipus attitude* by themselves obeying the pull of sexual attraction, and that where there are several children the father will give the plainest evidence of his greater affection for his little daughter and the mother for her son.[4] [But then he adds:] *But the spontaneous nature of the Oedipus complex in children cannot be seriously shaken even by this factor.*

(p. 333, my italics)

Obviously, no one can accuse Freud of ignoring the vital importance of the parents' contribution to the child's emotional problems, but he clearly felt that he should qualify his clinical observations on this matter, in order to avoid any temptation to abandon or dilute the tenets of the theories of instinctual drives and the universality of the Oedipus complex. But it is a fact that both metapsychology and psychoanalytical practice have had, from the very beginning, a place for extra-psychic reality, which has to be acknowledged and taken into account by mental processes, which necessarily have to adapt to it, as he clearly demonstrates in 'The two principles of mental functioning', which he considered to be only a 'few remarks on the psychical consequences of adaptation to the reality principle' (p. 226).

But all this requires a further probing into the concept of 'reality', which Freud takes for granted and leaves undefined – obviously under the assumption that we all know what reality is.

What is real, anyway?

The point of departure of psychoanalytic enquiry was the ordinary and socially shared conception of things, from which psychoanalysis was bound to depart. Consequently, consciousness was taken for granted as a given, intuitively known, since the Unconscious was the real mystery to be untangled, the Dark Continent to be explored.

Similarly, the concept of reality, usually identified with our sense perception of the material world, was taken for granted, since the focus of interest lay in the radically new concept of *psychic reality*, which derived from Freud's discovery that unconscious fantasies could be the determining factor of neurotic symptoms. Nonetheless, just as we know today that consciousness is a much more complex phenomenon than what we used to believe and deserves deep and ample research

(Ornstein, 1972), we should also enquire into the nature of reality itself, starting by questioning what we actually mean when using the term 'real'.

'Real' is whatever exists independently from our will, wishes, or thought, and that resists our attempts to modify it, thus requiring work and effort in order to introduce any changes in it, and sometimes proves to be impossible to change, in spite of our efforts.[5] In this sense, the material world is real: a brick wall is real because we cannot go through it as we may wish, but need instead to break through it with a pick or somehow wander about in order to find an opening. But not only material objects are real, but also other human beings, groups, institutions, and society. So are emotions, which in ordinary thought are usually considered 'unreal'. However, they have an existence of their own, we cannot create or destroy them,[6] and we can only control or modify them by means of an effort, which necessarily includes striving to name and understand them. All this is what makes them real.

Other instances of the real, which are not usually thought of as such, are symbolic systems, such as languages, laws, and theories. It is a fact that these exist in their own dimension – what Karl Raimund Popper (1972) called the 'Third World', as opposed to the First World of material events and the Second World of subjective experiences. They determine us and understanding and apprehending them is hard work, as anyone who has ever tried to study law, learn a language, or comprehend a mathematical theorem well knows.

Fantasy, on the other hand, is usually considered something false and unreal. But it was precisely Freud who discovered the enormous power held by unconscious fantasy over the life, thought, behaviour, and relations of human beings. Later, Melanie Klein showed us how fantasy draws its strength from deep emotional strivings (Klein et al., 1952).

Unconscious fantasy is, therefore, fully real, since it exists independently from our will, imposes on, and resists us, and we can only understand, control, channel, or modify it, albeit only partially, by means of an expenditure of work. This reality of fantasy stems from various sources. First, it is based on and expresses emotions, which, as we have seen, are always real. Then, there is the fact that fantasy constitutes a complex symbolic system, with its own organisation, which is as determinant and resistant to change as the grammar of a language, the logic of a legal code, a tradition, or a dressing code. In this, Jacques Lacan's (1966) work, based on the structuralism of Claude Lévy-Strauss, represents a major contribution on this matter.

There is yet another driving force of fantasy, which is the relational and social experiences and processes, and here we are bound to face some major problems, since this has always generated controversy in the history of psychoanalysis. Freud's concept of 'instinctual drives' (*Triebe*) derived from his perception that the symptoms he was inquiring were being driven by an impersonal current that stemmed from the demands of bodily life and entered into a sharp conflict with the patients' persona, which he called 'the I' (*das Ich*, usually translated as 'the ego').[7] It was indeed tempting, if we consider his positivistic and physicalist upbringing, to compare it with the concept of 'energy' in the Newtonian model of the Universe, and to conceive it as the material cause of symptoms (and later of all human experience and behaviour). It is this quasi-physical aspect of Freudian theory that has become the target of much criticism by the various relational and culturalist theories, which discarded the causal theory of drives and emphasised instead the concrete experiences of relating to other human beings and participating in social systems.

Nonetheless, as I have noted in a previous paper (Tubert-Oklander, 2015 [Chapter 14]), this seems to be a case of throwing away the baby together with the dirty bathwater. There is no doubt that the personal aspects of human existence play an essential part in the dynamics of our experience, thinking, feeling, and behaviour, as pointed out by object-relational, interpersonal, and self-psychological theories, but we still have to account for the impersonal side of our existence discovered by Freud. Although a major part of our wishes are highly personal, as acknowledged by psychoanalytical theory since 'Mourning and melancholia' (Freud, 1917e), there is certainly an impersonal dimension of sexual and aggressive wishes, which Freud (1915c) strived to explain by means of his hypothesis that the object 'is what is most variable about an instinct and is not originally connected with it, but becomes assigned to it only in consequence of being peculiarly fitted to make satisfaction possible' (p. 122).

Human beings are certainly also driven by mighty impersonal currents that clearly transcend the limits of their personal identities. An essential part of these currents stems from bodily existence and its unrelenting demands, but there is still another impersonal current that drives and orients us, and this is the pressure of the community we belong to, which also extends in time (as in transgenerational transmission and the history of families and peoples) and space (as in the case of the impact of institutions, culture, and politics) far beyond the apparent limits of personal existence (Tubert-Oklander, 2013a, 2014). Such issues were addressed by Freud in *Totem and Taboo* (1912–1913) and *Moses and Monotheism* (1939a).

Such social processes surround, go through, and determine us, exist independently of our thought and will, and can only be changed partially by means of a collective effort and long-time work. This makes them real enough. Consequently, it should be expected that they have an inscription in the unconscious, no less than the bodily processes traditionally acknowledged by psychoanalytical theory. Unconscious fantasy should then be considered to reflect *the whole of reality* – inner, outer, and symbolic – albeit in terms of the language of unconscious mentation – the primary process – which is in sharp contrast with that of verbal consciousness and communication – the secondary process. Hence, our daily work of making conscious the unconscious should include a painstaking exploration of all the various dimensions of reality, and contrast it with wishful thinking, as Freud's seminal paper indicates. But this is where trouble begins, as we shall readily see.

Real for whom?

The key concept here is that social currents and their impact on individual and group thinking, feeling, and acting are mainly unconscious. Hence, it is only natural that they differ from and contradict the conscious image that society and its members have of themselves, just as the individual's inner truth contrasts with that carefully censored and idealised image of him- or herself that Freud called 'the I'. This phenomenon, which resembles our well-known mechanism of rationalisation, was studied by Marx and Engels (1932 [1845]), in socio-political terms, under the name of 'ideology'.

Ideology, in this sense, is the false image of a society and its nature that its members have of it, both individually and collectively, and should be clearly differentiated from the dire reality it conceals. One can certainly take exception at some unilateral uses of this concept, but the fact remains that the true human motives are, more often than not, unknown by the subject – as our discipline has shown over and over again – and that there is no reason to assume that this should be any different in the case of social issues. Both individuals and groups are likely to define what is real for them, in terms of their own experiences, persuasions, and interests, and not be aware of the fact that they are actually constructing their reality through this definition (Berger & Luckmann, 1966). This is as true for patients as it is for analysts, politicians, psychoanalytical theorists, and ordinary citizens.

One would expect a psychoanalytical treatment to explore these issues, but the fact is that all our theory and practice has tended to omit them. We have therefore to face the problem of who is to define what is real and what is not. We usually leave this task to the analyst, but we should ask ourselves whether this is fair and, especially, if it works and how.

In this, the question of material reality is not usually an issue (with the exception of the analysis of psychotics), but it certainly becomes one when we have to deal with other aspects of reality, unless analyst and patient fully share – as they frequently do – a same conception of the world (Hernández de Tubert, 2009a). But when there are cultural, religious, or political differences between the two parties, these issues come to the fore, unless they are swept under the carpet by a categorical statement that the patient is 'out of touch with reality'. And, if this seems too strong a judgement of analysts' rationalisations, we should well remember the many occasions in which a theoretical difference was summarily dismissed by a whole group of analysts on the grounds that the dissenter 'was psychotic' or 'lacked sufficient analysis'.[8]

There is no way in which a psychoanalyst could carry out her or his interpretative activity without starting from a whole set of assumptions and prejudices, derived from personal experience, upbringing, the social context, training, theory, and the psychoanalytical tradition of which he or she is a part.[9] The patient also bases all her perceptions, thoughts, feelings, and expressions on a similar set of assumptions. The analytic dialogue confronts, identifies, verbalises, and enquires these assumptions and the similarities and differences between them. From such shared enquiry, a certain agreement may emerge, which is the basis of the parties' conviction about their findings (Tubert-Oklander, 2013b).

What just will not do is the common practice of assuming *a priori* that the way in which the analyst conceives things is the reliable version of reality, and that the patient's view is, when it differs from the former, 'unreal'. Such an approach would be tantamount to turning the analysis into a form of indoctrination, instead of an open enquiry that brings about liberation and freedom of thought.

We have by now reviewed the various kinds of reality, thus showing this concept to be much more complex than what it initially appeared to be. We have also seen that our conception of the real is by no means straightforward, that it brings about divergence and conflict, and that this requires a shared enquiry, discussion, and negotiation between patient and analyst, in order to reach the partial and temporary agreements that lead to a moderate conviction about the findings of an analysis.

Taking all this into consideration, we may well ask ourselves why we should deal with reality at all. Would it not be better for us to focus only on *meaning*, as some Postmodern versions of psychoanalysis would have it (Civitarese, Katz, & Tubert-Oklander, 2015)? Does reality matter at all for psychoanalysis? The answer is that it certainly does, as a consequence of the fact that our discipline has always focused on the search for truth, as we shall see in the next section.

The search for truth

Most psychoanalysts would agree that our practice involves such a search, but they would probably differ in the meaning they assign to the word. This is not only a problem for psychoanalysis, since philosophy has also had to deal, throughout history, with various concepts of truth. We shall presently see a brief review of what I consider to be the main ones (Tubert-Oklander, 2008b).

The first one is *semantic truth*, also called 'truth by correspondence', that is, the concordance between a thought or statement – a logical proposition – and a state of affairs which is independent of the subject. This is the usual scientific meaning of truth.

The second is *syntactical or logical truth*. In a symbolic system based on axioms and rules for combination, it is possible to infer certain consequences that are necessarily true, on account of their consistency with the rest of the system. This is the type of truth to be found in logic and mathematics.

The third kind is *pragmatic truth*, which identifies, following William James, Wilhelm Dilthey, and Charles Sanders Peirce, truth with what is useful. This implies that the validity of ideas depends on their capacity to orient our actions vis-à-vis the world we inhabit. Such stance, which has been heartily endorsed by Postmodernist thinkers, has the advantage of taking into account the impact of relation and context, and the disadvantage of forsaking the search for wider truths.[10]

The fourth one is *consensual or social truth*, which represents the general agreements, which are mainly unconscious, that the members of a certain community have about what is and what is not, what is possible, and what should be. This includes the customs, beliefs, and values that compound a *Weltanschauung* or Conception of the World. The fact that this is largely unconscious makes it a valid object for psychoanalytic enquiry, but it also generates many blind spots, as it is quite likely to be shared by analyst and patient alike (Hernández de Tubert, 2009a; Tubert-Oklander & Hernández de Tubert, 2004).[11]

The fifth possible sense is that of *expressive truth*, which is the concept of truth in the arts. This is based on the harmonious consistency between the expressed message, which creates an aesthetic impact, and its capacity to evoke and induce in the receiver emotional states akin to those that the emitter wanted to convey.

One last sense, which is clearly related to the previous one, is that of *narrative truth*. Here it is the consistency of discourse that generates the power of conviction of the narrative. In literature, this moves and makes the reader think, but in the humanistic sciences it also requires verisimilitude, which turns the reader into an active participant and convinces him of the validity of the story that has been told. In the particular case of *historical truth*, the narrative should also be based on established facts, derived from documents, testimonies, and evidences, without omitting any that might be relevant for the matter at hand.

All these forms of truth are characterised by their *power of conviction*, which means that we are dealing with a message (statement, interpretation, construction) that convinces both the emitter and the receptor of its validity. The experience of truth always gives us certainty, which may not be absolute, but good-enough – that is, adequate and sufficient – for a given context.[12] As Wilfred Bion (1962, 1970) suggests, this corresponds to a basic and primary need of the human spirit, which is to have at its disposal certain ideas that can be considered valid, at least for the time being, as a basis for thinking, relating, and acting. Although he emphasised emotional truth, this being the very gist of psychoanalytic enquiry, this need also includes the relational, social, political, and moral aspects of truth.

And what is the case of *psychoanalytic truth*? Sigmund Freud conceived it as a semantic truth, in other words, as a precise, complete, and reliable description of a state of affairs that took place independently of the observer's intentions and mental processes. In other words, it was for him an expression of the reality principle, which clearly corresponds to the ethos of natural science. Nonetheless, in the actual practice of the treatment method he created, both he and the many generations of analysts that came after him, up to our present days, have relied on a highly complex admixture of all the aforementioned forms of truth.

There is certainly a dimension of semantic truth whenever we give a name to a patient's feelings or to a shared emotional experience in the transference-countertransference field. But there is also a space for syntactic truth, not in the absolute sense of the formal sciences of logic and mathematics, but in our understanding of the inner coherence of the symbolic systems, starting with language, that determine our mentation, experience, and action, in the context of the analytic relation and dialogue. Besides, these very systems and their influence become an object for the analytic enquiry, as a part of the consensual truth that both allows patient and analyst to understand each other and then becomes an obstacle for further insights, unless they are themselves analysed.[13] Thus, the analytic dialogue, in which there is a confluence of thinking, feeling, and relating, generates a new kind of consensual truth, based on the shared analytic experience, an agreement that is fully convincing for both parties (Tubert-Oklander, 2013a).

And what about pragmatic truth? An interpretation is much more than a valid hypothesis: it is a verbal action, intended to produce a certain effect in both the receptor and the emitter. As Madeleine and Willy Baranger (2009) have suggested, insight is not an intrapersonal event, but a field phenomenon. A valid insight represents a reorganisation of the analytic field, and this is the validity of interpretations, in pragmatic terms.[14]

Expressive truth represents the capacity of the patient's and the analyst's utterances and other forms of expression to somehow convey and share the emotional experiences that generated them. When this effort is successful, this generates an aesthetic experience. This is the basis for empathic understanding in their dialogue.

Finally, narrative truth has always been basic for the analytic endeavour. Thus Freud (1895d) remarked, in the case of Elizabeth von R., that he found it strange that his case histories 'should read like short stories' and they lacked 'the serious stamp of science'. But he consoled himself 'with the reflection that the nature of the subject is evidently responsible for this, rather than any preference of my own' (p. 160). In other words, the results of an analysis should take the form of a good story, this being an essential part of their value of conviction, and this is not a mere adornment, but a basic requirement of the analytic enquiry.

But the very fact that the subject matter of our investigation determines the form of our interpretations and the findings of the analytic dialogue and relation imply that there is not a complete freedom for our thoughts and our agreements, but that they necessarily have to take into account *something* that exists independently from us, and this takes us back to the problem of reality.

In sum

What Freud's (1911b) great article taught us is one of the main findings of his clinical research: that the human being is torn between a basic need for truth and a desire to conceal it from himself and others, and replace it with a bowdlerised version that eschews the more distasteful aspects of human existence – individual, relational, and social. Since such aspects exist, in spite of our will, wishes, and beliefs, they are clearly a part of what we call 'reality'. But there are other aspects of reality that are not concealed, but are merely unknown, and yet remain unconscious unless they be enquired, interpreted, and constructed by the analytic dialogue. And yet this task must also overcome a resistance, which in this case is not fuelled by the effort to deny an unsavoury truth, but by the rejection of new ideas that would require a replacement or reformulation of old and well-known systems of mentation and relation. Such restructuring is painful and laborious, and therefore avoided unless imposed by the dire need to overcome a greater discomfort or suffering. This is perhaps the reason why psychoanalysis was discovered by a psychopathologist who was striving to alleviate neurotic suffering.

Consequently, the opposition and dialectic between the reality principle and the pleasure principle may be understood in terms of the contrast between truthfulness, on the one hand, and mendacity, self-deception, and laziness, on the other. Freud strove to explain this in terms of his grandiose project of constructing a metapsychology that was to go beyond his psychological discoveries to the material bases – which he believed to be biological – of all mental processes (Freud, 1898, p. 301).[15] Although nowadays many psychoanalysts do not share this project, and even sternly criticise it, none can ignore the momentous import of the discoveries that he put forward in these few fundamental pages.

Notes

1 I am using the non-standard term 'minding' as a neologism to refer to the processes of mind-building. This implies a conception of mind as a set of evolving processes for the construction of mental contents (what Freud, 1900a, called 'presentations'), processes that are steered by one or the other of the principles introduced by Freud (1911b) in the article we are now discussing. Nonetheless, I shall not discuss it further on this occasion.

2 Indeed, Freud does not speak of 'learning from experience', this being a term borrowed from Bion (1962). Nonetheless, I believe this to be a valid introduction, in this context, since learning from experience can only happen as a result of the operation of the reality principle.

3 There has also been much discussion about whether the newborn is really so out of touch with reality as this theory affirms, and this has led some authors to suggest that the reality principle is active from the very beginning, albeit in a primitive form, but good-enough for the baby to recognise the breast when it meets it (Fairbairn, 1952; Rycroft, 1962). Such a revision would bring about a theory of a life-long dialectic and complementarity of the reality and the pleasure principles (Rycroft, 1968) that I do not intend to discuss on this occasion.

4 This is probably the inspiration of Jean Laplanche's (1997) theory that the real basis of the original fantasies of seduction is the unconscious impact of adult sexuality on the baby. According to him, 'the breast transmits to the child a message and . . . this message is sexual . . . [since] the breast is firstly sexual for the mother, . . . [and] it forms part of her sexual life as an erogenous zone' (p. 660). But this would be a universal phenomenon, quite different from the idiosyncratic effect of family dynamics that Freud was describing.

5 This is, of course, my own definition of reality in terms of the resistance we find in it ('an object is something that objects'), but it is consistent with Freud's description, in which the principle of reality that rules the secondary process is contrasted with the hallucinatory wish-fulfilment of the primary process, which meets no resistance (Freud, 1900a, 1911b).

6 Of course, a material object can be destroyed, albeit with an effort, but emotions cannot; they can only be ignored, misnamed, or deviated, but they will still be there. This is indeed a difference between their kind of reality and that of the material world.

7 See Chapter 14.

8 Such was the case of the analytic group's reaction to Ferenczi's (1933) last paper. Various letters of the time qualify him as 'paranoid' and 'psychotic', on the sole basis that he actually believed his patients' memories of child abuse and that he dared disagree with Freud (Masson, 1984).

9 Hans-Georg Gadamer (1960) has shown this to be the case for all sorts of interpretation, in his major theory of hermeneutics.

10 See Appendix I on Analogical Hermeneutics.

11 See Appendix II on the *Weltanschauung*.

12 This concept of a partial, contextual, and temporary, but sufficient, truth is taken from
analogical hermeneutics (Tubert-Oklander & Beuchot Puente, 2008; also, in Appendix I).

13 This is indeed crucial: any new piece of insight, which opens new ways of understanding things, later becomes an obstacle, when it becomes an established knowledge, and
requires to be questioned and enquired again, in a process akin to Hegelian dialectics.
I believe this to be the meaning conveyed by Bion's (1967) puzzling statement that

> What is 'known' about the patient is of no further consequence: it is either false or
> irrelevant. If it is 'known' by patient and analyst, it is obsolete. . . . The one point
> of importance in any session is the unknown. Nothing must be allowed to distract
> from intuiting that.

(p. 272)

14 Understanding the analytic experience in field and process terms (Tubert-Oklander,
2017c) is part of a holistic conception of psychoanalysis (see Appendix III on Holism).

15 Freud (1898, pp. 301–302) clearly states, in this letter,

> It seems to me that the theory of wish fulfillment has brought only the psychologi-
> cal solution and not the biological – or, rather, metapsychical – one. (I am going
> to ask you seriously, by the way, whether I may use the name metapsychology for
> my psychology that leads behind consciousness.)

Part II

A fresh look

Chapter 8

The matrix and the bond (2017–2020)

The holistic theory of group analysis

Juan Tubert-Oklander

*In 2011, after the publication of the first book of the series on the Social Unconscious, edited by Earl Hopper and Haim Weinberg (2011a), in which I had participated with a chapter on Pichon-Rivière (Tubert-Oklander, 2011b), the editors invited me to write another chapter for their new book, which was going to be focused on the concept of the matrix. I readily accepted and started to work on a text on the stratification of the matrix. The production of this book, however, turned out to be much more complex and lengthier than was originally expected, so that it had to be split into two volumes (Hopper & Weinberg, 2016, 2017b): the first (which was actually Volume 2 in the series) was called **Mainly Foundation Matrix,** and the second (Volume 3), **The Foundation Matrix Extended and Reconfigured**. My own contribution was finally included in Volume 3, under the name 'The inner organisation of the matrix' (Tubert-Oklander, 2017a). But the manuscript turned out to be too extended for publication, so that I cut it down, following a suggestion by the editors, by eliminating the first part, which dealt with the general concept of the matrix, and leaving only the exposition of my own ideas. The omitted section now became the basis for the present chapter. A few paragraphs of what was then left out were included in the editors' Introduction to the volume (Hopper & Weinberg, 2017a), with my consent and their acknowledgement. The same Introduction also contained contributions by Dieter Nitzgen and Tom Ormay, so that it was actually an expression of group thinking, even though the final text was, of course, a creation of its authors.*

When we designed the outline of this book, we thought that we needed to write a new chapter to introduce the Second Part on group analysis, called 'A fresh look'. But then I remembered this previously unpublished text, and we decided that a revised and updated version of it, enlarged to include Pichon-Rivière's Theory of the Bond (since the original text focused only on the Foulkesian tradition), could well fulfil this function. And this is what we did.

One of the most significant contributions of S. H. Foulkes to the theory of group analysis was his concept of the *matrix*.[1] This was his way of tackling the problem of the group-specific factors and avoiding the pitfalls that result from the attempt to apply an unmodified theory of psychoanalysis to the group situation.

DOI: 10.4324/9780429055287-11

Mainstream psychoanalysis has traditionally identified with the individual paradigm of the human being that served as starting point of Freudian metapsychology, while usually ignoring the other transpersonal paradigm of collective mental processes that emerged in Freud's social writings.[2] This is unsurprising, since the founder of psychoanalysis never acknowledged that some of the concepts he introduced in his social enquiries were incompatible with the assumptions that underlay his standard theory-building strategy.

We psychoanalysts are basically therapists and, as such, we are always looking for a patient to analyse; without the patient, our skills become stale and ineffective. But who is to be the patient when we face a psychotherapeutic group? The easiest answer is to say, 'each of the individual members of the group is my patient'. From this perspective, analytic group psychotherapy becomes an application of standard psychoanalytic theory and technique to the conduction of the treatment of individuals in a group setting. This is the kind of group treatment that flourished in the United States at the beginning of group psychotherapy in that country (Wolf & Schwartz, 1962; Slavson, 1964).

The second answer is to conclude that 'the group as-a-whole is my patient'. Hence, by means of the simple trick of treating and interpreting everything that is being said by the group members as if it came from a single individual patient, and with the support of some misuse of the Gestalt hypothesis, the analyst had finally found his patient. This was developed in Britain at the Tavistock Clinic by Harry Ezriel (1950) and in Argentina by Grinberg, Langer, and Rodrigué (1957). Such authors found it easy to make this change from a group to a kind of super-individual, because they relied on the Kleinian concept of the unconscious phantasy (Isaacs, 1948; Segal, 1964), which was not restricted by the quasi-neurological implications of the ego psychology held by their US colleagues. But, in both cases, the psychoanalytic contribution to their work was limited to providing a set of pre-established theories and techniques, derived from the practice of bi-personal (so-called 'individual') psychoanalysis; there was actually no analytic enquiry of group phenomena.

The third answer, then, was to approach the group with the very same analytic attitude of curiosity and openness that Freud inaugurated when dealing with his patients and enquire whatever happened in the group situation. This would no longer be a mere application of psychoanalytic discoveries, theories, and techniques to the conduction of group treatments, but rather an analytic enquiry of groups that fully deserved the name 'Group Analysis'. In this approach, just as in standard psychoanalysis, the therapeutic aim became subordinate to the analytic investigation of what occurs in the clinical situation. This does not imply forsaking the therapeutic commitment to the patients, but rather a firm conviction that any direct striving to attain a therapeutic goal is unadvisable, and that the best way to treat the people who come to us is to help them to understand what it means working together in such group and to develop new ways of being with, relating to, and thinking with other human beings, in a climate of truthfulness, compassion, mutual trust, and co-operation.

Group analysis was introduced almost simultaneously in Britain by S. H. Foulkes (1946, 1948, 1964a) and in Argentina by Enrique Pichon-Rivière (1951, 1971a), although the latter called his theoretical and technical approach 'operative groups', rather than 'group analysis'. However, apart from some minor differences that we have expounded in a previous book (Tubert-Oklander & Hernández de Tubert, 2004), their coincidences are so great that it is quite obvious they are both speaking of one and the same thing. They both agree in their conviction of the essentially social nature of the human being. They also share a position about the role of theory in group analysis: that the true analytic stance in this matter is not to apply any preconceived ideas derived from the experience of bi-personal practice, but rather to develop new understandings and theories from the experience acquired in the group-analytic situation. And, since this clinical situation is one in which inter- and transpersonal factors and processes come to the fore, whenever its analytic enquiry needs help from other scientific disciplines, it should look for it in the social and humanistic sciences, not in the natural sciences, as Freud did.

Both pioneers strongly believed that there was no opposition between the individual and the group, that there was no need to choose one or another perspective, but rather that they were complementary, and we could not do without any of them. So, they oscillated between focusing on the individual and on the group. But how did they do it? How did they manage to carry through such conjuring trick?

What makes it at all possible is a difference in the ontological and philosophical assumptions that underlie ordinary thinking – both common-sense and scientific – and those of group-analytic thinking. Ordinary thinking is committed to the materialistic metaphysics that underlies the Newtonian model of the Universe: the World is a vast space in which there are only pieces of Matter, called 'objects', which have shape, volume, and mass, but are inherently inert, and a shapeless, volumeless, and massless Energy that acts on the objects through 'forces' that set them in motion, accelerate, decelerate, deform, or destroy them, since forces are inherently dynamic. This, and nothing else, is 'real', and the only way to know reality is through the sense organs and rational thinking. This was Freud's starting point ever since his *Project*, written in 1895 (Freud, 1950a).

This view of the Universe coalesces with the Cartesian belief in an individual, autonomous, and self-contained Subject, which is the basis of individuality. The subject is hence identified with the individual human organism, and particularly with its brain (Tubert-Oklander, 2008a [Chapter 1]). Starting from such assumptions, it is inevitable that one should conclude that a group is 'nothing but' an imaginary construction of its members, who turn their perception of their interactions into an idea of an actually non-existent supra-individual entity.[3]

Quite another picture emerges if one starts from a different ontology, one that includes not only material events, but also semiotic systems, communications, subjective experiences, relations, and meaning as real entities – 'real' here means 'capable of producing effects', as we have seen in Chapter 7. Then the group is no longer an illusion or just another name for the interactions between the individual members, but a reality in itself, albeit not a material reality, and group processes may now be seen as mental processes, thus severing the hitherto unchallenged alleged identity between mind and brain function.

This hyper-complex human reality, which includes intra-personal, inter-personal, and transpersonal processes, cannot be conceived, perceived, or thought from a single vantage point, and so requires multiple views in order to get some idea of the whole.[4] Such cognition is necessarily constructive and is ruled by the principle of the figure-ground distinction. Consequently, if one takes the individual member as the figure, the group becomes ground, the frame and context for the perception of the object that is thus constructed. On the other hand, if the group itself becomes the figure, the individual members turn into the ground. A similar phenomenon can be found in the perception of the group and the wider society to which it belongs. Hence, viewing, knowing, enquiring, and thinking about the human being becomes an active process of constructing images, thoughts, and entities, a process that necessarily includes the observer as a part of the field of enquiry.

Foulkes (1948) was well-aware of these problems, and he always emphasised that the group conductor was in a liminal position, both within and without the group, at one and the same time. This is what allowed him or her to integrate empathic understanding and rational explanation in a single interpretative knowledge. All phenomena that take place in the group were conceived by him as a multifarious network of communication that occurred, not only *within* the individual members (intra-personal processes) and *between* them (inter-personal processes), but also *around* them and *going through* them, pretty much like X-rays go through physical objects (transpersonal processes) (Foulkes, 1973). This network *was* human existence.

Pichon-Rivière's (1979) conception was quite similar: for him, individual and society form an indissoluble unit, a single dynamic field, because we all carry society within us, and society is made of individuals, who are also made by it and re-create it in each of them. Hence, 'One cannot think in terms of a distinction between the individual and society. It is an abstraction, a reductionism that we cannot accept' (p. 57, my translation). (Compare this with Foulkes's [1961] assertion that 'Both aspects, the individual and the social one, are not only integrated in our approach, but their artificial isolation – never found in actual reality – does not arise' [p. 148]. Also 'Each individual – itself an artificial, though plausible, abstraction – is basically and centrally determined, inevitably, by the world in which he lives, by the community, the group, of which he forms a part' [1948, p. 10].)

In Pichon-Rivière (1979), this took the form of his 'theory of the bond'. The *bond – vínculo* in Spanish, also translated as 'link' (Losso, Setton, & Scharff, 2017; Scharff, 2017) – is *not* the same as 'object relations', although it includes them. The human being is shaped by his or her multiple relationships – past, present, and anticipated or wished-for – with real external objects, with their own peculiarities and subjectivities, as well as the groups, communities, and culture to which they all belong – that is, the social, historical, and political context. All this is internalised and re-created in the inner field of the personality, forming what he calls the 'inner group'. This inner aspect of the bond is what psychoanalysis has studied extensively, under the name of 'object relations', but the whole bonding structure always includes the inner and the outer fields, in a perpetual dialectic relationship – and here 'field' does not only have physical or dynamic connotations, but also those of a football field: a space for groups to play (Tubert-Oklander, 2011b), and the play and dialogue within the inner group underlies the individual's mental processes and resonates with his or her outer relationships.

This approach led Pichon-Rivière (1971a, 1979) to formulate a novel theoretical development, which he called *Teoría del vínculo*. *Vínculo* is a Spanish word which means 'link', 'tie', 'bond', or 'relation'; it may refer to physical, logical, interpersonal, emotional, psychosocial, or legal connections. This term has been translated alternatively as 'link' or 'bond'. Nowadays the preferred English translation seems to be 'link', although 'bond' is probably nearer in its connotations to Pichon-Rivière's concept.

The connotations of the term 'link' are more frequently physical (like a link in a chain) or logical (like a connection between two things or situations, especially where one affects the other), but it may also refer to communications, travel, or computing. On the whole, this 'penumbra of associations' (Bion, 1962, p. vi) tends to be more concrete and impersonal. 'Bond', on the other hand, although it also has physical connotations (like ties, shackles, or structural connections), they may also be emotional (the bonds of love), legal (a contract), socio-political (as in bondage), relational (as in bonding), chemical (a force that joins two or more atoms and turns them into something new – a molecule), or economic (an interest-bearing document that implies a commitment). Hence, 'bond' seems clearly more adequate than 'link' to convey Pichon-Rivière's psycho-social concept. So how did 'link' become the preferred translation? It so happened that in the 1960s Wilfred Bion's (1959) article 'Attacks on linking' was translated into Spanish in Argentina as *Ataques al vínculo*, but the word *'vínculo'* was already familiar in Pichon-Rivière' discourse, and this led to the erroneous belief that it was a same concept. But that was not the case. Bion was referring to the mental capacity to join two separate thoughts, in either verbal or iconic form, and blend them into a new idea, this being in line with his Kleinian intrapsychic perspective. Pichon-Rivière's concept, on the other hand, was that of a hyper-complex and ever dynamic psychosocial organisation, which was intra-, inter-, and transpersonal at the same time. This is, of course, incompatible with a theory that focuses exclusively on the intrapsychic dimension. In any case, it was easy for the translators of Pichon-Rivière to English to turn *vínculo* into 'link'. In our book on *Operative Groups* (Tubert-Oklander & Hernández de Tubert, 2004), we had used 'bond', but 'link' seems to have prevailed, so that it appears that we shall have to live with this mistranslation, just as we learnt to live with Strachey's use of 'instinct' for *Trieb* (Tubert-Oklander, 2017b).

So, what is this bond or link? The author used the concept to refer to a dynamic structure that included: (1) a subject, (2) his or her object (which is really another subject) or objects, (3) their respective subjective experiences, (4) the mutual tie or relationship between them, 4) their histories, traditions, and beliefs, and (5) the whole group, social, political, cultural, historical, physical, and ecological context in which it takes place. This is a holistic field and process theory whose indebtedness to Kurt Lewin (1951) and Harry Stack Sullivan (1947) is quite obvious.

This way of thinking allowed the author to move effortlessly from the study of individual unconscious fantasy (which he conceived as a dialogue and interaction among internal objects – the *internal group*), the individual's personal and family history, his or her community's, and the whole country's social and political history and present situation (Tubert-Oklander, 2011b; Tubert-Oklander & Hernández de Tubert, 2004).

In 1965, Pichon-Rivière (1965a) wrote a case history that became a paradigmatic example of the way in which he understood what he once called the 'implacable interplay of man and the world' (1965b). It was an exercise in applied analysis – both psychoanalysis and group-analysis – a study in depth of the life and work of Enrique Santos Discépolo, the famous Argentine poet and tango writer, which included not only his personal and family history, but also the influence that the peculiar social and political developments of his time had on both the content and the social impact of his lyrics. In the chapter I wrote for the first book of Hopper and Weinberg's series on the Social Unconscious (Tubert-Oklander, 2011b), I expanded his analysis and showed how a full understanding of his argument required an exposition of one hundred years of Argentine history, which had left implicit, since he assumed (probably erroneously) that his readers and fellow-citizens would be familiar with them. This was a most unusual way of presenting a case study – at least in psychoanalysis, although there have been similar efforts by Erik Erikson (1950, 1958, 1969) and Vamik Volkan (Volkan & Itzkowitz, 1984). In the field of sociology, Reinhard Bendix's (1966) subtle and deep 'A memoir of my father' also represents a compelling effort to integrate the individual, social, and political aspects in a biographical study.

Now, Pichon-Rivière was never interested in formulating and using high abstraction concepts – what in psychoanalysis is called 'metapsychology'. His theorising took the form of a clinical theory of the enquiry and interpretation of human experience in relationships, groups, institutions, and society. Hence, the theoretical terms he introduced – such as 'bond' ('link'), 'inner and outer field', 'interplay of Man and the World', 'dialectic spiral', 'belongingness', 'pertinence', 'co-operation', 'task', 'referential schema', 'dialectic spiral', and others (Tubert-Oklander & Hernández de Tubert, 2004) – are experience-near and allowed him to continue developing his analytic work, without posing claims to universal knowledge. For him, theories were tools to be used in actual analytic operation, just as in Kurt Lewin's famous dictum, 'There is nothing as practical as a good theory'.

But Foulkes was not satisfied with remaining at this level of analysis. Although he introduced quite a few experience-near theoretical terms that he used in his clinic – for example, 'socialization through the group', 'mirroring', 'condenser phenomena', 'chain phenomena', 'resonance', 'translation', 'ego training in action', among others (Foulkes & Anthony, 1965) – he also felt the need for more abstract concepts that may account for these experiences. Thus, he introduced the concept of the *matrix* as a theoretical construct intended to bridge the apparent gap between the individual and the group, and to explain both the dynamics of the individual personality and that of groups, institutions, and societies. It also transcends the alleged opposition between 'biological' and 'psycho-social'.[5]

Foulkes's (1964b) tersest definition of the matrix is as follows:

> *The Matrix* is the hypothetical web of communication and relationship in a given group. It is the common shared ground which ultimately determines the meaning and significance of all events and upon which all communications and interpretations, verbal and non-verbal, rest.
>
> (p. 292)

In other words, the matrix is the *context* of everything that happens in a group, and it determines the meaning or meanings of such occurrences (Hopper, 1982, 1985, 2003a). But it is much more than that: it is a theoretical construct that purports to give a causal explanation of the events. The idea was to develop *a process theory of mind*; in other words, to break the old association between mind, on the one hand, and the individual and the organism, especially the brain, on the other (Foulkes, 1973),

> It seems difficult for many at the present time to accept the idea that what is called 'the mind' consists of interacting processes between a number of closely linked persons, commonly called a group. [p. 224] . . . The group-analytic view would claim that all these interactional processes play in a unified mental field of which the individuals composing it are a part . . . This network is a psychic system as a whole network, and not a superposed social interaction system in which individual minds interact with each other. This is the value of thinking in terms of a concept which does not confine mind, by definition, to an individual. [p. 226] . . . This enabled me to say that it is mental processes, not persons, that interact.
>
> (p. 228)

This is not to say that persons do not exist or that they do not have mental processes of their own before entering a group, which would be tantamount to a complete negation of the discoveries of psychoanalysis. Of course, whenever a few people meet to form a group, they start afresh a new network of communications, which is mainly unconscious, called the *dynamic matrix*. Each of them contributes with his or her personal structure, previous experience, ideas, and beliefs, and the influence of the other groups – past, present, and wished-for – of which she or he is a part of; this is the very basis of transference. But the point is that they are able to do this precisely because what we call 'the person' is also a matrix: the *personal matrix* – what Pichon-Rivière (1965c, 1979) called the 'internal group'. Hence, there is an interpenetration and resonance between the various individual matrixes, to form a new dynamic structure that does not reside in or belong to any one of them, but rather exists in between, goes through, determines, and is recreated and determined by them: the *dynamic matrix*.

This is also possible because both the group members and all the groups they belong to are also part of a wider social matrix, called the *foundation matrix*. Without it, there would be no possible communication between them,

> I have accepted from the beginning that even this group of total strangers, being of the same species and more narrowly of the same culture, share a fundamental, mental matrix (*foundation matrix*). To this their closer acquaintance and their intimate exchanges add consistently, so that they also form a current, ever-moving, ever-developing *dynamic matrix*.
>
> (Foulkes, 1973, p. 228)

This foundation matrix usually remains as ground, and only rarely becomes figure, whenever a cultural difference between the group members makes it problematic and brings it to the fore, as we shall presently see.

Now, why talk about the group 'matrix' and not the group 'mind'? This is still a matter of controversy; for instance, Earl Hopper and Haim Weinberg (2011b) recorded, in their 'Introduction' to Volume 1 of their series of books on the Social Unconscious (2011a, 2016, 2017b), their disagreement on the matter of accepting or rejecting the concept of a 'group mind'. For Hopper, the idea behind the introduction of 'matrix' was to avoid the personological connotations of the term 'mind' – namely, the assumption of an organised and unitary entity, with a conscious identity, purpose, and intention – in other words, a subject. This seems to me to indicate that there is a certain fear of falling back to the Cartesian subject, which had nonetheless already been lethally wounded by the discovery of the unconscious. In particular, those theorists that apply the concept of mind to the social system tend to represent a conservative ideology, which emphasises the integrity of the system and the use of homeostatic mechanisms to preserve it, so fostering the maintenance of the *status quo*.

This is, of course, a valid criticism, but it misses the point that our contemporary concept of mind is quite different from what it used to be in Modernism. First, no one can seriously maintain, after Freud, Nietzsche, and Marx, the Cartesian conception of a unitary, autonomous, and pristine subject. There is no doubt that human groups and societies harbour different interests, feelings, and points of view that must necessarily be negotiated, but so does the individual. Perhaps we should no longer speak of 'individuals', but of 'multividuals', of an inner society made of living parts that have to negotiate their agreements and disagreements, an internal group that follows a similar dynamics as that of the external groups it reflects and takes part into, as Pichon-Rivière suggested. This is, of course, one possible way of understanding Freud's (1923b) *The Ego and the Id*.

Another objection is that the group cannot have a mind, because it does not have a brain. This argument is precisely a consequence of one aspect of the foundation matrix: that of language and culture. In the English-speaking philosophical and scientific tradition, mind is usually conceived as a functional entity, something like an inner organ and intimately related to the brain, of which it is supposed to be an epiphenomenon. But in German, the corresponding terms are *Seele* (soul) and *Geist* (spirit), which carry very different connotations. Freud very frequently used *Seele* as interchangeable with *Psyche*, while reserving *Geist* for dealing with the supernatural or for 'the activating or essential principle of something' – as when he wrote about 'the scientific spirit' (der wissenschaftliche Geist). But he definitely resorted to the hypothesis of a collective mind (*Massenpsyche*) when having to explain archaic memories and the continuity of generations, as in *Totem and Taboo* (1912–1913),

> No one can have failed to observe, in the first place, that I have taken as the basis of my whole position the existence of a collective mind, in which mental processes occur just as they do in the mind of an individual. In particular, I have supposed that the sense of guilt for an action has persisted for many thousands of years and has remained operative in generations which can have had no knowledge of that action. I have supposed that an emotional process, such as might have developed in generations of sons who were ill-treated by their father, has extended to new generations which were exempt from such treatment for the very reason that their father had been eliminated. It must be admitted that these are grave difficulties; and any explanation that could avoid presumptions of such a kind would seem to be preferable.
>
> Further reflection, however, will show that I am not alone in the responsibility for this bold procedure. *Without the assumption of a collective mind, which makes it possible to neglect the interruptions of mental acts caused by the extinction of the individual, social psychology in general cannot exist.* Unless psychical processes were continued from one generation to another, if each generation were obliged to acquire its attitude to life anew, there would be no progress in this field and next to no development.
>
> (pp. 157–158, my italics)

Foulkes, whose native language and culture was German, had no trouble in conceiving the group as a *Massenpsyche*, as he shows in the following quotation:

> Looked at in this way it becomes easier to understand our claim that the group associates, responds and reacts as a whole. The group as it were avails itself now of one speaker, now of another [what Pichon-Rivière (1965c) calls the 'spokesman' for the group], but it is always the transpersonal network which is sensitized and gives utterance, or responds. *In this sense we can postulate the existence of a group 'mind' in the same ways as we postulate the existence of an individual 'mind'.*
>
> (1957, p. 118, my italics)

The fact that the word 'mind' is between quotation marks shows that Foulkes was as suspicious of the concept of the individual mind as of that of the group mind. He is indeed quite clear about it,

> This totally new phenomenon which they create I usually refer to as the 'context of the group'. I do not talk of a group mind because this is a substantivation of what is meant and as unsatisfactory as speaking of an individual mind. The mind is not a *thing* which exists but a series of events, moving and proceeding all the time.
>
> (1973, p. 224)

In other words, Mind is not a thing, but a process. This is akin to Marjorie Brierley's (1944, 1951) reformulation of metapsychology as a process theory, but Foulkes goes even further, when he asserts that such processes are not limited by the boundaries of the human organism, but extend all over the interpersonal and transpersonal dimensions.

A similar view has been advanced for both biology and the human sciences by the renowned anthropologist and epistemologist Gregory Bateson (1972, 1979). For him, the basic question is to distinguish between the world of substance (i.e., that of physical science, in which only 'forces and impacts' can be causes) and the world of form (i.e., of biology and the social sciences, in which a piece of information is a cause),

> The explanatory world of *substance* can invoke no differences and no ideas, but only forces and impacts. And, per contra, the world of *form* and communication invokes no things, forces or impacts but only differences and ideas. (A difference which makes a difference *is* an idea. It is a 'bit', a unit of information.)
>
> (1972, pp. 271–272)

From this definition of an idea stems a similar definition of mind as any organised system of ideas. Hence, the genoma, an ecological system such as a forest, a person's thinking, experience, and behaviour, a group, or a society are all minds. This is, of course, compatible with the idea of a group mind, and free from the criticisms of the ordinary reified concept of mind.

Weinberg's (Hopper and Weinberg, 2011b) disagreement with Hopper follows a path which is similar to Bateson's,

> [He] believes that in order to have a mind, a social system does not need to have a brain. It is sufficient for the members of a social system to possess brains and to interact with one another. In other words, the flow of energy and information *between* the members of the social system *is* the mind of the social system. Thus, the mind of the social system exists within the transitional space that is co-created by all the members of the system, and is a function of their interpersonal

relations and of their capacity for 'we-centric' space . . . Thus, he is prepared to refer to the mind of a social system, not only as a synonym for the culture and/or social organisation of a social system, but as a matter of substance.

(pp. xliv–xlv)

Now, these functional definitions of mind and the matrix leave out one of the main characteristics of mind, originally introduced by Aristotle, which the young Freud learnt in his classes of philosophy with Franz Brentano, a deep and creative Aristotelian thinker: its *intentionality*. According to Brentano, all psychic acts are *intentional* – that is, they tend towards something, which is its aim. Freud's clinical thinking always took this into account, although, at the time of theory building, he omitted any consideration of it and tried to build a strictly causal theory, which could be considered 'scientific', according to the positivistic requirements of his physicalist teachers. It is interesting to point out that Freud never mentions Brentano, although the letters of his student years show how deep an impression he made on the young man. Perhaps the religious aspect of Brentano – a former priest – clearly related to this teleological thinking, made him something of a shameful sin of youth for the older Freud (Domenjo, 2000).[6]

But if we take intentionality as an essential characteristic of Mind, it becomes obvious that this kind of living process is not just only a causally linked time sequence of events, but one with a direction and a goal, which give it a meaning. Living processes, in both biology and the human sciences, are not the result of linear causality, as the displacement of billiard balls on the table or planets in space, but of what cyberneticists call 'circular causality' – that is, they are self-regulated and corrected in order to attain their goal, and this requires an ongoing input of fresh information about the circumstances, the effects of their actions, and the response from other living systems. So, the group mind may not be conscious, but it has intentions that it tries to fulfil; however, since social systems are not homogeneous, neither are the intentions of the various subgroups, and this requires negotiation, which is one of the main functions of mind.

The concept of the matrix tried to avoid these problems, by conceiving the behaviour of individuals as the result of changes in the network, thus retaining a certain semblance of scientific causality. But the matrix is not just a structure, but an evolving process, as Foulkes clearly stated, and, if we include the fundamental concept of intentionality, there is no way to obviate a discussion of the assumptions, goals, beliefs, and values in the course of a group-analytic enquiry. This means also including the political aspect of human life.

Now, this theoretical approach is difficult to integrate with traditional psychoanalytic thought, which takes the individual subject as its starting point. It is clear that those theories that have a basis in the assumption of the primary existence of the individual isolate are quite proficient in studying its inner workings and experiences, but find themselves at odds when trying to explain how these individuals relate and communicate to each other over a seemingly unbridgeable gap. In this kind of thinking, human communication appears to be something like smoke signals passed between the inhabitants of different islands, and their mutual influence and emotional resonance is almost inconceivable.

On the other hand, those theories that affirm the primacy of the social and relational nature of the human being find it easy to account for communication, relationship, and social participation, but are in deep trouble to account for the unexpected existence of individuality. If we are all part of a network of subjectless collective mental processes, how does the individual subject emerge? And how are we to make the discoveries and concepts of psychoanalysis compatible with the field and process group-analytic theory of the matrix?

Both Pichon-Rivière and Foulkes have opted for a view that highlights a dialectics of inner and outer, individual and collective. Foulkes did it on the basis of Gestalt Theory, by postulating a figure-ground relationship between 'individual' and 'group'. Thus, he poses the following,

> When speaking of psychology or psychopathology we would do better to have in mind the composite total which embraces and contains all psychological processes in any given situation of study. We can focus on the group as a whole or on any one individual or individuals in their specific interactions: all that happens is meaningful from any point of view, and the different meanings dovetail. It is not the case that the one viewpoint is right and the other wrong. It is rather as if we took photographs from various positions. One picture may be better for certain purposes and the others less good, but all of them show what is true from the position from which they are taken.[7] However, the total process must always be defined from the total field. The relationship appears to be best understood in terms of figure and ground . . . Figure is that which we choose particularly to observe, that on which we focus, or what in impartial observation forces itself into the foreground.
>
> (Foulkes, 1973, pp. 230–231)

This passage is an excellent explanation of what we mean when we say that the findings of an analysis are not discovered but constructed through our enquiry. Nonetheless, 'constructed' does not mean 'invented'. Foulkes is no relativist, but a perspectivist. What we are observing is a hyper-complex human reality, which exists independently from us (see Chapter 7), but the views, descriptions, meanings, and understandings we reach are not pre-existent to our search, and the particular form they take depends on our vantage point and the instruments of our enquiry (what Bion, 1970, would call our 'vertex').[8] And, in the group-analytic situation, this is not only or basically provided by the conductor, but emerges from the group, through the group-analytic dialogue.

Pichon-Rivière, much in the same vein, approached this problem in terms of a dialectics between 'inner' and 'outer'. This is how he describes it:

We talk about internal bonds and external bonds, both integrated in a process of dialectical spiral. The bond, which is first external, then becomes internal, and then external again, and afterwards once more internal, and so on, thus configuring the notion of a boundary between inner and outer. This determines that the characteristics of a given person's internal world be completely different from those of other persons facing the same experience of external reality.

(Pichon-Rivière, 1979, p. 55, my translation)

But how are we to explain this essential confluence of inner and outer, individual and collective? Pichon-Rivière, who was never interested in developing an abstract theory of mind, did not explicitly approach this problem, but just took it for granted as an assumption that underlay his clinical theory and practice. It was left to his disciple José Bleger (1967, 1971) to spell out the theoretical consequences of his master's way of thinking. Bleger, who had had a Kleinian upbringing, postulated the existence of a third position, which antedated Klein's paranoid-schizoid and depressive positions. This he called this the 'glischro-caric position'. *Glischro* means viscous, and *karyon* means nucleus; hence, an *agglutinated nucleus*. In this position, there was no differentiation between inner and outer, subject and object, body and mind, male and female, or any other notion of difference. This state of mind he described with the term *Syncretism*, and the peculiar quality of its experience he called *ambiguity*. But he did not just consider it to be a primitive state of mind, prior to later developments, as in the Kleinian theory of mental development, but rather as a permanent organisation of minding, that coexisted, alternated, and complemented the other positions. As we have seen in Chapter 5, this development of Romain Rolland's and Freud's concept of the 'oceanic feeling' is compatible with the theoretical proposals of Hans Loewald (1951), Margaret Mahler (1968), Blanca Montevechio (1999, 2002) and myself (Tubert-Oklander, 2004a, 2004b, 2014).

Bleger (1971) conceived unconscious experience as having a syncytial organisation. A *syncytium* is defined as 'A single cell or cytoplasmic mass containing several nuclei, formed by fusion of cells or by division of nuclei'. In other words, it is a single protoplasmic mass that contains several or many nuclei. The metaphor suggests that a collective entity is continuous and homogeneous and contains the individual subjects, immersed in it, thus allowing a free flow among them, at the deepest level, while their differentiated parts have to communicate with other nuclei by undirect means.

In my own work (Tubert-Oklander, 2004a, 2004b, 2014), I have built upon Bleger and Montevechio's concept of syncretism, and introduced, in 2014, the proposal of a *Syncretic Paradigm*, that allowed an easy integration of individual, relational and group mental processes. In 2017, in the article from whose first draft the present chapter has been extracted, I developed it further to postulate a multi-levelled organisation of the matrix (Tubert-Oklander, 2017a).

But these ideas were indeed already implicitly contained in Pichon-Rivière's thinking. In his article 'Implacable interplay of Man and World' (Pichon-Rivière, 1965b), he writes as follows,

> In the individual dimension, situations of crisis are more frequent than situations of change, which the former may precede and prepare. Crises unleash anxiety states in the individual and constitute the zigzags of personal development in front of each achievement, operating as the cutting edge of change towards the final situation of being a man oriented towards, committed to, and actively adapted to reality. The subject establishes a dialectical relationship with the world and transforms things, from being in-itself-to being-for-itself. By means of a permanent praxis, as he is changed, he changes the world, in a permanent spiral movement.
>
> (p. 170, my translation)

And then he quotes John Donne's most famous quotation from *Meditation 17*, which says,

> No man is an island, entire of itself; every man is a piece of the continent, a part of the main. If a clod be washed away by the sea, Europe is the less, as well as if a promontory were, as well as if a manor of thy friend's or of thine own were: any man's death diminishes me, because I am involved in mankind, and therefore never send to know for whom the bell tolls; it tolls for thee.
>
> (Donne, 1624)

This is a most poignant metaphor that highlights the essential identity of the individual and the collective, of Man and Humankind. Islands do not really exist, they are only mountains whose essential continuity with each other, through the sea bottom is concealed by the deep waters from which they emerge. The same is valid for the individual subjects, who are built on the foundation of being-at-one, not only with all others, but with everything-that-is. This is the philosophy that underlies the concept of the bond, and the very spirit of group analysis.

Notes

1 Regine Scholz (2003, 2011, 2017) considers the foundation matrix to be an essential transpersonal concept, which subsumes the more partial ones of social unconscious and large group identity.
2 See Chapters 5 and 6.
3 This was Bion's contention in his 1955 article on 'Group dynamics', included in his book *Experiences in Groups and Other Papers* (Bion, 1961), in which he wrote:

> The belief that a group exists, as distinct from an aggregate of individuals, is an essential part of this regression, as are also the characteristics with which the supposed group is endowed by the individual. Substance is given to the phantasy that

the group exists by the fact that the regression involves the individual in a loss of his 'individual distinctiveness' (Freud, 1921c, p. 9), indistinguishable from depersonalization, and therefore obscures observation that the aggregation is of individuals. It follows that if the observer judges a group to be in existence, the individuals composing it must have experienced this regression.

(p. 142)

Strangely enough, this conclusion contradicts what he had previously expressed in his famous series of articles, originally published in 1948–1951 in *Human Relations*, Vols. I–IV, and later included in the very same book, called 'Experiences in Groups, I–VII'. There he had clearly shown, enquired, and theorised the unquestionable existence of group mental processes. This surprising turn in his discourse may be attributed to the influence of his later re-analysis with Melanie Klein and to the fact that, although this article had originally been published in *The International Journal of Psycho-Analysis* in 1952, it did not include this paragraph and its final version was written for its inclusion as a chapter in a book edited by Melanie Klein, Paula Heimann, and Roger Money-Kyrle (1955). Hence, it is fair to assume that the editors required this clarification, in order to make Bion's novel ideas compatible with Kleinian theory. However, in his 'Introduction' to his book, the author seems to recant from this rather dogmatic assertion, in the following more flexible terms,

> I am impressed, as a practising psycho-analyst, by the fact that the psychoanalytic approach, through the individual, and the approach these papers describe, through the group, are dealing with different facets of the same phenomena. The two methods provide the practitioner with a rudimentary binocular vision.

(Bion, 1961, p. 8)

4 See Appendix III on Holism.
5 'From the very beginning our biology is social and vice versa' (Scholz, 2017, p. 30) and 'Thus challenging the boundaries between the inside and the outside, the division between the realms of biology and the world of interactions, the matrix contains in essence an anti-Cartesian approach' (p. 33). These assertions clearly correspond, as we shall see, to Foulkes's and Pichon-Rivière's points of view. This is also our own, as we shall see in Chapter 16.
6 The name of the author I am quoting is Blanca Anguera Domenjo (2000), a psychoanalyst and historian from Barcelona, and here the paternal surname comes before the maternal one, according to Spanish custom. So, she should be quoted as 'Anguera', but I have kept her as 'Domenjo', because this is the way she appears in the PEP database.
7 This is similar to Mauricio Beuchot's (1997) concept of Analogical Hermeneutics (see Appendix I).
8 Bion (1970) defines his concept of 'vertex' in the following terms,

> The scientific or sophisticated approach tends to become confounded with the realizations its formulations are intended to represent. The point (.) and the line (–) are regarded as if they were analogous to representations of reversible perspective. Their significance therefore varies according to the point of view (or vertex) with which they are associated. Vertices may have as their approximate realizations various recognized disciplines such as religion, mathematics, physics, music, painting, and other arts.

(pp. 20–21)

Chapter 9

The British and the Latin-American traditions (2014)

The Social Unconscious and the large group part I

Juan Tubert-Oklander and Reyna
Hernández-Tubert

In June 2013, the authors participated as staff in the International Workshop 'Studies of Large Groups and Social Unconscious', which took place in Belgrade. A major part of this participation consisted in delivering a lecture on the articulation of the British and the Latin-American group-analytic traditions, with a special reference to Large Groups. The present article is a development of that lecture. As the result was too long for its publication in Group Analysis, it was divided in three parts, which correspond to this chapter and the next two. Here we compare the British and the Latin-American group-analytic traditions, exploring their similarities and differences, and make a brief presentation of the latter. This implies introducing quite a few terms that are foreign to those colleagues that belong to the Foulkesian tradition. Nonetheless, we make a case that this is indeed a form of group analysis, on account of its basic attitude, its underlying assumptions, and the process fostered by its practice.

The two traditions of group analysis

Let us start at the beginning. For S. H. Foulkes (1948, 1964a, 1990), the creator of group analysis, this was originally a form of psychotherapy: *group-analytic psychotherapy*, understood as an intensive form of treatment in small groups, conducted along analytic lines. But it most certainly was *not* an application of psychoanalytic theory and technique to the treatment of individuals in groups. It is rather a method and technique based on the knowledge and use of the group's own dynamics. In this, it can be seen as an extension of the analytic enquiry of human affairs that Freud initiated in a bi-personal setting, to a group and social context (Tubert-Oklander & Hernández de Tubert, 2004).

Freud believed that his method allowed him to investigate the structure and functioning of an individual psyche; hence, the name Psycho-Analysis. Nowadays, we tend to think that the smallest possible field of observation in a psychoanalytic treatment comprises two people, not one, thus emphasising the bi-personal and relational nature of psychoanalysis (Tubert-Oklander, 2013a), but yet the name stuck. So, when we started to analyse groups and social systems, it was only natural to speak of *Group-Analysis* and *Socio-Analysis*.

DOI: 10.4324/9780429055287-12

Group analysis or more specifically, group-analytic psychotherapy, is an intensive form of treatment in small groups. The term group analysis also includes applications of the principles both within and outside the therapeutic field. While fully based on psycho-analytic insights, it is not an application of psychoanalysis to a group but a method and technique based on the dynamics of the group. It is a therapy *in* the group, *of* the group and *by* the group, the group providing the context in which the individual person is treated. Intra-psychic processes are seen as interacting within the mental matrix of the group.

(Foulkes, E. T., 1984, p. 6)

This means that the therapist, now called the *conductor*, is not conceived as the active part in therapy, as a doctor who cures his patients, but rather as something like a catalyst, that is, an element that makes a chemical reaction possible and speeds it up, but without really being a part of it. The conductor is, at one and the same time, *in* the group and *out* of it (Foulkes, S. H., 1948). The underlying metaphor is that of the conductor of an orchestra, who convenes the musicians, trains them, helps them become a functional group, and takes them to the concert, but once the music starts it is the members of the orchestra who carry out all the work. The only remaining functions for such a conductor, during the performance, is to somehow modulate what the group is doing, and behold and enjoy it. Of course, in the case of the group-analytic conductor, such modulation is carried out through his particular position of being both in the group and out of it.[1]

Although group analysis in no way rejects or discards psychoanalytic discoveries and theories, it develops its own theories and techniques out of the group-analytic experience, just as psychoanalysis had developed its theories and techniques out of the psychoanalytic experience. In both cases, the starting point and touchstone of their theorising is the *analytic experience*, whether psychoanalytic or group-analytic.[2] Theory is necessarily the most variable aspect of the analytic edifice, since it comes about as an effort to account for whatever happens when two or more people meet in an enclosed space in order to 'do analysis'.

But the term 'group analysis' also includes the application of its principles to the conduction of non-therapeutic dynamic groups. Once again, this is not an application of the group-analytic theories, as derived from the experience of group-analytic psychotherapy, but of the group-analytic principles that allow the group and its conductor to enquire, interpret, and understand together their shared experience. Hence, just as therapeutic group analysis is not a mechanical application of psychoanalysis to the treatment of patients in groups, non-therapeutic group analysis is not a mechanical application of group-analytic psychotherapy to the conduction of other kinds of groups, but an integral part of the group-analytic enquiry of human life and experience in groups.

All this is fairly well known by now. What is not so well known is that there was another school of group analysis that developed simultaneously with and independently from the British group-analytic movement initiated by Foulkes. This was the Latin American school of psychoanalytic Social Psychology derived from the work of Enrique Pichon-Rivière (1971a, 1979). He was a Swiss-born Argentinian psychiatrist and psychoanalyst who came to a jungle area in North-Eastern Argentina at the age of three, was raised in a multi-cultural and multi-linguistic environment that included the influence of his French parents and the Guaraní Indians, and eventually became a physician and a psychiatrist who was a pioneer of psychoanalysis and group analysis in Argentina (Tubert-Oklander, 2002; Hernández-Tubert, 2017c).

Pichon-Rivière called his own approach to group analysis 'Operative Groups' (Pichon-Rivière et al., 1960). He did not call it 'Group Analysis', but that was what he did. He, like Foulkes, emphasised the primary social nature of man, the importance of group work, and the social, cultural, historical, and political determination of individuals, relationships, groups, communities, and institutions. He was also convinced that psychoanalytical theory and technique were an insufficient basis for working with groups, and that they had to be complemented by the knowledge derived from the Social Sciences and the Humanities, as well as by a whole set of new concepts that emerged from the group experience itself. He also conceived the therapeutic and learning processes that took place in the group to be something derived from the group members' active efforts, while the analyst, whom he called the 'coordinator', was something like a coach who would help them to make the best of their hitherto unknown resources.[3]

There were differences, of course. Pichon-Rivière defined an *Operative Group* as 'a group of people with a common goal, which they try to approach by acting as a team' (Bleger, 1961, p. 57, our translation). This he called the *group task* (Pichon-Rivière & Bauleo, 1964). A large part of the group work is intended to help the members develop the skills and knowledge that are needed for them to be able to operate as a team. The group therefore has a double task: trying to attain its goal (*external task*) and learning to operate as a team (*internal task*).

Now, Foulkes always emphasised that a group-analytic group does not have a task. In this, he was surely trying to dispense with the kind of purposeful organisation and efforts that define most ordinary work groups in society, so that they would not interfere with the emergence of the unconscious group dynamics by means of a *free-floating discussion*. But he also always conceived the group process in terms of an *ego-training in action* (Foulkes, 1964b), and that action would have necessarily implied intentionality, even if it were not in terms of the kind of concrete goals that are usually formulated in ordinary groups. So, this difference is probably to be found more in the terms and concepts used by either author to think-through their group experiences, than in the group experience itself.

Perhaps this divergence stems from the kind of group each of them took as the paradigm of their approach: Foulkes clearly started by exploring therapeutic groups, and only later turned his attention to non-therapeutic ones, while Pichon-Rivière originally concentrated on learning, institutional, and communitarian groups, which he called 'operative groups', from which he developed his concepts and techniques that were also to be applied to therapeutic groups. For him, a therapeutic group was conceived as 'an operative group that assumes the explicit task of attaining the healing of its members' (Pichon-Rivière, 1965c, p. 127, our translation).

A perhaps more substantial difference is to be found in their respective attitude towards interpretation. Foulkes did not consider interpretation to be a major contribution of the conductor, but rather that, once the group-analytic setting had been established and the group process set in motion, the conductor's main contribution would be to nurse this process, on the basis of her or his ability to take into account the whole situation, represented by the group and its boundaries. This he clearly stated in a letter to Juan Campos Avillar (1981), when commenting on the work of Grinberg, Langer, and Rodrigué (1957), another group of Argentine psychoanalysts, highly influenced by the Tavistock's Kleinian approach, who developed an exclusively interpretative approach, centred on the concept of a single group unconscious phantasy, which allowed them to take the group-as-a-whole as if it were an individual analytic patient. According to Foulkes they,

> . . . had not understood my point of view. . . . Their main misunderstanding is that they believe that I only provide interpretations to the group-as-a-whole, and that we emphasize solely verbal communication, while what I have always said is that what we do is to treat the individual in the context of the global situation, which is represented by the group and its boundaries.
> (Foulkes, quoted by Campos Avillar, 1981,
> p. 18, our translation)

Pichon-Rivière, on the other hand, conceived interpretation as a stimulus for thinking and reflection among the group members, so that it became for him the main contribution of the coordinator. Interpretation was intended to help the group overcome the primitive anxieties that hindered the members in their task, imprisoning them in stereotyped roles and sterilising the group's productivity. This he summarises as follows,

> The aims and purpose of operative groups may be summarised by saying that their activity is centred on mobilising structures that are stereotyped, as a result of the anxiety levels generated by every change (depressive anxiety for the loss of the previous bond and paranoid anxiety generated by the new one and the resultant insecurity). In the operative group, clarification, communication, learning, and the resolution of the task coincide with healing, thus creating a new referential schema [for the group and its members].
> (Pichon-Rivière et al., 1960, p. 120, our translation)

His interpretations were not, of course, traditional psychoanalytic interpretations of intrapsychic wishes, conflicts, and mechanisms, but rather reflections about the group's and the members' situation, assumptions, relations, and efforts, as well as on the way in which they tackled their task and related to it and to the coordinator. Such interventions did not usually look like interpretations, since they were frequently formulated by means of analogies; so, he could recount an event in a football match, a film, the words of a tango, or quote the popular long poem *Martín Fierro*, that everyone had read in elementary school. But, of course, it is true that he spoke much more in his groups than what Foulkes used to in his.

Besides, Pichon-Rivière, like Foulkes, did not conceive the group coordinator (conductor) as someone alien to the group, but as an analyst who should always include himself as part of the very same phenomenon he was striving to understand. Foulkes (1948) described, in his first book, 'the characteristic position of the Conductor: partly inside and partly outside the group' (p. 143). Pichon-Rivière (1965c), on his part, wrote that '*The coordinator included himself in the psychotherapeutic process,* thus attaining a change in the distorted image he had of the patients, as well as the distorted image they had of him' (p. 131, our translation, original italics).

In any case, there is still a difference in the approaches of the two schools of group-analytic theory and practice they initiated, albeit one that may well be cleared away by dialogue and mutual understanding. We shall further deal with this when discussing large group techniques.

There is certainly no question of priority here, since neither of them seems to have had any influence on the other. Foulkes started his first therapeutic group in Exeter in 1940, developed his approach to group-analytic therapy in the North-field Military Centre Hospital from 1943 to 1945, published his first book *An Introduction to Group-Analytic Psychotherapy* in 1948, and founded the Group-Analytic Society in 1952. Pichon-Rivière started his clinical explorations in the *Hospicio de las Mercedes*, the Buenos Aires psychiatric hospital, in 1936 (Zito Lema, 1975, 1976), and developed it in his work with non-therapeutic and therapeutic groups (Pichon-Rivière, 1951), until he managed to implement, together with a group of disciples and co-workers, in 1958, a social laboratory called the *Rosario Experience*, in which they tried to analyse a whole city (Pichon-Rivière et al., 1960).[4] These two traditions developed independently and with few contacts between them, since Latin-American group therapists still have little knowledge of the Foulkesian tradition, and there have been no English translations of Pichon-Rivière's writings, a limitation the two present writers tried to overcome when publishing, in 2004, our book *Operative Groups: The Latin-American Approach to Group Analysis* (Tubert-Oklander & Hernández de Tubert, 2004). Later, I published a chapter on Pichon-Rivière and the social Unconscious (Tubert-Oklander, 2011b).[5] We believe it is high time for these two group-analytic traditions to engage in a productive dialogue, such as the one that took place in Belgrade.

There is still the question of the name. It could be argued that the name *Group Analysis* should be used only to refer to the particular approach to analytic groups introduced by S. H. Foulkes and to the school and institution he founded. This would be to treat the term as a proper name and, of course, every person and group are entitled to choose their own.

Besides, Pichon-Rivière never talked of 'group analysis', but of 'operative groups'. Then, why not leave things as they are and avoid any confusion, by keeping their chosen names? Personally, we have tended, over our decades of writing, teaching, and practising, to restrict the use of the term 'operative groups' in favour of 'group analysis'. Why? Because we have found that speaking of operative groups always generates the misperception that we are talking about a particular kind of groups, to be distinguished from therapeutic groups, learning groups, focus groups, and the like, while Pichon-Rivière always used the term to refer to a whole conception of what groups are, how they function, and how they should be handled, quite apart from their manifest goals. The term 'group analysis' connotes a process, the underlying values, and its evolution, so we believe that it should be used to denote any kind of group theory, technique, and practice that shares its basic tenets (Tubert-Oklander & Hernández de Tubert, 2004; Tubert-Oklander, 2014).

Besides, there is room to argue that 'group analysis' is not a proper name, but a common name. The term was introduced by Trigant Burrow (1927) and later used by Karl Mannheim, before it was taken over by Foulkes in 1943 (Foulkes & Lewis, 1944). This being so, it seems only natural that we extend the use of the term in order to include other similar traditions and practices. This is, of course, a moot question, and we fully understand why someone raised in the Foulkesian tradition might object to the idea of qualifying the operative group approach as 'group analysis'. Nonetheless, our position, which is open to discussion, is that terms like 'psychoanalysis' and 'group analysis' are more fruitful when they refer to a specific field and a method of enquiry, than when they are limited to particular theories, techniques, or traditions.

The operative group approach

We shall now present an essential aspect of the way in which Pichon-Rivière and the tradition he initiated approached groups. Since he considered that a group is defined by the common task shared by all its members, their work together could be seen as a problem-solving activity, and the coordinator's function would be to help them attain the highest possible level of effectiveness in their operation, defined as 'operativeness'; hence, the name 'operative groups'.

Now, all of us approach new problems with a previous set of assumptions about the nature of problems in general and the way of understanding and tackling them. These we might qualify as 'prejudices', meaning 'judgements made before having all the relevant information', but this is inevitable: there is no way of approaching new things, if not in terms of old knowledge and habits. This we have seen in Chapters 5 and 7, in terms of Hans-Georg Gadamer's (1960) contention that every work of interpretation starts from a prejudice. The only way to avoid them turning into an obstacle for perceiving, conceiving, thinking, and dealing with novel situations is to become conscious of these assumptions, and this requires reflection and, in the case of groups, dialogue, as in Gadamer's approach to hermeneutics.[6]

Pichon-Rivière (1951) conceived this set of assumptions as a reference schema for thinking, and called it the *Conceptual Referential Operative Schema*, abbreviated as 'CROS' ('ECRO' in Spanish, the acronym for 'Esquema Conceptual Referencial Operativo).[7] This he defined as 'the whole of knowledge and attitudes that each of us has in his mind, and which he uses in working in his relation to the world and to himself' (p. 80, our translation).[8]

So, each of the members of the group, as well as the coordinator, comes provided with a personal CROS, which is the crystallisation of his or her life experience, and the internalisation of the collective schema shared by the groups, institutions, and society she or he belongs to. These disparate schemas, which are largely unconscious, are activated whenever a number of people get together in order to relate or do something.[9] At the beginning, this breeds *misunderstanding* and requires a special effort in order to turn it into *understanding*.

In this, the group coordinator's contribution is essential: her task should be to induce and help the group members to enquire into their various frameworks for thought, and to construct a common shared conceptual framework for their use in working together as a team; in other words, constructing a group CROS. This, for the author, can only be attained by means of interpretation. In the last interview he gave, just before his death at the age of seventy, Pichon-Rivière answered to the question of which are the operative tools of a social psychologist (the term he used to refer to what the present authors would call a group analyst) as follows: 'They are the same [as in psychoanalysis]; basically, interpretation given to groups. . . . [I]t is a discovery: what is implicit should become explicit' (*Actualidad Psicológica*, 1977, p. 1, our translation).

This is a consequence of the fact that a large part of the group members' CROS is unconscious for them. Hence, the coordinator's task is to interpret this – that is, to utter an explicit formulation of what, from her point of view, has previously been a set of implicit assumptions. This is not an easy task, since each one of them feels that his own personal assumptions about reality are necessarily true, that they are nothing but 'the way things are', and this breeds dogmatism. The mere discovery that other people perceive, think, and work from contrasting assumptions opens the way for the development of critical thought. So, one of the main tasks that a group has to face in order that its members be able to work together is to build a common group CROS (Pichon-Rivière, 1970; Tubert-Oklander & Hernández de Tubert, 2004, pp. 47–52 and 74–82).

Of course, the CROS is not merely an individual matter. We have already noted that it is largely the result of the internalisation of the collective schema shared by the groups, institutions, and society. As such, it is obviously determined by history, language, culture, ecology, economics, and politics. This is clearly related to Foulkes's (1964a) concept of the *foundation matrix*, Norbert Elias's (1939) and Bourdieu's (1972) *habitus*, and our present understanding of the *social unconscious* (Hopper, 2003a; Hopper & Weinberg, 2011a). In previous writings (Tubert-Oklander & Hernández de Tubert, 2004; Hernández de Tubert, 2004a; Hernández Hernández, 2010), we have analysed this in terms of the concept of the *Weltanschauung*, as a mainly unconscious psychological and social structure, to be enquired by means of analysis.[10] Nonetheless, a study in depth of these conceptual relations would require a full article of its own.

One major difficulty in analysing this collective aspect of the CROS is that it is not only unconscious, but also largely shared by the conductor and the members, inasmuch as they belong to a same social context. This makes it invisible, in principle, but it suddenly emerges when there is a crack in communication, as, for example, in a heterogeneous group in which there are people from diverse national, social, or ethnic origins.

This might seem to be an extremely intellectualistic approach to the group, but this is not the case, since for Pichon-Rivière there was no split between cognitive, affective, and conative functions – that is, between thinking, feeling, and acting. The assumptions we are talking about are not only those of the head, but also those of the heart and the body. The French philosopher Blaise Pascal (1670) once wrote that 'The heart has its reasons, of which reason knows nothing' (p. 127). This implies that there is a certain logic of emotions and intuition, which can be studied and talked about, just as there is an emotional basis of all our thinking processes, which has to be experienced in order that it may be known. So, in the operative group tradition there is no essential difference between therapeutic and non-therapeutic groups, since in both of them there is need for interpretation, emotional experience, and action, even though the subjects they are dealing with may be widely different.

This means that the group conductor in this kind of group is more than a convenor and a facilitator of the group process, but rather an active part of the dialogue that ensues.[11] This is why Pichon-Rivière used the term 'coordinator' or 'co-thinker', since she is thinking together with the group and participating in the development of group thought, which follows a spiral course, called the 'dialectic spiral' (Pichon-Rivière et al., 1960; Baranger, 1979).

A three-dimensional spiral is an apt metaphor for this kind of evolution, since it has a triple movement: (1) a *circular movement* that goes over and over again back to the same themes; (2) an *amplifying movement*, which determines that each new circle does not go back exactly to the same point, but is wider and more encompassing than the previous one, and (3) an *ascending motion* that makes it go further as it goes round and expands. The result is something like a cone, resembling a tornado, which revolves, expands, and ascends as it evolves (Tubert-Oklander, 2013a, 2013b). But, of course, a tornado also advances over the country, and this determines a *fourth movement*: thought and dialogue in the dialectic spiral do not only go over and over on the same themes, amplifying their coverage in each successive circle, and gradually attaining a higher (or deeper, depending on the metaphor) understanding, but they also *advance* – that is, move over to new problematics, covering new grounds.

A particular kind of operative group, created by Alejo Dellarossa (1979), an Argentine psychoanalyst and group analyst, who was a disciple of Pichon-Rivière and also teacher of one of us (Tubert-Oklander), is what he called *reflection groups*. These he introduced as a teaching practice at the Institute of Group Techniques of the Argentine Group Psychology and Psychotherapy Association. The training course for group therapists was intended for those professionals working in public mental health institutions. All of them had had previous studies and experience in individual psychotherapy and were already in some personal treatment, so it was not feasible to require them to enter a therapy group in order to acquire a personal group experience. Hence, it was decided that they should be provided with the experience of participating in a dynamic group, which nowadays we would conceive as a form of non-therapeutic group analysis. These were the reflection groups.

What is a *Reflection Group*? It is an operative group formed by members of an institution, who meet in order to think together about their experience of belonging and working or studying in that organisation. In this case, they were groups of students of the Institute who were to discuss their experience of being, studying, and learning in it.

Tubert-Oklander was a member of one of those first reflection groups, which was coordinated by Dellarossa (there were two others, which met simultaneously and had other conductors). Unlike what happens in therapy groups, the emphasis was on thinking, not on feeling, although it was not a rigid, logical thinking, but a free-flowing discussion, which was every now and then punctuated by the conductor's interpretations that referred it to what was happening in the institution and the group, in theoretical terms such as those the students were learning in their seminars. Dellarossa believed that in therapy groups the process should move from intellectualisation to deep feeling, but that in a reflection group the direction is reversed, from an initial immersion in an intense group regression, towards an ever-growing detachment and conceptualisation, in which the members recover what had been momentarily forgotten (repressed) – that is, the concepts they had been studying in their readings and classes.

Years later, when Dellarossa presented his paper on 'Reflection groups', he defined such a group as 'a context which becomes text'.[12] In other words, the organisational structure, dynamics, values, and assumptions that underlay everything that happens in that institution cease to be part of the perceptual ground (context) and become a figure (text), when they are taken as the subject of the group's discussion. And this effort is introduced and fostered by the conductor's interpretations, which remind the group members that they have forgotten the agreed-upon task, in their fascination with the intense emotional experiences that emerge in the group.

All this obviously has a bearing on our enquiry of the Social Unconscious and the conduction of Large Groups, as we shall presently see.

Notes

1 This was Foulkes' (1948) metaphor, but it has its limitations, as all analogies. José Luis Tubert (2021, email of February 19, 2021), a professional musician and music teacher, points this out in the following terms:

> The analogy of the conductor of an orchestra is not fully accurate. The task of a good conductor during a concert is quite different. You see, a musical score is a partial text that must needs be interpreted, because it only takes note of some aspects of what has to be turned into sound, while all others depend on the interpreter's judgement. This as a consequence of the limitations of the notation language and procedure. But if each of the instrumentalists made his own interpretation of what

is written in his score, the overall result would be chaotic. That is why the conductor has to interpret the piece and ask each of the players to do what he feels and thinks to be necessary to realise that interpretation he is listening to in his inner self. Many aspects are worked through in the rehearsals, but others are only defined at the time of the concert. The conductor imagines an interpretation and does whatever it takes to have the players respond to that interpretation. During rehearsals, he conveys it by means of words and singing, but some aspects can only be conveyed by means of gestural language. And this is what he uses during the concert to induce in the players or pluck from them that interpretation born from his own understanding of the piece.

I feel that a better metaphor for what you are trying to say would be that of a theatre director, who works the text through with the actors during the rehearsals, but who no longer directs during the actual performance, when the play is fully in the actors' hands.

These metaphors obviously demand a deeper examination, which will have to be left for a later occasion.

2 This epistemological stance was originally posed by Sándor Ferenczi and Otto Rank (1924) in their book *The Development of Psychoanalysis*, in which they stressed the unique importance of shared emotional experience as the only basis for conviction about the findings of an analysis, as well as for testing psychoanalytic theories. For them, subjective experience, and not behaviour, was the subject matter of psychoanalysis. We believe that the same may be held in the case of group analysis and the group-analytic experience.

3 For Pichon-Rivière (1971a) there was an essential identity of the processes of learning, therapy, an communication, which were but the various aspects of a single dialectical process that followed an ever-widening and ascending spiral course (Tubert-Oklander & Hernández de Tubert, 2004).

4 More about this in Part II of this series of articles (Chapter 10).

5 Since we first published this article, there have been other publications in English on Pichon-Rivière (Losso, Setton, & Scharff, 2017; Scharff, 2017; Scharff, Losso, & Setton, 2017; Tubert-Oklander, 2017b).

6 See Appendix I on Analogical Hermeneutics and Appendix II on the *Weltanschauung*.

7 'CROS' is the English acronym we introduced in our previous book (Tubert-Oklander & Hernández de Tubert, 2004), as a translation of the Spanish 'ECRO'.

8 In other words, what we call our Conception of the World or *Weltanschauung*.

9 And, since this does not include only cognitive assumptions, but also emotional, relational, and action schemata, this is, of course, also the basis for transference-countertransference processes.

10 See Appendix II on the *Weltanschauung*.

11 Here we feel that the term 'conductor' is more appropriate, since it refers to the generic function of initiating, fostering, and modulating the group's enquiry of its own thinking processes.

12 It is interesting to note that this suggestive formulation, which was part of Dellarossa's oral presentation in the Buenos Aires Association, in 1976, was lost in the published version in his 1979 book.

Chapter 10

A context that becomes a text (2014)

The Social Unconscious and the large group part II

Juan Tubert-Oklander and Reyna Hernández-Tubert

This chapter is the second part of our Belgrade lecture. In the previous chapter, we compared the British and the Latin-American traditions of group analysis. Here, we discuss the conception of the Social Unconscious in both traditions showing their essential coincidence. Then we turn to the Group-Analytic Large Group, defining it, describing its various types and functions, and providing some examples of them. In particular, we present Pichon-Rivière's 1958 'Rosario Experience', which became the original model for his conception of the operative groups. We have left the exposition of our own approach to large groups for the third and last part of the presentation, in the next chapter.

The Social Unconscious in both traditions

The status of our concept of the *Social Unconscious* is something to be discussed. On the one hand, it is a simple name for a much needed and awaited project: the full inclusion of the social dimension in the psychoanalytic and group-analytic theories and practices. As such, the term 'Social Unconscious' denotes two different but mutually related ideas.

First, there is the fact that the social context and processes have an impact on and a representation in the unconscious of individuals, and that they constitute a motivational force which is at least as powerful as instinctual drives (Tubert-Oklander, 2015 [Chapter 14]). This means that they are a necessary theme for analysis in both bi-personal and group treatments. And second, that there is an unconscious dynamics of social processes, which should then be conceived as mental in nature, even if they have no definite subject (Tubert-Oklander, 2014). This shows, as Foulkes insisted, that a mental process need not be related to an individual brain, as when he wrote,

> To me it does not seem difficult to accept that communication, verbal or otherwise, can take place, from one mind to the other with complete disregard of whether the brain substance is located in one or other skull of the participants.
>
> (Foulkes, 1967, p. 18)

DOI: 10.4324/9780429055287-13

This makes such unconscious social processes a subject to be enquired by means of analysis, although we still have to determine what sort of technique would be adequate for the task at each level of complexity – groups, communities, institutions, national states, international relations (Hernández de Tubert & Tubert-Oklander, 2005).

Other writers, such as Earl Hopper (2003a) would take exception at any suggestion of a 'group mind', which he considers an undue extrapolation to the social level of concepts that are only adequate to refer to the psychology of individuals. Hence, he would rather seek support in the social sciences than in any functionalist concept of 'mind'. His definition of the Social Unconscious is as follows,

> The concept of the social unconscious refers to the existence and constraints of social, cultural, and communicational arrangements of which people are unaware: unaware, in so far as these arrangements are not perceived (not 'known'), and if perceived not acknowledged ('denied'), and if acknowledged, not taken as problematic ('given'), and if taken as problematic, not considered with an optimal degree of attachment and objectivity.
>
> (p. 127)

This obviously has much to do with the socio-political concept of 'ideology', but it clearly rejects the organismic connotation of the notion of a 'group mind',

> It is misleading to assume that people have unconscious minds in the same sense that they have complex brains; it is more appropriate to assume that people are unconscious, pre-conscious and non-conscious of much thought, feeling, fantasy and even sensation. Similarly, social systems do not have 'unconscious minds' or any kinds of mind, and the use of the concept of the social unconscious should not be taken to imply otherwise. After all, social systems are not organisms and the notion 'group mind' is rather misleading. Nonetheless, whereas we have come to accept the validity and utility of the concept 'unconscious' for phenomena originating in the body, we need a concept like the 'social unconscious' in order to discuss social, cultural and communicational constraints
>
> (pp. 127–128)

Clearly, much depends on our definition of 'mind', as pointed out by Haim Weinberg (2015; Hopper and Weinberg, 2011b, pp. xliv–xlv). From our point of view, it is nonsense to say that social systems *have* a mind, whereas social systems *are* mind, in at least one of its manifestations. But, in order to be able to think and say this, one should have to strip the word 'mind' of the functional and organismic connotations it has in English. The German terms *Geist* (spirit) or *Seele* (soul), which were those that Freud used, are much more adequate to refer to living complex symbolic systems and processes, such as those that occur in individual subjectivity, interpersonal and group relations, and social entities.[1]

On the other hand, Hopper's criticism is warranted, since the term 'Social Unconscious', especially when preceded by the definite article 'the', suggests that we are referring to a thing or entity, some sort of a specific system that differs from other kinds of 'unconscious'. Should we then speak of an 'individual unconscious' and a 'group unconscious', in terms of their spatial extent, of a 'present unconscious' and a 'past unconscious', in those of their temporal reference, or of a 'sexual unconscious' and a 'relational unconscious', as to their central themes?

The problem with the word 'unconscious' is that it is both an adjective – that is, the name of a quality – and a noun – the name of an entity. Hence, when Freud discovered that most of one's mental processes were unknown to the subject – that is, qualitatively unconscious – it was easy to fall into the misperception of taking this discovery as the manifestation of some kind of object or system, a thing that was somehow 'inside' the individual and which was the cause for many things that happened to him. Then, one could say that one 'has' an unconscious, just as one has a heart, a liver, or a brain (Tubert-Oklander, 2004c). This might seem an improbable way of thinking, but in fact it became the subject matter of a whole school of psychoanalytic thought – that of Ego Psychology.

Yet, just like Hopper, we think we may well use this term, since its assets far outweigh its liabilities, as long as we remember that we are not talking about a particular *system*, but about a *problematics* – that is, a whole set of theoretical and practical questions that urgently demand to be tackled, responded to, and dealt with by psychoanalysts and group analysts alike,

In Foulkes's thinking, the primary social nature of mind was never in question; it was indeed the starting point of his theorising and his therapeutic method. He always thought of group and social processes as something to be interpreted and insisted on the need for taking into account the social context of whatever happened in a group-analytic session. For instance, James Anthony (2010) tells us that once, when he presented, at an international group meeting, the history of a group of psychopathic and borderline mothers who had at various times consciously threatened to kill their children, Foulkes criticised him for not having 'taken into consideration the historical and Hitlerite era in which they had lived' and that he felt Anthony 'had not followed group analytic lines' (p. 84).

However, in actual practice, Foulkes selected the members for his therapeutic groups in such a way that insured that they shared a common *foundation matrix* – that is, he chose,

> . . . patients talking the same language against the same background of national feeling and participating in all the imponderables that go to make a pattern of culture [. . . and] other shared conditions, such as age, sex, religion, social background, intelligence, education, profession, marital status.
>
> (Foulkes & Anthony, 1965, p. 65)

This kind of group would seem to be designed in order that the inner contradictions of society remain invisible and do not become an outstanding figure in the group-analytic experience and hence a subject for the group-analytic enquiry, as it would happen if the various members came from different collective contexts and represented contrasting sets of values and conceptions of the world.

Now, there is a rationale for this policy. In such homogeneous groups, social and political issues are not likely to come to the fore, and the focus of the discussion will most probably centre on personal, emotional, and interpersonal conflicts, which is, after all, what is expected to happen in a therapy group, even though it leaves out a large portion of what is actually happening. If the group members are expected to think-through and solve their personal problems, without calling into question the society they have grown and live in, this would be quite appropriate. But, if we believe that a fuller mental health requires becoming conscious of the nature of society and its contradictions, we should strive to have our groups as heterogeneous as can be tolerated by the members, the conductors, and the institutional setting.

This was Pichon-Rivière's (1969) stance on the matter; one of the basic laws of his technique was that 'the greater heterogeneity in the members and the greater homogeneity in the task bring about a greater productivity' (p. 151, our translation). He always thought his theory and practice in social, historical, cultural, and political terms, which he considered to be an essential part of an individual's life and relations.

For instance, when he made an analysis of the personality, works, and public figure of Enrique Santos Discépolo, the famous Argentinian poet who wrote some of the most popular tangos of the first half of the Twentieth Century, he studied not only his family history as an early orphan, but also the plight of the large number of European immigrants, such as his family, who came to Argentina looking for a fortune that never came about. And, in understanding the enormous success of his tangos, characterised by their despairing and bitter lyrics, he saw him as a spokesman for the whole population's disbelief and despair as a result of many decades of authoritarian regimes and having had a most popular president deposed by a military coup (Pichon-Rivière, 1965a). Indeed, when one of us (Tubert-Oklander, 2011b) wrote an expansion of this analysis, he was forced by the very nature of the subject to review one hundred years of the political history of Argentina, which Pichon-Rivière had tacitly assumed to be well known by his readers.

Discépolo himself was quite aware of this confluence and resonance of his own feelings and creativity, on the one hand, and the vital and emotional plight of his public, on the other, when he said,

A song is a piece of my life, a suit that is looking for a body that fits it well. The more bodies there are for that suit, the greater will be the success of the song, since, if everybody sings it, it is a signal that all of them are living it, feeling it, that it suits them well.

(Discépolo, quoted by Diez, 2010, our translation)

This is the very same idea as Pichon-Rivière's (1965c) concept of the individual as a spokesperson or talebearer for the group, inasmuch as he reveals its secrets. In his groups, he always considered any individual expression to be the representative of his or her personal history, conflicts, and relations – what he called a *vertical interpretation* – and of the present situation of the group and the wider social context – this being a *horizontal interpretation*. Any interpretation, in order to be comprehensive enough, should be made simultaneously in the vertical and horizontal directions.

Both Foulkes and Pichon-Rivière thought in terms of an essential unity of the individual, the group, and society, and conceived these terms to be abstractions constructed from the indivisible human experience. For them, mental processes were neither coextensive with the limits of the organism, nor an epiphenomenon of brain function. Foulkes once wrote,

> . . . to us intra-psychic does *not* convey 'intradermic' . . . and we look upon the dynamic processes in the group not from the outside, but from inside, as intra-psychic dynamics in their interaction.
>
> (Foulkes & Anthony, 1965, p. 21)

Pichon-Rivière (1965b), on his part, described a perpetual dialectic of the inner and the outer, which is the very stuff of human existence. This he synthesised in his concept of the *bond* (sometimes translated as 'link'), which refers to both inner and real, actual relationships. There are two psychological fields in the bond: there is an *inner field* and an *outer field* – and here 'field' does not only have physical or dynamic connotations, but also those of a football field: a space for groups to play. So, there are internal and external objects, and an internal and an external group, as well as an internal and an external aspect of the bond. Hence, the bond is the complex relational structure made up of the person, the other(s), their mutual relation, and their whole social, political, historical, cultural, and ecological contexts (Pichon-Rivière, 1979).

The internal bonds correspond to what psychoanalysis calls 'internalized object relations' and the external bonds to interpersonal and group relations. They are both integrated in a dialectic spiral process, by means of which that what was originally external becomes internal, and then external again, and so on. There is a fluid interchange between the two fields, which helps to establish the differentiation between the inside and the outside, while at the same time keeping a deep continuity between them. Hence, the individual and society form an indissoluble unit, a single dynamic field and process,[2] because we all carry society within us, and society bears the imprint of the multiple individuals (Hernández-Tubert, 2017c).

Of course, there is a division between subjects and objects, but it is based on a split in the original human experience, a split that may only be transcended by a process of reflection that allows the individual to reframe his or her identity feeling,[3] in order to include its collective dimension, thus becoming what Earl Hopper (2000) calls a *citizen*. This new status is equivalent to what Erich Fromm (1958) termed the *revolutionary character*, defined as a mature, reflective, critical, and responsible member of the group.

This is not only a question of individual dynamics, but also of the political organisation and functioning of the group, since people cannot take such roles if society does not give them an assurance that citizenship is indeed available, and this is a political process. But even if this were the case, the individual members of the society still would have to be or become willing and able to assume citizenship and to do whatever is necessary to ensure that such roles actually exist and persist within a democratic society (Hopper, 2000). This is where group analysis, particularly through participation in large groups, has much to offer,[4] since such willingness and ability, which necessarily also require a conscious knowledge of at least some of the unconscious aspects of society, should be developed through what Foulkes (1964a) called *ego training in action* and what Pichon-Rivière (1969) conceived as the conjunction of *belonging, cooperation,* and *pertinence* in carrying out the group task (Tubert-Oklander & Hernández de Tubert, 2004).

The group-analytic large group

When we talk about 'large groups', we do not refer to the kind of numerous groups we may find in society, such as multitudes, crowds, audiences, mobs, assemblies, hosts, clans, and the like; not even Freud's 'primal horde' and certainly not institutions. We use the term to refer to the *Group-Analytic Large Group*. This means that a number of people – let us say, more than twenty and up to a few hundred – meet with a conductor or conducting team in order to enquire and think-through their experience of being, relating, and doing something together. Hence, it is always a *reflective group* and it is not self-managed, since there is always someone or some people who assume the responsibility of convening and conducting the meetings. Hence, even if the particular way in which they choose to do so happens to be self-effacing, the fact that they are in charge is inescapable.

These groups vary according to their general aim. They may either be: (1) *problem-centred large groups*, (2) *experience-centred large groups*, (3) *therapy-centred large groups*, and (4) *research-centred large groups*.

The problem-centred large group

This kind of group is not too popular among Foulkesian group-analysts, since it would seem to be too goal-directed for their tradition. Such groups meet in order to discuss some problem that affects the participants, either as members of a pre-existent group, such as an institution or a local community, or as members of a wider class of persons with a common interest, such as a profession. The conductor or conducting team are there to help the group and its members to discover and learn a novel way of working as a team and dealing with problems. In the operative group tradition, the coordinators would observe and interpret the various referential schemes that are active in the group, helping the members to identify and analyse them, and to negotiate a new group CROS[5] that may be the basis for their working together more effectively. They would also point out and foster the discussion of any obstacles that emerge and hinder the group in carrying out its task. Such obstacles may be related to the *affective* basis of the group dynamics (for instance, unconscious conflicts and defences), to the *cognitive* basis of the group discussion (prejudices, misunderstandings, rigidity, dogmatism), and to the *conative* aspect of their work together (difficulties in passing from conceptualisation to action, interacting, negotiating their interests, coordinating their efforts, or developing the necessary skills). When the process evolves as it should, the group passes from an initial *confusion* and *attacks on the task*, to a *dilemmatic formulation* in 'either-or' terms, which later becomes a definite *problem* that may be now tackled, and finally turns into a *project* that may be carried out by the group, without the coordinators (Pichon-Rivière & Bauleo, 1964; Tubert-Oklander & Hernández de Tubert, 2004, pp. 37–42).

But in spite of the fact that Foulkes always emphasised that a group analytic group has no task, there is at least one occasion in which he suggested something quite similar to Pichon-Rivière's idea of the group's *Project*. This was in his first book, *Introduction to Group-Analytic Psychotherapy* (Foulkes, 1948), when discussing the dual position of the conductor *vis-à-vis* the group, of being both *in* and *out* of the group. The result of this is that

> . . . the group is integrated but leader-centred *as a group* . . . [and] *within* this configuration . . . the group can still be individually leader-centred . . . or truly group-centred.
>
> (p. 143, original italics)

But, when the group members do not only meet when the conductor is present, as is the case of natural groups, families, institutions, or members of a same community or profession, a new evolution may take place and

> . . . the leader can eventually make the group comprise himself and his function within itself, thus it becomes truly group-centred. *Here this is represented by his reference to an aim beyond the boundaries of the group, which embraces the whole group alike including its leader.*
>
> (p. 143, my italics)

This is precisely the definition of the group project. In our previous book on operative groups, we discussed the evolution and results of a reflection group with the whole staff of a psychoanalytic therapeutic community, which lasted five years and helped the group improve their problem-solving resources in the day-to-day handling of their work, as well as the power and economic relations between management and labour [Tubert-Oklander & Hernández de Tubert, 2004, pp. 197–208].

The experience-centred large group

This is aimed at providing the participants with a living learning experience of the nature and dynamics of such a group, of the difficulties it faces, and the various solutions that are attempted during the sessions, as well as the social forces that are in action in its functioning. The group members are expected to come out of the experience with a greater knowledge and understanding of what groups are, how they function, what drives them, and what sort of mechanisms they use. They should also have a direct knowledge of the workings of the Social Unconscious, and what impact it has on individuals, relations, and groups.

This sort of large group is perhaps the most widely known, since it is used both in our training courses, as a way to offer the students a living group experience, and in our congresses, in order to provide it to the larger professional community. Alejo Dellarossa's (1979) original reflection groups were precisely intended to offer such an experience to the students in a group psychotherapy training program. They were conceived, however, as small groups. The whole course initiated with forty-five students, who were divided into three seminars of fifteen each, called Seminars A, B, and C. There were also three Reflection Groups, called 1, 2, and 3, and they were made up of five members from each of the three seminars. The idea was that each of the reflection groups would resonate with whatever was happening in the three seminars, and thus give the students a more or less accurate picture of the workings of the whole institution and the way they affected the learning processes. Nowadays, we would rather have a single large group, including all the students, and perhaps even the teachers and the administrative personnel, so as to turn it into an institutional analysis. But if the idea were to limit the aims of the group to providing the students with a dynamic group experience, the large group should only include them. This is an example of how the setting of the group determines the kind of phenomena that are more likely to emerge in it, this being an example of a *situational approach*.[6]

In the British tradition, the members of the professional team that is in charge of the experience are conceived more as *convenors* than as *conductors* (de Maré, Piper, & Thompson, 1991), and this determines a more passive and self-effacing stance, which expresses their faith in the group processes and the capacity of the group members to turn by themselves the original intense emotional experience, usually laden with hate, into productive thought. The Latin-American tradition, on the other hand, requires a more active participation by the coordinators, conceived as co-thinkers, who should plant the seeds for the growth and development of group thought, by means of interpretation. However, in both the aim of the Large Group is, as Pat de Maré suggested, *thinking together and developing a group thought* about such issues as concern its members, which are typically of a social and political nature (Tubert-Oklander, 2020c).

From the temporal perspective, these groups may either be *intensive* or *continuous*. The kind of experience-centred large groups that are offered to the attendants in conferences are, of course, always intensive, usually lasting not more than four days, with daily meetings. They may be open to a limited number of participants, determined both by the size that is considered adequate by the conducting team and by the capacity of the premises, which usually means something between fifty and one hundred and twenty members. But they may also be conceived as a group experience for all the attendants to the conference, and this implied, in the largest group we have been in, during the Dublin European Symposium of Group Analysis, more than 500 members.[7]

The experience-centred large groups used in training are usually continuous, at least during a predetermined period, and they are smaller – not more than fifty members, and sometimes twenty to thirty, which would be qualified as a 'median group'.

The therapy-centred large group

These groups are necessarily continuous and smaller – usually median groups.[8] They meet regularly at appointed times, in most cases once a week, but sometimes two and even three times a week. They are most frequently carried out in an institutional setting and with severely disturbed patients. They are regularly either closed groups or slow-open groups, and they also require a greater participation by the therapists than the experience-centred groups. There have been, however, experiences with much larger groups, which functioned as open groups, meaning that new members might join at any time and that none of them was obliged to keep any continuity in their attendance.

One such group we had the opportunity to observe was that led for forty years by Jorge García Badaracco (1990) in Buenos Aires. It was a Large Multi-Family Group, in the context of a psychoanalytic therapeutic community, which included psychotic patients, their families and significant others, psychiatrists, nurses, therapists, and the conducting team. Even though it was not conducted on group-analytic lines, the dynamics and the sheer size of the group were most impressive and, surprisingly enough, one could witness enormous advances in the most severely ill patients. The original group, which functioned in the therapeutic community, had over one hundred members and met once a week. Later, after the community disappeared – which unfortunately seems to be the fate of therapeutic communities worldwide – he continued with a group of chronic patients and their families, who had been in treatment for a long time, of about fifty members, which met once a month in the Argentine Psychoanalytic Association.

The therapeutic results with these large groups are usually excellent. Yet, they are not very frequently used, partly on account of the lack of sufficiently trained group analysts for their conduction, and mostly of the mistrust that the medical establishment has towards such methods.

The research-centred large group

These groups are usually combined with some of the previous three, since the participants in such a group are attracted to it by some other need, be it problem-solving, experience-based learning, or therapy. So, research becomes possible only inasmuch the large group responds to a need of the participants. This is similar to what happened with psychoanalysis, which was able to investigate the depths of human experience only on account of the therapeutic aim of the treatment.

Pichon-Rivière's Rosario Experience (Pichon-Rivière et al., 1960) was a research-centred large group, conducted by a staff of psychoanalysts and group therapists, all of them his disciples, led by him. This was organised by the Argentine Institute of Social Studies, which he had founded, and several schools and departments of the University of Rosario. The staff prepared for it by working as an operative group, coordinated by the leader, and they then travelled by train to the City of Rosario, where this social laboratory was to take place. There had been previous advertising there, inviting everyone, both professionals and ordinary citizens, to attend. The participants were several hundred,[9] including university students and teachers, boxers, painters, insurance brokers, workers from the port, employees, homemakers, and some prostitutes – that is, a wide sample of the citizens. The whole experience was organised in a spiral sequence, which oscillated between plenary meetings, small heterogeneous groups, staff meetings, small homogeneous groups, and new plenary meetings. The sequence was as follows:

1 *First Plenary Meeting*, with an introductory lecture by the General Coordinator, Enrique Pichon-Rivière, explaining the organisation and aims of the workshop and introducing a few ideas to serve as a stimulus for the following discussion
2 *First Session of Small Heterogeneous Groups*, fifteen of them, conducted by a team made of a coordinator and one or two observers. The session was four hours long
3 *First Staff Meeting* with the General Coordinator, in order to evaluate and discuss the work done up to that moment, with a special emphasis in what had transpired in the small groups
4 *Second Session of Small Heterogeneous Groups*, with the same participants, in which the conducting team acted in accordance with what had been discussed in the Staff Meeting
5 *Second Staff Meeting* in order to analyse the further experience of the Heterogeneous Groups
6 *Second Plenary Meeting*, held the next day with an even larger attendance. Pichon-Rivière gave the participants a feedback of what had happened and emerged in the Small Groups. But there had been a radical mood change: the audience no longer kept a passive stance, but they now worked and discussed as a group, a large group, of course
7 *Session of Homogeneous Groups*, twelve of them: five on psychosomatic medicine, three on psychology, one of boxers, one on statistics, one of painters, and one of insurance brokers. The composition of these groups reflected the nature of the schools that sponsored and hosted the event (Medicine, Economics, Statistics, and Psychology) and Pichon-Rivière's lifelong interests and contacts (art and sports)

8   *Third Staff Meeting* with the General Coordinator, in order to discuss what
     had happened in the groups
9   *Final Presentation by Pichon-Rivière*, with the members of the Heteroge-
     neous and Homogeneous Groups

After the formal termination of the experience, the staff continued to analyse
it in the Institute, and it was expected that some of the small groups that had
been formed during the workshop would continue working on their own. In other
words, that the group work that had been done might turn into a project.

In the Rosario Experience, the participants had various motives for attending.
For the conductors of the Heterogeneous Groups, it was obvious that a number
of the participants had come looking for a therapy that was not available in their
city at the time. The members of the Homogeneous Groups were mainly interested in dealing with some problems of their respective professions. Many of the
large number of people who attended the plenaries were looking for some sort
of knowledge and experience that might help them to orient themselves in the
labyrinth of social life.

But for the organizers and staff, the whole experience was research-centred.
Pichon-Rivière himself made a curt comment on this during the train trip from
Buenos Aires to Rosario. His young disciples had a great confidence in him, but
they were anxious and plagued by gloomy forebodings. His acid answer was:
'If, by the time we take the train back, they throw horse-shit at us, this will mean
that, when a group like ours does in Rosario whatever we end up doing, they get
horse-shit thrown at them' (Carpintero & Vainer, 2009) In other words: 'Whatever
comes out from this experience shall be a piece of knowledge, and a valuable
one'. This mocking remark calmed down the group.

The Rosario Experience took place in 1958, but Pichon-Rivière had been
exploring his group approach since 1936 (Zito Lema, 1976), and started to conduct what he later called 'operative groups' in 1948 (Pichon-Rivière, 1951).
Yet the name and the formal conception that underlay this practice were finally
attained at this moment, and published in 1960 (Pichon-Rivière et al., 1960).

The Belgrade International Workshop, in which the first version of this text was
read, took place in June 2013, exactly fifty-five years after the Rosario Experience, with an international staff of senior group analysts, convened and coordinated by Carla Penna and Marina Mojović. This was explicitly conceived and
organised as a re-edition of that historical model. Of course, no experience can
ever be repeated, since there are always new people, time, place, social and historical context, and circumstances. Nonetheless, this workshop was a recreation, in a
new century, of the spirit of its model, albeit with the benefit of fifty-five years of
the collective group-analytic experience. There were, of course, similarities and
differences, which we will discuss when dealing, in the third and last article of this
series, with the wider context of the large group.

This kind of structured approach, which somehow resembles Kurt Lewin's
Social Laboratories and the corresponding work style of the Tavistock Institute of

Human Relations, is in a sharp contrast with the Large Group tradition developed by members of the Group-Analytic Society, as we shall also see in our following chapter.

Notes

1 In General Systems Theory and in the work of Gregory Bateson (1972, 1979), it is indeed possible to conceive groups and societies as organisms and mental entities, no less than ecosystems, such as a forest, a pond, or the coexistence and interrelation of several species.
2 See Appendix III on Holism.
3 This is only the cognitive path to the re-integration of experience, but there are others, based on emotion, action, or intuition, such as those offered by art, mysticism, or religion.
4 One particularly illuminating example of this is Marina Mojović's (2015, 2016) Serbian Reflective Citizens' Project.
5 Acronym for *Conceptual Referential Operative Schema* (see Chapter 11).
6 The situational approach is further discussed in Chapter 11.
7 See Chapter 11 for more about this group.
8 Roberto Schoellberger (2013) defines 'the Median Group [as] a setting with 12–30 participants, in clinical practice 17 is the ideal number. It is small enough to promote the identification process and to get to know each other personally, and it is large enough to be a social dimension.' (p. 118).
9 The number of participants quoted in the various reports differs, but, considering the number of small groups reported in the original paper, it must have been something between two and three hundred, since quite a few people attended the plenary meetings, but did not participate in the small groups.

Chapter 11

Listening to the voices in the wind (2014)

The Social Unconscious and the large group part III

Juan Tubert-Oklander and Reyna Hernández-Tubert

In this third part of our Belgrade lecture, we expound our own conception and practice of the group-analytic large group and discuss our coincidences and differences with those of the British group-analytic tradition. On the whole we are more active in our participation as conductors of a large group, and we give our reasons for this. In this comparative discussion of the two approaches, we rely on the experience of the large group that took place during the Dublin Symposium. Our basic approach to the conduction of large groups consists in creating the conditions and giving an initial stimulus for the inception of a group dialogue. Then, we listen carefully, with an analytic attitude, looking for the emergence of a reference to a possible underlying conflict or concern. If this is not taken by the group, we retrieve it, with an explorative intervention or an interpretation. Then we listen again. We conceive the various, frequently disjointed, interventions by the group members to be 'voices in the wind', fragments of an unsaid collective discourse that we, as coordinators, have to construct and turn into a cogent formulation that may be returned to the group, in order to foster a reflective thinking that may then proceed by itself.

Voices in the wind: our own approach to the large group

It should be quite clear by now that our way of understanding and conducting a Large Group is necessarily a hybrid of the two traditions we have been expounding all along. This is pretty much in line with one main feature of Latin-American culture, in general, and Mexican culture, in particular, which is *Mestization* (Beuchot, 2003; Tubert-Oklander & Beuchot Puente, 2008). Our nations have emerged from a clash and pairing of contrasting peoples, cultures, languages, and races. It was only natural that our way of experiencing, understanding, thinking, and practising both psychoanalysis and group analysis were to be as hybrid as we are (Tubert-Oklander, 2011a, 2011b). In the case of Pichon-Rivière, he was reared and formed, since the age of three, within the confluence of three contrasting cultures and languages. His first language was French, which was spoken by his parents; the second was that of the Guaraní Indians, learned from his father's foreman, and the

DOI: 10.4324/9780429055287-14

third one was Spanish, which he only learned on entering elementary school (Zito Lema, 1976).

However, he was, from that time on, forever split between two conceptions of the world. One of them stemmed from his European roots: it was strictly rational-istic and found its expression in scientific research. The other was derived from his contact with the Guaraní culture, which was magical and mythical, and it was expressed in his love for poetry and his passion for surrealism and the uncanny poems of Lautréamont. It was only when he found psychoanalysis that he was able to reconcile these two worlds (Pichon-Rivière, 1971a, pp. 7–12; Zito Lema, 1976; Tubert-Oklander, 2002).

So, our approach to the Large Group is Foulkesian and Pichonian, Latin-American and Mexican, psychoanalytic and group-analytic, psychological and sociological, intellectual and emotional, but, on top of all that, it is our own.

Although our way of working with groups is certainly more active than is usual in the British tradition, and includes organised workshops, such as those convened in Rosario and Belgrade, we shall now discuss it in the particular instance of the kind of groups that regularly meet in group-analytic conferences. This means an Experience-Centred Large Group, made up of people who are mostly not familiar with each other, which meets for a very short period during a conference.

The first point to be made is that we do not believe starting the group with a maximum of ambiguity and uncertainty to be at all necessary or advisable. Strik-ingly enough, that was Foulkes's (1975b) point of view, when he wrote that start-ing a group with a minimum guidance from the beginning produces phenomena such as panic, fear, and bewilderment, which are usually considered to be inherent to the group, but which he viewed merely as a consequence of the abnormal situ-ation into which the group is put. And then he added,

> By contrast, I have always felt that, having convened the group or having offered therapy to the patients in such a group, I ought to help them, espe-cially at the beginning, to understand what is hoped for or expected from them and why – not by the way of lecturing them but by way of experience. In this way one keeps anxiety at a tolerable level.
>
> (p. 43)

What did he mean by helping the members to understand 'by the way of experi-ence' what to expect and what was expected from them? What he actually did was to be present and clearly in charge, and demonstrate, through his attitude and interventions, what sort of group this was going to be. Nonetheless, although we agree with him that no amount of lecturing can do the job, we still feel that the group members are entitled to receive a minimum of information about where they are, why, what for, and what they are to do; at least, if we are to invoke the members' conscious cooperation and intelligence.[1] This is what we psychoana-lysts do when we establish what we call the 'analytic contract', and it has never interfered with the development of the analytic process.

So, we never start a Large Group without identifying ourselves as the conductors and giving a brief idea of what we are going to do, why, and how. This may be done through a brief written text, which may be distributed previously to all the attendants and/or read by one of the conductors at the beginning of the first session.[2] It also frequently implies naming a general theme for our discussion. But, if there were no explicit theme for the group, this would be tacitly derived from the theme of the whole conference, as it was in the case of the Large Group held during the Survivor Syndrome Workshop (Hopper & Kreeger, 1980).

Then, we would remain silent, waiting for the group to start some interchange. If the group's response were a complete paralysis and stubborn silence, we would make some simple interpretation of anxieties that may have been unleashed by the beginning of the group. When the silence had been overcome, we would expect some admixture of confusion and paranoid anxiety to emerge. We would listen carefully, until we identified some intervention or interventions by one or several of the members that seemed to offer a way out of the group's present predicament. Then we would make some interpretation that collected the various voices heard, in terms of what we deemed to be the group's present problem and the various solutions that had been suggested for it, including those that seemed to be regressive and defensive, and those that fostered a development in the group. After that, we would once again listen.

This sort of intervention that aims at mustering the intellectual resources of the members is clearly in line with Pichon-Rivière's (1971a) *Operative Groups* and Dellarossa's (1979) *Reflection Groups*. It is also the model for all our work in these groups. This means listening carefully to the few phrases and fragments of speech that stand out of the melee of the group – 'melee' being a term used for a disorganised, violent, and close free-for-all fighting encounter. This we conceive as 'listening to the voices in the wind', until one can reconstruct an underlying discourse, which has no subject and belongs to no one in particular, and to all those present at the same time. But, when this is put into explicit words, the group and its members may appropriate it and turn it into an object of enquiry and a tool for thought. Then the melee becomes an assembly that is ready to tackle the task of dealing with the group's problems.

The voices in the wind speak, more often than not, of the problems in society. This reminds us of one of Bob Dylan's well-known songs, called *Blowing in the Wind*. There the singer asks, over and over again, about the contradictions, injustices, and crimes that flourish in our society, and gets always the same ambiguous reply, that the answer is blowing in the wind. What does this mean? Did the poet want to tell us that such questions are futile? Or did he suggest a more subtle and elusive idea, that the response that he sought was not something concrete to be thought, but an ever-flowing process to be intuited? We would rather favour this last interpretation.

Now, if we accept the proposition that there is no definitive answer to the problems of the group, but a multifarious and fluid complexity that eludes any attempt to capture it with our conscious and rational thought, there are two possible ways to tackle the problem of making sense of whatever is happening in the Large Group.

The first of them is to reject from the very beginning any kind of formal leadership by the conductor or conductors. This was the course heartily endorsed by Pat de Maré (de Maré, Piper, & Thompson, 1991), who had a full confidence in the group's own resources, which would be mobilised if the conductor gave up his invested role of being 'he who knows and thinks' – corresponding, of course, to Lacan's (1973) *sujet supposé savoir* (the supposed subject of knowledge). Hence, he preferred to conceive his role as that of a *convenor*, who provided the space, the time, and the circumstance for people to get together and strive to become a thinking group. The path for them to travel was of course rough, turbulent, and infused with hate, which should be turned into thought, by means of dialogue. And this should be achieved by the group itself, without any conducting from the convenor or convenors.

The other way to approach the Large Group, which is the one we practise, requires a more active participation by the conductors. In this, we consider that one conductor is never enough for dealing with the intense anxieties and conflicts that are unleashed in the Large Group context. Consequently, we fully agree with the decision taken in the case of the Dublin Large Group, which included 568 participants, to have a three-person conducting team (Ahlin, 2010, 2011; von Sommaruga Howard, 2011). However, our conducting style is quite different from theirs, as we shall soon see.

In our way of conducting these groups, we use not only interpretations, but also *constructions* of what we believe is being expressed in and by the group. In this formulation, we follow Freud's (1937b) distinction between an *interpretation*, conceived as a partial tentative explanation or assignation of meaning to some particular expression by a patient (or group), and a *construction*, understood as a more complex theory that purports to account for what has been discovered and interpreted during the treatment. In the case of Freud's clinical work, this referred to a reconstruction of the patient's forgotten past, which he assumed to be strictly true in all its details, but this is not the only way to do it or to interpret the results.

The *constructions* we do in our work with groups (and note that we do not speak of 'reconstructions', because we in no way assume that they existed before we created them) are elaborate formulations that try to make sense out of the fragmentary and disjointed expressions that emerge in the sessions. These are the 'voices in the wind', which are hardly heard in midst of the cacophony of the group process, and which would appear to be nothing but a senseless noise, until we do something with them, by taking them as fragments of an unknown or yet unformulated ongoing discourse.

When thus seen, our constructions would seem something akin to the reconstructive work done by forensic anthropologists, palaeontologists, or archaeologists; this is the way Freud thought of it, but there is a major difference in our view of the process. These professionals carry out a kind of detective work, aimed at finding out the appearance and structure of something pre-existent that has been destroyed or deteriorated, but here we are dealing with what Donnel Stern (1983, 1997) calls 'unformulated experience', albeit in this case it is a collective experience that has to be 'signified' – that is, turned into signs, in the semiotic sense of the term – so that it may acquire a meaning for those involved in the experience.

Giving a meaning to an unformulated experience is not the same as revealing something that had been hidden or interred, nor as reconstructing from the remaining pieces something that had once existed as a whole. It is more a question of finding the right expression for an intuition, something akin to the work of a poet, who strives to find the right language and expression that may realise and convey an intuition she or he has and is trying to capture and share with others. It is therefore a work of interpretation, in its hermeneutical sense (Gadamer, 1960; Tubert-Oklander, 2009, 2013b).

To interpret implies placing a text within a relevant context, in order to give it a new meaning that goes beyond that which appears at first sight (Beuchot, 1997). But here we do not have a text to begin with, but only fragments of something that might become a text, so our work as interpreters also involves the very construction of a possible text to be interpreted. In this, interpretation and construction go hand in hand.

Now, the keyword in this is 'relevance': the context in which the text is placed (or constructed) must be relevant. What does this mean? *A relevant context is one that highlights some aspect of the underlying unformulated emotional, relational, and social collective experience that we are trying to enquire.* So, even if there are more than one alternative constructions, contexts, and interpretations for any given situation, not all of them are equally valid: some of them are better, others not so good, some are poor, and yet others are outright bad, in terms of their ability to give a form and a meaning to the formless living experience that we are trying to think-through.

Consequently, our construction and interpretation of the unknown discourse in the group is not *the* construction-interpretation, but *a* possible one among quite a few others. Then, the group members may well criticise, discard, modify, relativise, substitute, or build upon it. Sometimes it is one of the members who proposes a first interpretation or construction; in this case, we would wait to see what the rest of the group does with it and, if it were violently attacked or summarily discarded, we would intervene with an interpretation of how the prevailing anxieties prevent the members of the group from considering a perhaps valuable contribution by one of them.

The result is the inception of an *interpretative dialogue* that may shed a light on the chaotic and confusing experience that we are all sharing. So, it is not so much a question of discrete interpretations that may turn out to be right or wrong, but of an *interpretative process* (Tubert-Oklander, 2006b, 2013a, 2014) that gains a momentum of its own and follows an ever-expanding and forward-moving spiral course, as suggested by Pichon-Rivière (1971a).

Now, there is still one essential point in our conception of the Analytic Large Group. This sort of group is not adequate to deal with either the intimate experiences and conflicts of individuals or the complexities of interpersonal relationships.

On the contrary, it may teach us much about inter-group relations, when we witness the formation of subgroups, and about the workings of society. Social issues are very much present in the group's dynamics and unspoken discourse, but more often than not they are repressed and unutterable. This is the process that Hopper and Kreeger (1980) called 'equivalence'. It is then up to the conductors to be alert for any expression of or reference to current social events and conflicts, and salvage it, by means of an interpretation, if the group fails to take the implied hint and turn it into a theme for discussion.

In this, there are of course diverse points of view. When we participated in the Dublin Large Group, in 2008, we were impressed by the unquestionable presence in the sessions of social, political, institutional, cultural, linguistic, racial, and gender issues, and surprised that the conductors did not address them explicitly (Hernández-Tubert, 2009 [Appendix IV]).[3] We inferred that this should probably be a conscious decision on their part, intended to offer the group the widest possible breadth for the expansion of its own capabilities and resources. And indeed, there was an evolution, during the four sessions, towards a more explicit expression of the underlying conflicts.

However, we still wonder whether such a large group – the largest we have ever participated in – would find the time it needed for carrying its process of working-through to a completion, in the four brief sessions it had at its disposal, without the conductors' intervention. Of course, this kind of reflection does not have an end, and it may well be argued that the individual members carried home with them the questions raised in the group, for their personal working-through – as we did. Nevertheless, from our own perspective, we would still think that an attempt by the conductors to integrate and reflect upon the many themes that emerged during the Large Group could have enriched the experience and made a further use of the group's resources, to the advantage of its members.

In the case of this particular large group, we would probably have commented on the anxieties generated by the great number of members, their many differences, the process of generational replacement that was taking place in the Society, the fact that both the Presidency and the Organizing Committee were in the charge of women and that they were not British, and the vertiginous growth and variegation of the Society. We would have tried to identify the prejudices and defensive manoeuvres mustered against such anxieties, and the obstacles to communication that were thus generated, and we would have also pointed out the impediment to the group's enquiring and thinking that derived from the fact that most members were striving to participate, not as individual human beings, but *as group analysts*, thus assuming the role of a professional identity, which barred the enquiry of our participation in and responsibility for a social process. All of this, of course, would be based on the many expressions provided by the group members during the sessions, and would be offered as a stimulus for further discussion.

Much later, when we had access to the published versions that two of the three conductors wrote about this experience (Ahlin, 2010, 2011; von Sommaruga

Howard, 2011), we confirmed our impression that their protracted silence was a conscious strategy. This was clearly stated by von Sommaruga Howard (2011), in the following terms:

> We spent many hours together before, during and after the symposium pre-paring for and metabolizing the material. *Our explicit group-analytic inten-tion was to refrain from leading but to encourage leadership from within the group.* Keeping to this stance was challenging in an environment where it was difficult to discover who was responsible for conducting.
>
> (p. 329, italics added)

> Our conducting approach coupled with our forced anonymity did not pro-vide a beacon of hope for the future and frustrated the universal desire for charismatic hierarchical leadership. We could only accompany the group and think alongside everyone while seeking to encourage a friendly atmosphere: Koinonia.
>
> (de Maré, Piper, & Thompson, 1991) (p. 337)

She also pointed out that there was a systematic attack on their leadership, which they were exercising in their own way, an intolerance of their shared leadership in an unfathomable threesome, and a demand for a male-style hierarchical leader-ship, instead of

> soft voices, an acceptance of a more receptive leadership, complexity and organic relationship-building through cooperation, and sharing the earth's resources of the feminine.
>
> (p. 339)

It is also obvious, from her subtle analysis of what happened in the group, that the conductors were well aware of the social and political context of the group pro-cess. So, why not share this work of thought with the group? We know the answer is that such decision is based on the conviction that it is the group which should carry out this task, and the conductors should not usurp it in search, perhaps, of a narcissistic satisfaction. But we still feel that the wish to avoid charismatic leader-ship and the fear of its dire consequences may have taken us to the other extreme of abdicating our responsibility towards the group.[4]

Nowadays, after carefully studying von Sommaruga Howard's (2012) account of the large group she conducted in 2007 in Napier, at the annual conference of the *Aotearoa* New Zealand Psychotherapy Association, we have come to a fur-ther understanding of our different perspectives. It seems to us that she views the large group that takes place in a conference as an episode in an ongoing process in a professional community. This is quite clear in the case of the New Zealand Association, where she has regular twice-yearly visits, usually attends the annual conference, where she contributes a workshop, and also conducts a once-yearly large group workshop that has become a regular calendar event. Such ongoing work with the members of the Association provided an opportunity for a protracted working-through of all that had been stirred up by the large group but could not be resolved at the time. Besides, the next year she was invited to present a one-year-on-thoughts on the experience in the opening plenary of the following conference, which was also published in the NZAP Journal Forum (von Sommaruga Howard, 2007), as a previous version of her 2012 article. This implied offering the community a detailed construction of what had happened in that particular large group.

This perspective shows the large groups that take place in conferences, not as isolated occurrences, but as episodes in a more extended trans-personal process. This may work well for those who attend the conferences and participate in the large groups every three years. But what about those group members who are first-timers and may not come again to such events? How are they to carry out a productive working-through of the experience? Should we not do something to help them with this most difficult task?

Our own view of such groups is to deal with them as a one-shot affair, which needs to have an aperture, a development, and a closure. This requires that the conductors actively contribute to an initial working-through of the experience, by means of interpretations and constructions, in order to help the individual members to leave the group in the best possible condition to tackle their posterior working-through, which might also take the form of a dialogue with other participants and colleagues.

In any case, there seems to be no definitive solution to the question of which of these two positions we should adopt. It might turn out to be mainly a question of temperament, tradition, and personal experience, as suggested by Meg Sharpe (2008), whose conclusion, after comparing her experiences with a number of large groups with conductors with different styles, theories, and techniques, was that,

> There is no fixed prescription for the right style of large group leadership. It is no easy task, and anxiety is inevitable and necessary. . . . I believe that conducting a large group is more an art than a science, which defies conventional academic analysis. . . . Experience is the only real teacher, and humility on the part of the leader is an indispensable asset.
>
> (pp. 300–301)

Nonetheless, this does not exempt us from the duty of studying and comparing their respective processes and results. Such research is not easy, but it is necessary, and remains to be done.

One final point to be made is that we would never put an end to a Large Group session without making some sort of closure, usually in terms of a recapitulation of what has happened and what we seem to have been talking about. We believe that this is a way to protect the participants, or at least the more fragile among them, from the danger of acting out, after the session, the intense emotional experiences we have all undergone in it.

In the same vein, we would not finish such a group, after several days of work, without suggesting that we carry out an evaluation of the work we have done together and the experiences we have shared. This would be done by the members of the group, but the conductors should also convey their own thought about it. Quite frequently, such an evaluation emerges spontaneously but, if the conducting team does not validate and pursue it and interpret the resistances and obstacles that usually hinder it, the opportunity may be lost.

In sum, our position is to emphasise the conductors' responsibility for the safety and integrity of the group members, as well as for the creation of the adequate conditions for the group to tackle its task, and the monitoring and nurturing of the group process. We believe that this may be done without curbing the group's use of its own resources and creativity or imposing our own ideas and points of view.

Analysing the total situation

It should be obvious, by now, that our approach to the conducting of large groups demands that we take into account and interpret the total situation. This means including the whole social, political, and institutional context in our understanding, interpretations, and constructions, but it also implies considering the conducting team and the whole organisation of the conference as a part of the group field. Difficult as it surely is, we cannot analyse the matrix unless we do it as fully as we possibly can. Analysing half a matrix, as classical psychoanalysis used to do when focusing exclusively on the patient's internal processes, is necessarily misleading (Tubert-Oklander, 2013a, 2014).

A large group always takes place in an organisational setting. This may be an educational, economic, political, professional, social, or mental health institution, or a conference, and this implies power structures, conflicts, negotiations, lobbying, personal and group interests, manipulations, and, more often than not, secrets. All these have an impact on what Stiers and Dluhy (2008) call the 'organisational unconscious'. Hence, it is inevitably part of the matrix and should be duly analysed. But how are we to do it?

For instance, von Sommaruga Howard (2011) tells us that, during the Dublin Large Group, an organisational secret was revealed during the first group session, in which the members were frantically discussing the technical problems that impeded communication between them – namely, the impossibility of seeing and hearing each other. This erupted when someone suggested a tiered setting, an arrangement that had been repeatedly required by the local organising committee, until they were told flatly that it could not be afforded, in spite of the fact that the number of participants, and consequently the revenues, had increased substantially. This is how the author tells it:

> Then a bombshell was dropped, 'Tiered seating – let's be serious!' The Group-Analytic Society (London) committee decided that tiered seating could not

be afforded. This was news to us. I felt disempowered. 'Who is in charge – really?' I asked myself again.

As in wider society, exactly who decides where money should be spent is often opaque and difficult to discover. Now, it was quite transparent that the decision about seating had been taken by the London Society behind the scenes. Discovering the origins of this decision for the first time had the flavour of a multi-national corporation that ignores individual governments to ensure bottom line profits without concern for the local environment or the welfare of local workers. In the Forum afterwards the symposium treasurer, who was also the London society's treasurer, explained that the symposium sub-committee had been faced with two options, either to spend the surplus on providing tiered seating or to provide the London society with an increase in funds and the local society with a five-fold boost to its funds.

(pp. 331–332)

So, during the first day of the Large Group, the conductors suddenly found out that the Society had decided, unbeknownst to them, to deprive this activity of a most needed support, on account of financial considerations that were never acknowledged. What could be the impact of such information and the way it was obtained on the members, the conductors, the unconscious dynamics of the group, and the matrix? And what should be the conduct of the conducting team, pinpoint this particular event and suggest that the group analyse it, or ignore it and go on enquiring the emotional processes and experiences in the group?

This is not an easy decision. In this case, the information became explicit, but quite often the conductors manage to identify the emergence of an institutional conflict that is neither explicit nor perceived by the group members. Should they interpret this or let it go, since it has not been openly formulated? There is always a tendency to keep the secrets, just like in a family, but this is nothing but following the popular – and most certainly un-analytic – lore of 'let sleeping dogs lie' and 'what the eye does not see, the heart does not grieve over'. Of course, there is no love lost in institutions for group conductors who insist on analysing such matters.

One final point is that a conference or workshop, no less than an institute, has an inner organisation, a spirit, and a way of being, and this certainly influences the small, median, and large groups that take place in it. For example, Pichon-Rivière's Rosario Experience (Pichon-Rivière et al., 1960), which we have discussed in the previous chapter, was conducted by a charismatic leader, who defined the ideology and perspective of the work to be done, and his students followed him on the basis of their trust in him. It was his leadership that ensured the cohesiveness of the team and the consistency of the work done in the various groups; it was also he who synthesised and drew the conclusions of the experience.

The Belgrade Workshop was conceived, as we have seen, as a recreation, explicitly inspired by the Rosario Experience. Nonetheless, it was not a mere repetition of what those people did in Argentina, fifty-five years ago, but a new development, which incorporated the various traditions of the British group-analytical school (small, median, and large analytic groups), the Social-Dreaming Matrix, and the Tavistock Human Relations approach.

Such heterogeneous complexity was bound to generate some tensions and uncertainties, both in the participants and in the staff, but they were worked-through by means of the systematic use of our group-analytical instrument.

In Belgrade, the two organisers-convenors, Marina Mojović and Carla Penna, recruited an international staff of senior group conductors of various persuasions, in order to work together on a basis of faith in our capacity for conjointly enquiring, thinking-through, and dealing with conflicts and differences. This is, after all, the main task for any analytic group: to explore together our similarities and differences, and turn them into a matter for dialogue.

There was also an effort to articulate, compare, and integrate our two traditions: the Foulkesian Group-Analytic tradition and the Latin-American Pichonian one. The latter was represented by one of the convenors, Carla Penna from Brazil, and the present authors, and our lecture was an attempt to contribute to this integration. The organisation of the workshop also reflected this duality, since it included small groups and a large group, in terms of the British tradition, and reflection groups, in those of the Latin-American one.

The large group had been planned as a traditional group-analytic one, since it was decided that Earl Hopper and Haim Weinberg would conduct it, but when Earl had to excuse himself, on account of some health concern, Juan Tubert-Oklander replaced him. The two co-conductors then decided to include Reyna Hernández-Tubert as a silent observer – a role that does not belong to the British tradition, but which was usual in Argentina in Pichon-Rivière's time (Marrone, 1979).[5] So, in the end, the conducting team was once again a threesome, and the three of us discussed and thought-through each of the large group sessions in the interval between them.

An unexpected result of this impromptu solution to the problem created by Earl's absence was that we could compare our respective ways of understanding and conducting a large group, and found out that they were indeed different, but could complement each other.

Now, this particular organisation of the Belgrade Workshop, together with its accidental beginning, determined a climate that was quite different from that of the Rosario Experience. The fact that there was no formal leader (although, in fantasy, the role of the yearned-for charismatic leader may have been invested on Earl's absent figure) generated a particular dynamics, in which the obvious divergence in the understanding and conducting style of the members of the staff introduced a heterogeneity in the experience that contributed to its richness, but also to a certain feeling of confusion that was manifested in the various groups.

What all this shows is that the group conductors have to look far beyond the apparent boundaries of the Large Group, in order to be able to understand and interpret the feelings, relations, actions, and thoughts that surface during the sessions, and this includes the conductors themselves, their team, and their institution.

For instance, in Belgrade we found out, particularly in the reflection group we co-conducted and in the final plenary evaluation of the workshop, that many of the local participants – who represented the majority of the attendants – who had had some information about Pichon-Rivière and the Rosario Experience, mainly through the concepts that we had summarised in the first part of our book (Tubert-Oklander & Hernández de Tubert, 2004), were expecting to be introduced to the secrets of a particular technique that they would then be able to replicate in their country. It was then necessary to point out to them that no group experience could ever be replicated out of its original social, cultural, and historical context, and that there was no such standard technique that might relieve us of our commitment to think our own thoughts and take our own decisions. And this is not a question of techniques, but of the construction of a group-analytic identity, in terms of prolonged study, learning, and personal reflection. Obviously, this is something that is hard to hear and to accept, but it is basic, if we are to become group analysts, instead of merely applying the theories and techniques of group analysis.

Notes

1 Donald Winnicott (1958b) discusses the question of conscious cooperation by the analysand in 'Child analysis in the latency period'. There he says that

> The difference [between Anna Freud's and Melanie Klein's approaches] is largely a matter of conscious or unconscious co-operation. . . . With very intelligent children *we need to be able to talk to their intelligence, to feed their intelligence*. It is sometimes a complication when we are doing work with a child and the child feels that something is going on, and yet has no intellectual understanding of what it is all about. In any case *it would seem to be a pity to waste the intellectual understanding of the child, which can be a very powerful ally*, although of course in certain cases the intellectual processes may be used in defence, making the analysis more difficult.
>
> [pp. 119–120, our italics]

Since the members of our large groups are likely to be very intelligent adults, should we not lean on their intellectual understanding and conscious cooperation in unravelling the highly complex situations that emerge during a large group?

2 This was the procedure followed by Haim Weinberg and Juan Tubert-Oklander at the beginning of their conduction of the Large Group in Belgrade.

3 This analysis on the Dublin Large Group is based on a text by Reyna Hernández-Tubert (2009), published in *Contexts* and reproduced here as Appendix IV, in which she did a personal reflection on the experience of this Large Group.

4 The next three paragraphs were not part of the original publication but represent our present reflections on the matter.

5 The inclusion of silent observers, for both training and research purposes, has also been a common practice in Italy, and has been shown to also have interesting therapeutic possibilities (Pinto & d'Elia, 1980; Cappiello, Zanasi, & Fiumara, 1988). Foulkes himself used to include trainees and distinguished visitors in his groups, at the beginning of his group-analytic practice (Foulkes, 1948, pp. 149–151).

Chapter 12

The politics of despair (2008)

From despair to dialogue and hope

Reyna Hernández-Tubert

*In 2008, we participated in the 14th European Symposium of Group Analysis that took place in Dublin. There, I read this paper, which was later published in **Group Analysis** in 2011 (Hernández-Tubert, 2011a). This gave me an opportunity to develop the idea that despair is not just an individual phenomenon, as usually conceived by psychoanalysis, but a relational and social one, as conceived by group analysis. There is a collective form of the syndrome of the unwelcome child, described by Ferenczi (1929), which stems from a fracture between the individual and society, this being the result of an inadequate social organisation and conception of the world. Such approach obviously requires a critical view of our present society, its institutions, its philosophy, and its politics. When this paper was originally read in the Symposium, some colleagues, particularly those from the former Eastern block, objected to what they felt to be a piece of socialist propaganda. However, my criticism, valid or not, is directed to the contemporary Modern Weltanschauung, in both its Western individualistic and Eastern collectivistic forms. I firmly believe that social and political change must needs be complemented by spiritual change, in the inner dimension of our beliefs, values, relations, and emotions, and here psychoanalysis and group analysis have a lot to say, as long as they do not abstain from social and political criticism.*

Despair, dialogue, and desire

The theme of our Congress – 'Despair, Dialogue and Desire: The Transformative Power of the Analytic Group in the Movement from Despair to Desire through Dialogue' – poses a striking relation between three concepts that we should clarify, as a starting point for the discussion that follows.

Despair is something more than the mere absence of hope; it implies utter helplessness, dire anguish, and, when it turns into desperation, also wild and reckless impulsive action, or total apathy. It is the outcome of a crisis in human relationships, both at the interpersonal and the transpersonal – that is group, institutional, and social – levels.

This way of understanding the concepts derives from the relational conception of psychoanalysis and group analysis, which poses that we are constituted and develop as human beings, and feel, think, and act as a result of our relationships – past, present,

DOI: 10.4324/9780429055287-15

and anticipated or yearned-for in the future – with other human beings and with the collective entities formed by them, such as groups, families, institutions, communities, and culture. Proper development and the physical and emotional welfare of people depend, to a large extent, on the existence and quality of these relationships.

When a person has had, during his or her life, loving and gratifying personal and social relationships, he or she develops what Erik Erikson (1950) called 'basic trust'. This we might also call 'faith', meaning a deep and enduring conviction that existence is good and life is worth living, in spite of its inevitable sufferings and disenchantments. On the other hand, when there is a fracture in a relationship that should have been trusting, caring, and containing, especially if it is a dependence relationship, the result is the emergence of despair, called by Erikson 'basic mistrust'. This happens in the primary mother-baby dyad, in couples, in friendship, and family relationships, and in the relation between individuals and groups, on the one hand, and the wider society to which they belong, on the other.

But what is the relation between despair and *desire*? The latter is an expectation of and yearning for something good to come. Whoever founders in despair becomes unable to desire, since he or she is convinced that there is nothing good to be found in the future. Consequently, the passage from despair to desire may only come about through a healing process, and this requires that the person have the experience of a relationship whose characteristics correspond to what he or she has lacked or lost in life: reliability, compassion, understanding, solidarity, and care. Such a relation can never be one-sided, since it demands a mutual recognition and understanding; hence, we may well summarise it as a *dialogue*.

Therefore, the human process that we are describing is *the transition from despair to desire through dialogue*. When the despairing subject manages to establish new stimulating and nourishing relations, in terms of mutual respect, understanding, recognition, and care, he or she begins to recover his or her lost – or perhaps never previously developed – capacity for desire.

The fracture between the individual and society

In facing the complex problem of the relation between the individual and society, there are two opposite philosophical positions: one which poses an intrinsic opposition between the individual and society, and another which highlights the essentially social nature of the human being.

On the one hand, we have the political philosophy developed by authors such as Hobbes, which poses that there is an essential opposition and conflict between the individual, driven by primitive and selfish passions and desires, and society, which demands that he or she renounces them, as a requisite for social life, which is indispensable for survival. This is the perspective taken by Freud (1930a) in *Civilization and Its Discontents*. Thus, Hobbes (1651) argued, in his *Leviathan*, that men in their natural state are 'solitary, poore, nasty, brutish, and short' (p. 186), and therefore require a strong sovereign to impose order and avoid bloody war between them.

On the other hand, we have a contrasting philosophical view, which considers the human being to be essentially social, as a result of a primary and unavoidable need to relate and belong to the community, in order to fully develop his or her nature. Human existence is intrinsically relational, so individual life can only occur through a relation with others and in a community setting, and it can only be fully understood when taking into account its collective context.

Such perspective comes from Aristotle and was later developed by Rousseau, Hegel and Marx. For them, the antagonism between the individual and society is not a primary phenomenon, but the result of an inadequate and unfair society, which we should strive to improve (Greenberg & Mitchell, 1983). In Rousseau's (1762) words, 'man is born free, and everywhere he is in chains', and these chains are what we should break.

In psychoanalysis, this conception of the human being is found in relational analysis and group analysis. It is not the case, however, of having to choose one of these two polar views, but rather of finding an analogical medium between them. There is no doubt that the human being needs to relate with his or her peers, and that this is a primary need that cannot be reduced to the pleasure-seeking and utility motives, which were the only ones recognised by Freud in his social writings. But it is equally true that human relations always imply conflicts, to a greater or lesser degree, and that there are no ideal societies. Consequently, community life depends on our capacity and skill to negotiate the conflicts of interest that arise between individuals and groups, as well as the inevitable contradictions between the individuals' yearnings and desires, on the one hand, and society's requirements, on the other. Such conciliatory efforts are frequently successful, thus allowing transitory periods of harmony between society and the individuals and groups that compose it.

But what happens when this is not accomplished, or perhaps not even attempted by the members of a society? Then there is a fracture between individuals and society, which breeds despair.

Society influences the individual in several ways. Other human beings have an inevitable impact on the development and functioning of the personality; this is the gist of object relations theory and interpersonal psychoanalysis. On the other hand, there is also an imprint of social, institutional, political, and cultural reality on the individual's behaviour and subjective experience. But there is still another aspect of the person's relation with the group and social matrix of his or her existence, since the latter is taken as an object, and the resulting bond may be compared to the mother-baby relationship (Hernández de Tubert, 1997, 2006b). It was Bion (1952) who pointed out that the adult, whose dependence on the social system is as great as that of the baby vis-à-vis its mother, must needs intuit its presence and feel similarly helpless and dependent towards it.

The object relation established by the individual with his or her environment – both the social system and the non-human environment (Searles, 1960) – is a container-contained relation. What does this mean? Wilfred R. Bion (1962) suggested that the mother acts as a container for the baby's physical and emotional needs, and especially for its unbearable anxiety. The baby projects its painful emotional experiences into the mother, who receives, suffers, and symbolises them, and then turns her understanding of her child's suffering into a specific action that aims at solving it (Tubert-Oklander et al., 1982; Tubert-Oklander, 2008c). She also helps the baby to 'name' its emotional experiences, by means of her consistently suitable responses, whose perceptions become signs for these experiences. This is the beginning of symbolisation.

Social institutions and the community-as-a-whole have a similar function towards the individual. The social system should respond to the basic needs and sufferings of individuals and groups, in the first place, by recognising their existence, and then by carrying out the necessary actions in order to solve them. On occasions, this is materially impossible, but even then, recognition is essential for the sufferers, so that they may feel real and existent in the eyes of their community. In this, the adult is, as pointed out by Erich Fromm, 'by the very conditions of his existence . . . even more helpless than the child' (1975, p. 176, my translation). Therefore, whenever the community and its institutions stop acting as a container for individuals and groups, this generates a traumatic experience, which may be compared with the baby's experience of a failure in maternal function.

Such failures may be classified in several categories: (1) when the social system fails to contain, nurture, care for, and protect the individuals, as in the case of the lack of assistance and compassion towards the victims of poverty, disease, natural catastrophe, social turmoil, economic crisis, violence, or war; (2) when there is a blatant attack by the authorities or privileged social groups on minorities, or even on the bulk of the population, as in the case of social repression, war – both internal and external – racism, genocide, or persecution; and (3) when there is a perversion of the social system, which feigns to uphold current social values and laws, while actually breaking them, as in the case of corruption, chicanery, and mendacity by the authorities (Hernández de Tubert, 1997, 2006b).

The impact of this failure to comply with what I deem to be the essential functions of the social system towards the individuals and groups that compose it is quite similar to what we can observe in children, whenever the adults who are responsible for their care neglect, forsake, or abuse them, lie to them, act in bad faith, or deny what is happening before their very eyes. This reaction was described in 1929 by Sándor Ferenczi, in his paper 'The unwelcome child and his death instinct'. He then observed, in adult patients who had been mistreated and rejected in childhood, a syndrome composed of severe depression, suicidal and self-destructive ideas and behaviour, extreme psychosomatic disturbances, and a nihilistic philosophy. He suggested that the treatment of such patients should consist in allowing them to regress to a dependence relation with their analyst, who should then respond with understanding, care, and love, thus giving them an opportunity to experience, perhaps for the first time, the benefits of a normal childhood, which would then compensate for their original lack of it (Hernández de Tubert, 1999b).

In the past few decades, we have witnessed the emergence of a collective version of this syndrome, which may be ascribed to the failure of the social system and its leaders to fulfil the containing, nourishing, and protecting function towards the individuals and groups that compose it, especially those which are underprivileged, disempowered, and helpless, as we shall now see.

The blind alley of the present world

In our present world, there has been a sharp turn away from the belief that the community is in any way responsible for the welfare of its members, and especially for those who are deprived, disadvantaged, infirm, marginalised, or helpless. There is, instead, an upsurge of a ruthless ideology of savage ferocious cannibalistic competition that drops the losers on the way, which has lately been called 'neo-liberalism'. Such ideology represents a conception of existence as a perpetual contest, in which, for some of the players to win, all others have to lose. Only winners are considered to be of any value and capable of assuming responsibility for their family's and their own welfare and security – and no one else's. Losers, on the other hand, are irresponsible and despicable beings, who deserve nothing but indifference, in the best of cases. Consequently, any claim for social responsibility towards and the attention and care of the underprivileged is rejected as inadequate, and even immoral, since it implies 'giving a reward for laziness and ineptitude'.

This position, vaguely based on a misunderstood Darwinism that interprets social problems in terms of the 'survival of the fittest', is a latter development of the bourgeois capitalist view that flourished with the Industrial Revolution. In its present form, it leans on neoclassic economic theory, which emphasises the maximisation of economic benefit and market self-regulation as the foundations for the progress and development of any given society, measured in terms of its wealth-generating capacity.

This brings about the most severe consequences for human life. On the one hand, it promotes a ruthless cannibalistic competition for economic success that summarily discards all those who do not fit into the system. This implies a fracture in the very fabric of society, by leaving behind the time-honoured values of solidarity, compassion, and care for other human beings. It thus fosters self-ishness and the utter lack of concern for those who are not a part of a person's inner circle of relations – his or her family and, to a much lesser extent, friends. Children learn, early in life, that if they are going to get a place – for instance, at school – they will have to manage to do whatever it takes to leave others out of it. Obviously, this is not the way in which things are presented in their elders' mani-fest discourse, but in fact they learn that others must lose, so that they may win. Sometime afterwards, this is to be repeated in the search for a job.

On the other hand, with the enormous present development of monopolistic globalised capitalism, an ever-growing sector of humankind has become negligible and disposable, since it comprises the unemployed, who do not contribute to the accumulation of wealth and can neither engage in the unrestrained consumption that sustains it. Therefore, they are not taken into account in governmental planning and services, and their material, emotional, and spiritual needs find no response from the community. Hence, their predicament is quite similar to that of the 'unwelcome child', described by Ferenczi (1929), who comes as an unwanted guest in its own family.

The result is despair, crass materialism, a relentless exploitation of sensuality, egotism, cruelty, and ultimately violence. Extreme deprivation and the lack of future prospects quench the capacity for love (Fromm, 1956), and people lose sight of their hearts' longings, which are substituted by mere whims, whether material or sensual. When the belief in the very possibility of love and happiness is lost, all that remains is a wild and wanton quest for stimuli and possessions, and outbursts of uncontrolled rage whenever they are not available or when, having attained them, the feeling of dissatisfaction persists.

Consequently, this essential disturbance of existence and relationships is to be found not only in the victims of the system, but also in its beneficiaries. Of course, those who are underprivileged, marginalised, and ignored suffer the greatest lacks, not only because they cannot satisfy their primary needs, but also because they cannot possess those goods that the prevailing culture considers to be the only ones worth desiring. This is compounded by the fact that the same culture holds them guilty for their unfortunate situation. Blaming the victims for their victimisation is always an act of utter cruelty, both in the cases of rape and the sexual abuse of children, and in those of discrimination, unemployment, and total lack of solidarity and compassion by society. The consequence is that those who cannot find a social space to inhabit and develop in – as in housing, schools, hospitals, or the workplace – end up feeling inadequate, inferior, ashamed, and guilty for not having that which has been denied to them.

But even the winners, those who have attained the kind of professional, economic, and social success required by the contemporary conception of the world, also feel deeply dissatisfied and frustrated. Such apparently paradoxical result stems from the fact that the goods that culture has declared to be the only goals worth striving for do not satisfy the deepest human needs and, since the latter have been discarded as absurd and non-existent, this makes people incapable of finding a way out of this trap. Consequently, since they cannot think of an alternative, they indulge in a feverish rush for more of the same – more money, more sex, more power, more thrills, more food, more drugs, more danger – which is never enough, since it is merely a plug that can never fill an inner void, like a baby's dummy, which cannot nourish its physical and emotional needs.

This is a desperate situation, with no visible way out, and we are all in it. For a long time, the critics of the capitalist system – socialists, communists, and anarchists – believed that the answer would be found in a change in social structure, especially in laws, institutions, the state, and the production and distribution of wealth. But, ever since the collapse of the so-called 'real socialism' of the former Soviet bloc, it became apparent that external change is not enough, if one keeps the assumptions and the *Weltanschauung* of Modernity, since dire experience showed us that attempting to develop socialism in these conditions only brings about a state capitalism. Obviously, political change must needs be complemented by spiritual change, in the inner dimension of our beliefs, values, relations, and emotions, and here psychoanalysis and group analysis have a lot to say.

The way back

In this collective dehumanising process, the only way back to a shared humanity is through *dialogue*, understood not only as an interchange of ideas, but also as a way of relating to, cooperating with, helping, and ultimately loving each other. People will only recover their capacity for hope and desire, when they meet again as equal subjects, as fellow human beings, in an intersubjective relationship.

Ferenczi (1929) posed this kind of encounter in his concept of the therapeutic regression, in the treatment of those patients who have been severely traumatised by their childhood experiences. In his last paper, called 'Confusion of tongues between the adults and the child' (Ferenczi, 1933), he emphasised the vital need for the analyst to speak with the truth, no matter how painful it might be for both parties, thus transcending what he called the analyst's 'professional hypocrisy'. Some later psychoanalysts, identified with object-relations theory, such as Donald Winnicott (1954, 1955–1956) and Michael Balint (1968), salvaged from oblivion this theory of the regression to dependence and the provision of actual care by the analyst, which might compensate for the original lack of such care in infancy. But these emphasised almost exclusively a unilateral model of relation, posed as similar to the mother-baby relationship. The more recent developments of relational psychoanalysis (Aron, 1996) highlight, instead, the fundamental importance of mutuality between the patient and the analyst, in an approach which is more akin to Ferenczi's original research.

Here we should ask what might be the application of these ideas to group analysis. Psychoanalytic enquiry of and interventions in these phenomena have been curbed by the intrinsic limitations of the bi-personal setting, and by the methodological strategy of restricting all enquiries and explanations to the intrapsychic field, conceived as identical with the intra-personal dimension. Group analysis, instead, has a setting that allows the observation of all sorts of interactions between the group members, as well as that of the manifestations of social, cultural, and political phenomena in the group field. In the theoretical dimension, group analysis remains a study of the intrapsychic, but without restricting it to the intra-personal domain, since it conceives the inter- and trans-personal processes as mental phenomena that transcend the limits of the individual subject. This necessarily includes the study of its political, social, and historical dimensions, which have been largely omitted by classical psychoanalysis, as convincingly demonstrated by Malcolm Pines (1998).

This is why the group-analytic device is especially adequate for the enquiry of and corrective intervention in the pathologies derived from social phenomena, albeit this may be more easily attained in median groups, than in small groups (de Maré, Piper, & Thompson, 1991). Obviously, group analysis as a profession cannot modify by itself the social pathologies in their collective dimension, but it might well be part of an interdisciplinary effort to contribute to their solution, an effort that must also, of course, include a political dimension. But what it can do, with its present resources, is to help various individuals and groups to become conscious of the situations they are in and their consequences for their existence, and act in ways that tend to solve them. Group analysis is particularly effective in helping human groups – whether they be natural groups, whose members have a relationship before, during, and after the intervention, or artificial groups, specially convened for the occasion – to explore new possible ways of relating and coexisting.

In therapeutic groups, we are able to interpret and explore the social, cultural, and political dimensions of the personal experiences of its members, as well as those of the group. The recognition of the fact that many of their problems and conflicts are not a personal construction, but an expression of collective phenomena of which they are a part, has a liberating effect, putting an end to the guilt of not being able to do what society denies them, thus giving them a greater freedom of thought and action. And all this happens in the context of a group whose very existence and operating style contradict the prevailing conception of the world.

In the usually larger groups that convene on special occasions, such as workshops, laboratories, and conferences, group analysis can offer the attendants a novel experience of enquiring and thinking together about relations and social life. When the members bid farewell and go back to their everyday contexts, they carry with them a greater capacity for becoming conscious of social facts and their consequences for individual life, as well as for rational cooperation in a peer group.

Finally, in the case of natural groups – families, work teams, institutions, communities – group analysis helps their members to understand better what it means to live and work together, the influence of their place and affiliations in the wider social context, the nature of their problems, and the best way of dealing with them as a group. Thus Enrique Pichon-Rivière (1971a) always emphasised the need to analyse the object relation that the group develops with its assumed task. In family groups, for instance, he tried to help them to become an efficient work team, whose task was to attain a mutual support in order to aid in the healing of its sick member.

It is worth noting that the type of personality change that can be expected as a result of this kind of group work is akin to what Erich Fromm (1958) called the 'revolutionary character', in a little-known paper retrieved by Earl Hopper (2000, 2003a). Fromm defines this character as follows:

> The revolutionary character is the one who is identified with humanity and therefore transcends the narrow limits of his own society, and who is able, because of this, to criticize his or any other society from the standpoint of reason and humanity. He is not caught in the parochial worship of that culture in which he happened to be born in, which is nothing but an accident of time and geography. He is able to look at his environment with the open eyes of a man who is awake and who finds his criteria of judging the accidental in that which is not accidental (reason), in the norms which exist in and for the human race
>
> (Fromm, 1958, pp. 162–163)

Hopper (2000) points out that this revolutionary character is another way of talking about the mature person, understood as someone who has managed to transcend the limitations of his own environment and origins, to reflect about his own psychic life, interpersonal community and identity, and that of others, and who is willing to take the risk implied by trying to change the very social circumstances that moulded him as a human being.

All this corresponds to the cognitive dimension of perception, thought and decision making, as well as to the conative dimension of rational action. But this ripeness in relationships also requires an emotional evolution, which allows the subject to treat all other persons as similar subjects and develop the skills that are needed for shared cooperation, compassion, understanding, and solidarity.

Such a development is remarkably similar to that intended by the early Christian communities. Consequently, Patrick de Maré chose their term *Koinonia* to refer to this evolution. *Koinonia* is a form of non-possessive and non-passional love that binds the members of a community, a communion reached by means of an intimate co-participation, which could well be expressed as 'brotherhood' (de Maré, Piper, & Thompson, 1991). This proposal of building a community whose members are bound by love is still as revolutionary as it was two thousand years ago.

This kind of bond is indispensable for a full and satisfactory community life, as well as for that grand project for the conduction of social affairs that we call 'democracy'. This is the reason why Hopper (2000) has chosen to use the term 'citizen', for those who have developed such a capacity.

On the other hand, the experience of a mutual and cooperative dialogue and relation that these groups foster, offers a way to help to heal the dire consequences that the severe collective pathology I have described has for the individuals and groups, which strive to develop and live, in spite of it.

In sum, dialogue, understood as a mutual, affectionate, rational, and cooperative relationship, is the only thing that may help us to transcend despair and recover our lost capacity for projecting ourselves into the future, by means of desire.

Part III

Bridging the gap

Chapter 13

Ferenczi and group analysis (2019)

Juan Tubert-Oklander

*Some time ago, I was invited to contribute a chapter for a collective publication on Sándor Ferenczi, on the subject of 'Ferenczi and group analysis'. I was intrigued by this suggestion. This seemed clearly to be a task for me, being a psychoanalyst, a group analyst, and a long-time student of Ferenczi's life and work, but I had my doubts. Ferenczi, like Freud, did never work with groups and, unlike his teacher and friend, did not theorise about society, so there seemed to be no way in which one might argue that he had somehow participated in the inception of group analysis. Nonetheless, I still felt that Ferenczi's underlying conception of psychoanalysis was much more suited to the theory and practice of group analysis than Freud's, and that had certainly influenced my own understanding of this discipline. So, I set out to explore the possible relations – past, present, and future – between his work and group analysis. The results were illuminating and turned into the present text. However, the editors of that collective endeavour felt that my piece did not agree with the spirit of their project. They had expected an academic study of Ferenczi's texts and documental evidence proving that Ferenczi had had an influence on the emergence of group analysis, and I rather chose to discuss the relevance of his thought and practice for the problematics posed by group analysis. My own hermeneutic approach to the interpretation of texts is to establish a dialogue with the text and the author, as can be seen in Appendix I of this book. I believe that analytic texts should be read in the same way we listen to a patient, that is, they should be read analytically. All this was, of course, incompatible with an academic project, so I withdrew my manuscript and finally had it published in **Group Analysis** in 2019 (Tubert-Oklander, 2019b). My final conclusion was not only that Ferenczi's work is relevant to group analysis, as conceived and practised nowadays, and probably had some influence, direct or indirect, on its founders, but also that it has a bearing on the future development of this discipline and on our conception of the human being.*

Sándor Ferenczi did not work with groups, yet his thinking and practice can be conceived, not only as a major influence on the origins and development of group analysis, but also as a seminal source of ideas for its further development today. The initiators of group analysis – S. H. Foulkes in Britain and Enrique

DOI: 10.4324/9780429055287-17

Pichon-Rivière in Argentina – did not explicitly quote Ferenczi, although they undoubtedly knew his work. But in this field, as in many others in psychoanalysis, Ferenczi's influence has seeped unrecognised into so many new developments in our discipline.

Ferenczi did not write much about groups or society, although he was keenly interested, from the beginning of his career, even before meeting Freud, in the social and political consequences of what we call nowadays sexual diversity. Deeply committed with his liberal-socialist ideology, he fought, from 1902 onwards, for what we presently call 'gay rights', arguing that 'homosexuality is not a disease, but a psychic disposition'. He actively participated in the International Humanitarian Committee for the Defence of Homosexuals created by the German sexologist Magnus Hirschfeld, whose main aim was to attain a reform of criminal law, which qualified homosexuality as a crime and imposed severe punishments on its practice. In this, his attitude contrasted with Freud's, who sympathised with the committee, but refused to be associated with its call for legal reform (Stanton, 1990, pp. 10–11).

He firmly believed that society and its values and prejudices played a major role in psychopathology, and that psychoanalysis should free patients from the dire consequences of a repressive education. This set him on a path that was to become inimical to the orthodox psychoanalytical rejection of all environmental influence.

Ever since his very first psychoanalytic paper, 'The effect on women of premature ejaculation in men' (1908a), he showed a keen interest in mutual unconscious influence in relationships, thus paving the way for an interpersonal approach to psychoanalysis. In this text and his other 1908 article on 'Psychoanalysis and education' (1908b), he emphasised the educational origin of the restraints imposed by the human environment on the child's developing personality. Of course, Freud (1908d) had already discussed this in his '"Civilized" sexual morality and modern nervous illness', but only in terms of 'the injurious effects of our "civilized" sexual morality' (p. 204). Ferenczi, on the other hand, claimed that a misguided education induced a repression of the child's perception of his own experiences and his capacity to think for himself. He compared this to a hypnotic injunction that 'render[s] a hypnotized man, when awake, unable to perceive or recognize certain visual, auditory or tactile stimuli, so nowadays is mankind educated to *introspective blindness*' (1908b, p. 288). This leads to collective disturbances, such as 'clinging to meaningless religious superstitions, to traditional cult of authorities, to obsolete social institutions, [which] are *pathological phenomena of the folk-mind*' (p. 282, my italics).

Consequently, in his approach to psychoanalysis, social facts have a bearing on psychological facts and vice-versa, and this implies a constant interchange and mutual influence between individual and collective processes, inner and outer, psychological and social. This is, of course, one of the basic tenets of group analysis, which requires that social facts be given as much attention as the psychological. In psychoanalysis, such a dialectical approach to the relationship between inner and outer processes, individual and group, was developed by Fairbairn (1952; Clarke & Scharff, 2014), who had met Ferenczi in the 1929 Oxford Psychoanalytic Congress and was clearly much impressed by his thought (Fairbairn, 1929).

But his major contributions to the emergence of group analysis – which are still not fully recognised – are his conceptual and technical revolutionary innovations, which paved the way for the quite similar approaches of the British Independent Tradition of Object Relations Theory, Interpersonal Psychoanalysis, Psychoanalytic Field Theory, and the contemporary school of Relational Psychoanalysis, all of which are fully compatible with and complementary to Group Analysis.

These innovations, which he developed in a series of papers written between 1928 and 1932 (Ferenczi, 1955) as well as in his *Clinical Diary* (1985), centred on the essential unity and mutual interchange between the clinical phenomena we have learnt to describe as 'transference' and 'counter-transference'. However, this concept of the constant dialectic between the subject and the other had been implicit, as we have already seen, in his first papers, and was explicitly theorised in his articles on 'Introjection and transference' (1909) and 'Stages in the development of the sense of reality' (1913a).[1]

Group analysis is quite different from the mere application of the theories and techniques derived from the practice of bi-personal psychoanalysis to the treatment of patients in groups. It rather implies approaching the study and conduction of groups, both therapeutic and non-therapeutic, with an analytic attitude, striving to understand and interpret whatever occurs in them, and constructing new theories and techniques on the basis of the group-analytic experience, just as psychoanalysis has done on the basis of the bi-personal psychoanalytic experience. This idea that psychoanalytic theorising must be based on the analytic experience was first formulated in Ferenczi's 1923 book with Rank, *The Development of Psychoanalysis* (Ferenczi & Rank, 1924).

Group analysis also relies heavily on the social sciences – sociology, anthropology, and political science. This creates the major problem of articulating and building bridges between the 'internal' and the 'external'. In this, Ferenczi's emphasis on the fundamental importance of actual relations with other significant persons, such as the primary caregivers, the family, the analyst, and society, and his description of the dynamic interplay of transference and countertransference anticipated the theoretical developments of group analysis. He introduced the holistic concept of the unity of transference and countertransference, and of the family and the child (Ferenczi, 1928a). This implied an underlying but yet unformulated field theory, which is basic for group analysis.[2]

Field theories differ from ordinary causal theories in that they pose an atemporal organisation of data, which explains all occurrences in a certain event space, which is called a 'field', as the result of the mutual influence of all significant factors that are simultaneously present in that space. Hence, events in a field are determined by its overall organisation, instead of the linear sequence of events postulated by causal theories (Katz, Cassorla, & Civitarese, 2017;

Tubert-Oklander, 2017c). This allows us to study the interdependence of multiple factors which would be ordinarily considered heterogeneous and incommensurable ('comparing apples and oranges'). A psychological field may, according to Kurt Lewin (1951), include personal experiences, such as feelings, thoughts or desires, and interactions, as well as social, political, biological, geographical, and even climatological factors. It is obvious that this approach is fully consistent with Ferenczi's emphasis on the fusion of the analyst's and the analysand's mental processes (1985), the integration of social and psychological facts, and the mutual articulation of psychology and natural science (1924). This is the essence of Enrique Pichon-Rivière's concept of *vínculo*, which has been translated ad 'link' or 'bond'. The bond is a complex dynamic structure, which includes the subject, the object, their mutual relationship, and the whole physical, social, cultural, political, and ecological context (Pichon-Rivière, 1971a, 1971b, 1979; Tubert-Oklander, 2017b; Tubert-Oklander & Hernández-Tubert, 2014a; Losso, Setton, & Scharff, 2017).

But this essential unity and mutual interchange of 'inner' and 'outer' also needs to be accounted for in psychological terms, if we are to integrate these novel concepts with our previous knowledge, and this is where Ferenczi comes to our aid. His most important theoretical contribution postulated an originary undifferentiated state of mind, which he called 'Thalassal', from which all other mental states, experiences, perceptions, and thoughts evolve, and which remains present but unseen, underlying the more differentiated states. *Thalassa* is the Greek name for the sea. Ferenczi chose it because his book, called *Thalassa: A Theory of Genitality* (1924), was a bold bioanalytical speculation about the phylogenetic trauma suffered by all those living beings that were forced to adapt to a new life on earth, when the ocean waters receded. All organisms living in the water do not need a physical contact between the sexes in order for their gametes to meet and fuse; they can be set free in the watery environment and their conjunction is left to chance. But when life migrated to an earth and air environment, mating became an urgent need. So sexual behaviour, and particularly coition, are a consequence of the biological trauma of having lost the aqueous environment and an expression of an urge to return to it.

But what is true at the phylogenetic level is also true in ontogeny. Viviparous animals, such as human beings, which develop a prenatal existence in a liquid environment within their mother's body, resembling the originary form of life in our planet, also have an urge to return to the womb, and this is acted out in coitus. Psychologically, the human drive for joining bodies and fluids with a mate symbolises both the individual's urge to return to the mother's womb and that of the species to go back to the ocean.

Now, this line of thinking sounds quite strange because it oscillates between biology, psychology – particularly, psychoanalysis – and a most daring speculation about the origins of life on Earth. (Sigmund Freud [1933c, p. 228] said of Ferenczi's book that 'it was perhaps the boldest application of psycho-analysis that was ever attempted'.) But what allowed the author to make such wild flights of imagination was his most original approach to epistemology, which conceived that natural science and psychology should interpret one another, and that 'all physical and physiological phenomena require a meta-physical (i.e., psychological) explanation and all psychological phenomena a meta-psychological (i.e., physical) one' (Ferenczi, 1924, p. 4).

It seems that Ferenczi's bioanalytical essay – just as other bold attempts to integrate the physical and the psychical, as Freud's 1895 *Project* (1950a) – may be read in two quite distinct ways (Beuchot, 1985). There is a *literal* reading, which takes it as a depiction of actual physical events, and a *metaphorical* one, which conceives it as an analogy that attempts to clarify much more obscure and hyper-complex mental processes, a veritable origin myth of the emergence of Mind. Of course, Ferenczi would have argued that there is no need to choose between the two.

So, no matter what one might think about the author's bioanalytical efforts, of Lamarck's theory of the inheritance of acquired characteristics – which was wholeheartedly accepted by Freud and Ferenczi, and generally rejected by present-day biologists – and of Haeckel's Biogenetic Law ('ontogeny recapitulates phylogeny'), there remains the idea that Mind starts from an undifferentiated original state, that such a state somehow persists in the more mature states of being, and that there is a yearning, perhaps a drive, to return to it. In this, Ferenczi's approach differed from Freud's (1930a), who conceived what he called the 'oceanic feeling' as a primitive state of mind, characteristic of infancy, which should be left behind with growth and development, and that only persisted in adulthood in pathological conditions.

In the human being, this is what makes possible the appearance of 'Thalassal regressions', which are the basis of sexuality, creativity, art, religion, and social life. This is yet a much-needed concept for the full development of group-analytic theory, which is still to be incorporated into it. For the major question for such theory is how the articulation of individual and collective mental processes occurs. This finds a possible answer in the idea that there is a basic undifferentiated phase of mentation, which is not only a primeval state, but also a constant and pervading presence, underlying and constituting the base for the more differentiated mental processes, in which there is no such thing as discrimination between self, others, and the whole environment.[3] The consequences of such a hypothesis are still to be explored, and they may offer the key to a much deeper understanding of the individual-collective dialectic.

This is clearly related to the Aristotelean conception of Man as a primarily social being, a social animal – the *Zoon Politikón* – which underlies both group analysis and the various relational approaches to psychoanalysis. In Ferenczi's conception of the psychoanalytic situation, this primary undifferentiation silently underlies the more apparent analytic dialogue, which requires a differentiated definition of self and other. Thus, he writes in his *Clinical Diary* (1985),

> It is as though two halves had combined to form a whole soul. The emotions of the analyst combine with the ideas of the analysand, and the ideas of the

analyst (representational images), with the emotions of the analysand; in this way the otherwise lifeless images become events, and the empty emotional tumult acquires an intellectual content.

(p. 14)

In the very same way, several apparently differentiated individuals are submerged into a holistic group process, which can be studied and interpreted in itself. And this is possible because they were not just individuals to begin with, but part of a common whole that includes, not only them, but also their whole context – social, political, historical, legal, geographical, architectonic, climatic, and ecological.[4] The group field – both in group analysis and in traditional psychoanalysis, which can be thought as a two-person group – is not generated by the meeting of the parties: it was already there before they ever met. And all this is fully consistent with Ferenczi's approach to the interpretation of human affairs and the implications of his Thalassal theory.

Group analysis was born almost simultaneously in two quite distant places: in Britain, through the work and thought of S. H. Foulkes (1948, 1964a, 1990), and in Argentina, with those of Enrique Pichon-Rivière (1971a; Tubert-Oklander & Hernández de Tubert, 2004; Losso, Setton, & Scharff, 2017; Scharff, 2017). The term 'Group Analysis' was coined by Foulkes and is still identified with the Group-Analytic Society he founded, while Pichon-Rivière referred to his own theory and technique as 'Operative Groups'. Nonetheless, their approaches are strikingly similar, in spite of some formal and theoretical differences that may be derived from their respective psychoanalytical traditions and sociological influences, so that they may well be conceived as two forms of one and the same endeavour (Tubert-Oklander & Hernández-Tubert, 2014a [Chapter 9]).

Both authors had to deal with a same theoretical problem, that of transcending the spurious opposition of individual and collective psychology. Pichon-Rivière (1971a, 1979) resorted to the interplay of introjections and projections posed by Kleinian theory, the concept of an 'internal group', derived from Fairbairn's study of internal objects, Kurt Lewin's field theory, George Herbert Mead's social psychology, and Marxist sociology, as well as introducing the numerous new concepts he created in order to account for the group experience. Foulkes, on the other hand, was a red-blooded Freudian, but in his work on groups he relied on Kurt Goldstein's holistic theory of the organism and the nervous system, the sociological theories of the Frankfurt School and his friend and colleague Norbert Elias, and also on a series of concepts derived from the group-analytic experience. His main theoretical contribution was his concept of a group and social *Matrix*, which contains, suffuses, and determines the life, thoughts, feelings, and relations of all the individuals embedded in it.[5] The group is for him a gossamer network of relations and meanings, and individuals are just the nodal points in such a network. (Foulkes, 1964a, 1990; Hopper & Weinberg, 2016, 2017b).

As already pointed out earlier, neither of them quoted Ferenczi, although they must have been cognisant of his work, which was a required reading in all courses of technique at the time. Yet, it was Ferenczi who might have provided a much-needed element for their theorising, with his Thalassal theory. This book, however, is perhaps the least known and understood of his writings, on account of its great complexity and the fact that it is quite inimical to our present-day scientistic *Zeitgeist*. Ferenczi's silent contribution to the very bases of group analysis has since gone largely unnoticed, just as it was for many years in the case of the numerous developments in psychoanalysis that passed for new, albeit they were truly a revival of the revolutionary ideas and technical experiments of this forgotten master, whose memory had been radically repressed on account of Freud's utter rejection of his last contributions and their incompatibility with the orthodox point of view.[6] It is quite possible that Foulkes and Pichon-Rivière might have been unconsciously influenced, like so many generations of analysts and authors who failed to quote Ferenczi as a precursor of what they felt to be their new ideas of their own, by what Ferenczi would have called a collective 'introspective blindness' of the very fact that he had existed, worked, thought, and wrote about and taught psychoanalysis. This was, of course, a symptom of a repressed conflict within our professional community, a 'pathological phenomenon of the folk-mind', which took several generations to be acknowledged and worked-through by part of its members.

This is most certainly an interpretative hypothesis, but this is what analysis – both psychoanalysis and group-analysis – is all about. One of the peer reviewers of this paper posed a most important question, in the following terms: 'It could have being helpful to know better on which basis it is supposed that Ferenczi's thoughts gave origin and development to group analysis'. This is perfectly valid when theories are studied in academic terms, but I am making no such claim. The common-sense conception of thinking that prevails in the scientific and academic discourses view ideas as a production of individual brain processes and assumes that the influence of some person's thoughts on another's can only come about through some kind of visible communication, by means of speech, writing, or actions. But the analytic trend initiated by Freud, when he posed the existence of an unconscious communication between analyst and analysand (1912e), and of collective mental processes that underlie the hyper-complex phenomenon of cultural evolution (1912–1913, 1939a), call into question such assumptions. In analysis, we assume the existence of trans-personal mental processes that precede, surround, pervade, and determine individual thought. This can be found, for example, in Bion's (1967, 1970) concept 'thoughts in search of a thinker", and in Ogden's (1994) 'analytic third', as well as in Foulkes's (1973) 'matrix'.[7] New ideas are not personal creations, but the crystallisation, through the work of an individual or a group, of unformulated collective thoughts that are incubating in the social unconscious of a community and shape its *Zeitgeist*.

Hence, I do not claim that Ferenczi's ideas gave origin and development to group analysis. What I actually think is that a new conception of human existence was brewing unnoticed and found an expression in parts of Freud's enquiry, as well as in Ferenczi, Goldstein, the Gestalt theorists, Marx, the Frankfurt school,

Sullivan, Foulkes, Pichon-Rivière, and many others. This common theme was a holistic view that rejected the ordinary dilemmatic oppositions of inner/outer, subject/object, individual/group. Foulkes and Pichon-Rivière, who initiated the two great schools of group analysis, were both psychoanalysts, and it is a fair assumption that they must have received some influence from his thought, either directly or indirectly, consciously or unconsciously. In any case, they were certainly attempting to tackle the very same problems that occupied him, and the traditions that stemmed from their partially overlapping work can only profit from the belated incorporation of his ideas, practice, and experiences.

Now that we have recovered him from the no-man's land of banishment and imposed inexistence, it is high time for us to dig into the unexploited veins of these abandoned workings (Ragen & Aron, 1993). I strongly believe that the riches that are still to be found there will provide many of the missing pieces of the work in progress that is the group-analytic theory and practice, and build the much-needed bridges between psychoanalysis and group analysis. As the other peer reviewer aptly put it, 'Hopefully "introspective blindness" will give room to "creative awareness"'.

Notes

1 This dialectic had been anticipated by a number of Freud's clinical observations but was excluded in his formal theorising. For instance, in his Introductory Lecture XVI on 'Psycho-analysis and psychiatry' (Freud, 1916–1917), he clearly showed that a married woman who developed a delusion of jealousy after receiving an anonymous letter saying that her husband was having an affair with a younger woman, had herself unconsciously induced a malicious housemaid to send it, by an apparently chance comment that 'it would cause her the greatest unhappiness if her husband had a love affair with a young girl' (p. 251). There are many such observations in Freud's works, on the mutual unconscious influences between human beings, but in his formal theory, he stuck to an individual paradigm that explained experience, thought, and behaviour exclusively in terms of internal processes.
2 See Appendix III on 'Holism'.
3 This is what I have called, in a previous publication (Tubert-Oklander, 2014), the 'syncretic paradigm'.
4 Once again, this is Pichon-Rivière's notion of *vínculo*. Of the two possible translations of the term, 'bond' is by far much more adequate than 'link' (Tubert-Oklander, 2017b). The connotations of the word 'link' are physical (the links in a chain), logical, and communicational. The penumbra of associations of 'bond' are relational, emotional (the bonds of love), legal (marriage bonds), economical (government bonds), socio-political and historical (bondage, serfdom). Hence, 'bond' is a word that better conveys Pichon-Rivière's meaning. Nonetheless, the term 'theory of the link' has become the usual translation of *teoría del vínculo*, so most probably we shall have to live with this mistranslation, as we did with the use of 'instinct' for *Trieb*.
5 See Chapter 8].
6 Michael Balint (1968) presents a thorough analysis of the strange phenomenon of the virtual excommunication of Ferenczi, his ideas, and his memory from the psychoanalytical movement in his book *The Basic Fault*.
7 See also Chapter 8.

Chapter 14

The wind and the tide (2013–2020)

On personal acts and impersonal currents in human life

Juan Tubert-Oklander

In 2003, I met Lewis Aron in New York, during the Winter Meeting of the American Psychoanalytic Association. We found out that we had many things in common, particularly our shared interest in Sándor Ferenczi, and we started a lively epistolary interchange. As a result, I attended the Third Annual Conference of the International Association for Relational Psychoanalysis and Psychotherapy, held in Santa Monica, CA. There I heard Lew's participation in a panel, in which he referred to the relational criticisms of Freud's theory of instinctual drives. After that, during the discussion from the floor, I found myself saying that, quite apart from the mechanistic theory of drives, there was perhaps in Freud's concept an implied reference to the lived experience of being driven by something alien to one's will. This was a new idea to me and brewed in my musings and emerged in my classes and discussions during quite a few years. It was only in 2013 that it turned into a paper I read in the 11th Annual Conference of the IARPP, held in Santiago, Chile, in the same panel in which Reyna Hernández-Tubert (2015) read the paper that became Chapter 2 of this book. It was later published in 2015 in the **Canadian Journal of Psychoanalysis** *(Tubert-Oklander, 2015).*

Here I explore the idea that, even though Freud's concept of drives as natural causes of behaviour is no longer acceptable for the relational perspective of psychoanalysis, it nonetheless conveys an intuition of the experience of impersonal currents, derived from the body in human existence. To this I added another source of impersonal currents that stemmed from our belonging to the social context. This might be a way to integrate a valid aspect of Freud's theory with our present relational and psychosocial perspective.

Relational, intersubjective, and social approaches to psychoanalysis have usually begun by rejecting Freud's theory of instinctual drives. This seems fully appropriate, if one considers only metapsychology's ultimately failed attempt to turn psychoanalysis into a natural science and use the drives, as an explanatory principle, to find a 'cause' for human experience, thinking, and behaviour. Human life cannot be explained away and reduced to just another physical phenomenon, discarding completely its experiential, hermeneutic, personal, relational, and intentional dimensions (Guntrip, 1961; Home, 1966; Klein, 1976; Rycroft, 1985).

DOI: 10.4324/9780429055287-18

Freud consciously dreamt of turning his creation into a hard-core rationalistic and positivistic science, and strived fruitlessly to attain this goal, but another part of him was driven by deep strivings, yearnings, and perceptions of a completely different nature, and this duality was inevitably reflected in his grand creation: psychoanalysis, which has always been a hybrid and contradictory product (Tubert-Oklander, 2008a [Chapter 1]; Tubert-Oklander & Beuchot Puente, 2008).

For many years, I took exception at the whole theory of drives, but then I began to wonder whether this was not throwing the baby away together with the dirty bath water. Perhaps, below and beyond his physicalist theorising, Freud was referring to something else, an obscure intuition of the unknown aspects of human nature.

Relational approaches to psychoanalysis emphasise the *personal* nature of human experience, thought, and action (Guntrip, 1961; Mitchell, 1988, 2000; Tubert-Oklander, 1997). Where Freud saw them as discrete events, the *effects* of previous and underlying *causes*, relational analysts, starting with Ferenczi (1955, 1985), saw them as the intentional acts of a person, directed at other persons with whom he or she relates. As these other people do the same, the result is a continuous process of mutual influence, both conscious and unconscious. The very idea of the existence of impersonal causes that drive the individual, quite apart from his or her intentions, was deemed to be an anachronistic remnant of an outdated conception of science.

But this view leaves something out: the fact that we frequently feel our acts, reactions, emotions, and opinions not to be something we can choose, but rather that we are being carried away by a momentous current that does neither spring from ourselves nor from any identifiable person, an experience of being *driven* by an impersonal force or influence. Freud tried to explain it in terms of physical causality, perhaps in order to control and neutralise the uncanniness of such experiences, but I believe this to be the basic intuition that underlay his theories of instinctual drives.

In Freud's approach, these deep currents sprang from the experiences of our own living flesh, such as being invaded and commanded by lust or bodily anger. Certainly, this view is consistent with the experiences conveyed by many of our patients, who frequently have a conscious or unconscious view of themselves that is similar to Freud's conception of human nature. This is that the human being is set in motion by uncontainable, impersonal, beastly, and selfish drives, which only seek their satisfaction, without any consideration for other human beings.

It is true that this is the behaviour of a part of the personality of our neurotic patients, but, as Fairbairn (1952) and Kohut (1982) pointed out, this is itself a psychopathological phenomenon, the result of the fragmentation of the total personality that ensues as a consequence of traumatic experiences, in the context of early personal relations. In other words, from this point of view, if a person behaves according to the Freudian theory's motivational model – that is, seeking the mere discharge of unpleasant organic tensions, by means of consummatory acts with merely functional and infinitely replaceable objects (Freud, 1915c) – we would have to think that something bad has happened to him, severely distorting his personality.

Although this is a valid criticism, we should perhaps consider whether we are not missing something essential with this argument. Let us then dispense with the causal deterministic view and the ethical conception of some sort of 'bad blood' in the human being and see what is left of this theory. Could there be, apart from this conception, some influence of our living body on our experience, thinking, and behaviour? Not only the erotic and aggressive desires, which are frequently experienced in the body, but also yearnings for a meaningful relation with another human being, from which stems all our relational approach, and the very experience of being-in-the-body. Certainly, there are widely different experiences in the bodies of a child, an adolescent, a youth, and adult, or an elderly person, a man or a woman, healthy or sick, pregnant or not, and so on.

But all this may be experienced in two different ways. We may live them as expansive or intentional movements that spring from the very centre of our being, or experiment them as currents that carry us away, beyond our will. This is possibly the experiential content of the Freudian theory of drives: the fact of feeling *driven* by these impersonal currents that transcend us.

But, even then, there is an essential difference between feeling these currents as foreign, hostile, and dangerous, and keeping a perpetual war against them, as posed by the Freudian theory, or to live them as warm and friendly currents one may surrender to, let be carried away by, and enjoy the pleasure of the unique feeling of power this brings about.[1] This is akin to the experience that Emmanuel Ghent (1990) called 'surrender'.

This is so, but it is not the only instance of such currents that feed human experience, thinking, and behaviour. The other source of impersonal driving forces comes from having been shaped into human existence by and being a part of social systems, such as family, community, institutions, State, race, history, and culture. This is the world of values, customs, laws, traditions, and kinship. These new impersonal driving currents act on, in, and through the person, with his or her affects, yearnings, and strivings for relations and meaning in life, and set the basis for all personal experience, thought, and action, as postulated by S. H. Foulkes (1948, 1964a, 1990) and Enrique Pichon-Rivière (1971a, 1971b, 1979), the pioneers of group-analysis.

Such perspective corresponds to the study of what we call the Social Unconscious (Hopper, 2003a, 2003b; Hopper & Weinberg, 2011a, 2016, 2017b). This concept does not refer to the existence of a particular mental system, different from other 'unconsciouses', but to an unconscious dimension, which includes both the imprint of society in individual mental processes and that of individuals on collective mental processes (Tubert-Oklander, 2014; Tubert-Oklander & Hernández-Tubert, 2014a, 2014b, 2014c [Chapters 9, 10, 11]; Weinberg, 2015).

In the same way that bodily existence generates currents that go through, determine, and carry away people, so does society, no less unconsciously than the former. Thus, for instance, a male patient and a woman analyst may meet, relate, and interact automatically according to the conventional definition, in the culture they both belong to, of what is a man or a woman, and which are the adequate or mandatory forms of relation between genders (Hernández de Tubert, 2006c). And all this is unconscious for both of them, and hence needs become the object of a deep psychoanalytical inquiry, so that it may be perceived, identified, named, thought, and worked through.

Quite on the contrary of what is usually said in our professional milieu, these motivational elements are not 'merely conscious', and not even preconscious, but fully unconscious. Far from being a superficial, well-known, and controllable aspect of the human being, the imprint of society is the deepest stratum of the unconscious (Tubert-Oklander & Hernández de Tubert, 2004).

This is shown by an everyday clinical experience. When we interpret to a patient that some of her or his perceptions, feelings, thoughts, or behaviours is not an expression of free choice, but the acting out of certain norms, ideas, values, or scenes that had been written long before he or she was born, we obtain the very same scandalised response that we get when we interpret unconscious libidinal or aggressive wishes, or childhood traumatic experiences. It seems that we human beings cling tenaciously to the unwarranted belief that we are wholly in control of our thoughts and our behaviour, and hence violently reject any suggestion that we might be determined by forces and currents which seem alien to us.[2]

However, in the same way that the acceptance of the living experience and the demands of our body allows us to put an end to our battle with that part of ourselves, also the acknowledgement and acceptance of the fact that we are all unavoidably children and part of the society that bred us and to which we belong finalises a long-time conflict. Consequently, when we stop denying our subjection to these social currents that also drive us, we acquire the possibility of thinking and even taking a critical stance towards them. This gives us a greater freedom, as well as an acceptance, acknowledgement, and tolerance towards the ways of living, feeling, thinking, and acting of the members of other cultural groups (Beuchot, 2005). This particular form of maturity corresponds to what Erich Fromm (1958) named the 'revolutionary character' and Earl Hopper (2000) called 'being a citizen'. Such an evolution is, of course, much more likely to occur in group analysis than in bi-personal psychoanalysis.

A pregnant metaphor to depict and symbolise these aspects of human life is that of the wind, the tide, and the vessel. The self is a sailing vessel with a structure, a captain, a crew, and a cargo; the weightless wind that blows the sails corresponds to the social currents, while the tide, deep, dark, and thriving with invisible life, corresponds to the ever-expanding forces of bodily existence. Life is a permanent negotiation of all these elements, in order to make the trip feasible, fruitful, and happy.

The captain of a sailing ship knows well that he can neither create, nor control the currents that power his ship, and that these can only be very partially forecasted. He needs, however, a thorough knowledge of the ways of tides and winds, as well as of the assets, liabilities, and capacities of his vessel and his crew, in order to be able to take them through storms and tempests, luminous days and dark nights, strong winds and dead calm, and reach safely their destination.

Just like a seasoned captain knows how to wait for the tide and other motions of the sea in order to start and continue the vessel's journey, and to anticipate and use the blowing winds to power the ship, the person has to incorporate and deal with the bodily and social currents that underlie, surround, and go through him or her, in order to accomplish that eventful voyage called Life. And here our profession has a lot to offer for the welfare and growth of those people who decide to ship with us in that great adventure we call Analysis.

Addendum (2020)

I have not dealt, in the present article, with Freud's (1920g, 1930a) second theory of drives, in which he introduces his conception of the Life and Death Drives, since it would require a much lengthier discussion that I intend to develop on a later occasion. This theory surely avoids the mechanistic assumptions of his first theory of drives (Freud, 1915c), but it still conceives the drives as the efficient causes of behaviour, and not as lived experiences. This was Freud's attempt to explain the duality of love and hate, of creation and destruction. Nonetheless, we still find it to be unsatisfactory, since it places Life and Death on a same standing, albeit affirming the ultimate primacy of death and destruction. In our own view, which we explicitly state in Chapter 16, life is the central concept, the driving force, which always displays a dual nature of love and hate, creation and destruction, but it is a single ever-expanding principle. Of course, this is a moot question, since the opposing positions on the matter are based on previous assumptions that are a part of one's Conception of Life.[3]

Notes

1 Donald Winnicott (1960b) described the difference between experiencing sexual and aggressive wishes as a part of the ego that strengthens it, or as something external that has a violent impact on it. Thus, he wrote,

> It must be emphasized that in referring to the meeting of infant needs I am not referring to the satisfaction of instincts. In the area that I am examining the instincts are not yet clearly defined as internal to the infant. The instincts can be as much external as can a clap of thunder or a hit. The infant's ego is building up strength and in consequence is getting towards a state in which id-demands will be felt as part of the self, and not as environmental. When this development occurs, then id-satisfaction becomes a very important strengthener of the ego, or of the True Self; but id-excitements can be traumatic when the ego is not yet able to include them, and not yet able to contain the risks involved and the frustrations experienced up to the point when id-satisfaction becomes a fact.
>
> (p. 141)

But here he was trying to maintain the Freudian theory of drives as the biological basis of motivation and integrate it with the theory of the development of the self that he was introducing. This is quite different from the point of view I am putting forward. (See Chapter 3.)

2   At least, this happens in our contemporary Western culture, bent on an individualistic conception of the human being. Other cultures conceive such impersonal currents as the will of the gods or as manifestations of a spiritual invisible world.

3   See Appendix II.

Chapter 15

Beyond psychoanalysis and group analysis (2019)

Juan Tubert-Oklander

In 2018, I received an invitation from the Management Committee of the Group Analytic Society International to deliver the 2019 Annual Foulkes Lecture. I immediately accepted, not only because this is a great honour, this lecture being the society's most important annual academic event, but also because it offered me a privileged opportunity to share with a sympathetic group of colleagues the ideas Reyna and I had been working on since our very first conversation, in November 1992, about the dire need for a new paradigm of the human being. We both believed that Freud's thought leaned on a series of assumptions about reality, knowledge, and human nature that were at odds with the radically new perspective his discoveries had brought about.

Having both had a training and practice with groups, before going through a psychoanalytic training, it soon became apparent that we had incorporated psychoanalytic thought, theory, and practice in terms of an understanding that differed from that of those teachers, fellow students and colleagues who lacked the group experience. The first of these differences was a staunch conviction on the essentially social nature of human beings. This led us to reject, or at least qualify, those views that focused exclusively on intrapersonal processes. For us, the minimal field of observation required in order to understand any human event consisted of two people, not one, and it also demanded to take into account the wider social, cultural, historical, political, and ecological contexts. This made us sympathetic towards the interpersonal, relational, culturalist, and intersubjective versions of psychoanalysis, and also, of course, to group analysis.

Group analysis implied a major overhaul of psychoanalytic theory and practice and, in this, Foulkes's and Pichon-Rivière's contributions were as revolutionary as Freud's had been in his time. But, just as he had been hobbled by his previous assumptions, these pioneers were still burdened by part of their psychoanalytic inheritance.

In Foulkes, this was particularly noticeable since, as Dalal (1998) has pointed out, in his work there is a juxtaposition of an adherence to his classic Freudian upbringing, with a wholly novel interpersonal and transpersonal theory of Mind. In Pichon-Rivière, his rejection of the theory of instinctual drives, plus his adoption of a socio-political perspective, led him to distance himself from orthodox psychoanalysis and to call his own approach 'social psychology'. This

DOI: 10.4324/9780429055287-19

we deem to be a mistake. What we need now is to develop a new paradigm of the human being that integrates the discoveries, insights, and views of analysis – both psychoanalysis and group-analysis – with those of the Humanities and the other sciences – biological and social – that study the human being.

This is bound to be a holistic theory that transcends the traditional boundaries that separate and isolate the various disciplines.[1] It should therefore be a collective interdisciplinary and transdisciplinary enterprise, based on an open and fruitful dialogue among all students of human nature. And here the group-analytic tool can be a major asset for attaining mutual understanding.

*The lecture was well received and had two excellent official commentaries by Regine Scholz (2019) and Earl Hopper (2019). It was later published in **Group Analysis** (Tubert-Oklander, 2019d), as well as my response to both commentaries (Tubert-Oklander, 2020b).*

First, I wish to thank the Managing Committee of the Group-Analytic Society International for bestowing upon me the honour and giving me the opportunity to address you by delivering this 43rd Annual S. H. Foulkes Lecture, this being our society's major annual academic event. It is also an occasion to reflect on what we have been doing with the legacy of our founder and the direction in which group analysis is moving nowadays.

Group analysis is most certainly a fruitful development of that momentous enquiry of human nature and experience inaugurated by Sigmund Freud, but we all know that it is not a mere application of the theories and techniques of psychoanalysis, but an analytic enquiry in itself. Foulkes (1948) created group analysis as an exploration of human life in groups, carried out by the members of a group under the guidance of a conductor who maintained an analytic attitude vis-à-vis the group and put on hold his theories and assumptions in order to observe and understand whatever was happening in the session. Thus, group analysis was able to formulate its own concepts and theories, derived from the group-analytic experience, in the same way as psychoanalysis did with the bi-personal psychoanalytic experience. Hence, I have maintained for quite a few years now, that psychoanalysis and group analysis are but two aspects of the wider field of *analysis* (Tubert-Oklander & Hernández de Tubert, 2004). This precludes any hierarchical evaluation of both disciplines. Besides, group analysis can be seen as a quite successful attempt to transcend some deficiencies of traditional psychoanalytical theory and practice, derived from the exclusion of environmental factors, such as actual relationships with real people and the impact of the social, cultural, and political contexts. This accounts for the affinity of group analysis with the Independent Group's Object Relations Theory, Self Psychology, and the relational and intersubjective approaches to psychoanalysis.

Fourteen years ago, I had a conversation with Malcolm Pines, during the long interview Reyna Hernández-Tubert and I did with him, which was later published in *Group Analysis* (Tubert-Oklander & Hernández-Tubert, 2011), in which we discussed, among many other things, the relationship between psychoanalysis and group analysis. I then said I had a feeling that group analysis is what psychoanalysis should have been, but never was. Malcolm assented and said,

> I always said that psychoanalysis is slowly moving to where it should be, which is group analysis, and, through relational psychology and self psychology, it's moving in that direction.

(p. 10)

So, why the title of this lecture, 'Beyond psychoanalysis and group analysis'? If psychoanalysis and group analysis are but two aspects of a single field and the latter represents an improvement and further development of the former, is there any need to go beyond them? I shall now explain why I believe there is.

Freud made a revolutionary discovery: that the greatest part of our experiences, feelings, thoughts, motivations, beliefs, capacities, and intentions are unknown to us and beyond our conscious control; this he called 'the unconscious'. He also found that many of them are not only unknown by, but shocking and unacceptable to our conscious mentation, so that we make a purposive, but also unconscious, effort to ignore and forget them; this he called 'repression'. These discoveries, which do not only apply to individual human beings, but also to interpersonal relations, groups, institutions, communities, nations, international relations, and Humankind as a whole, should have brought about a major revolution in epistemology and our conception of the human being, but such evolution was stalled by Freud's adherence to several assumptions that were an essential part of his *Weltanschauung* or Conception of the World.[2] These were: (1) materialistic metaphysics, (2) the Cartesian subject, (3) deterministic positivism, (4) neutral objectivism, and (5) rejection of teleology (Tubert-Oklander, 2020a). In sum, this implied the individualistic paradigm and the misguided attempt to turn the discipline he had created into a positivistic science, framed in the model of the natural sciences (Tubert-Oklander, 2008a [Chapter 1]).

The *individualistic paradigm* takes the individual organism as the starting point and material basis of all mental activity. This implies identifying the mind with the brain and the unwarranted assumption that all mental processes must happen 'within' the individual, thus summarily rejecting any claim to the existence of collective mental processes. If mind is merely an epiphenomenon of brain function, how can there be something like group mental processes? A group has no brain, any more than it has a 'group liver', hence there is no such thing as a 'group mind'. Consequently, all the mental phenomena to be studied by psychoanalysis are perforce internal, what is usually known as 'intra-psychic'.

Nonetheless, this prejudice did not prevent Freud from initiating, in some of his social writings, such as *Totem and Taboo* (1912–1913) and *Moses and Monotheism* (1939a), the study of collective mental processes (Hernández de Tubert, 2008 [Chapter 5]). What he did not do is extract the inevitable consequences of these studies and include them in his formal theory. This is one of the contradictions between his practice and discoveries, on the one hand, and the formal theory he was trying to develop, under the name of 'metapsychology', on the other (Tubert-Oklander, 2008a [Chapter 1]).

Foulkes strove, from the beginning of his work with and thinking about groups, to transcend these limitations of Freud's thought. Thus, he wrote, in his first book, *An Introduction to Group-Analytic Psychotherapy* (1948), the following lines:

> Each individual – itself an artificial, though plausible, abstraction – is basically and centrally determined, inevitably, by the world in which he lives, by the community, the group, of which he forms a part.
>
> (p. 10)

The very same stance was taken by Enrique Pichon-Rivière (1971a, 1979), the founder of what I deem to be an alternative and independent Latin American school of group analysis (Tubert-Oklander & Hernández-Tubert, 2014a [Chapter 9]), in these terms:

> One cannot think in terms of a distinction between the individual and society. It is an abstraction, a reductionism that we cannot accept, because we carry society within us.
>
> (Pichon-Rivière, 1979, p. 57, my translation)

Both authors affirmed, in all their writings, the primary and essential social nature of the human being, and Foulkes went even further, in questioning the assumption, derived from materialistic metaphysics and common-sense thinking, that only matter and energy are 'real', and that any other alleged entity is either non-existent or an epiphenomenon of material processes.[3] From this point of view, 'mind' is nothing but an aspect of brain function and social processes are only a consequence of individual psychology. But Foulkes wrote, in 1967, that

> To me it does not seem difficult to accept that communication, verbal or otherwise, can take place, from one mind to the other with complete disregard of whether the brain substance is located in one or other skull of the participants.
>
> (Foulkes, 1967, p. 18)

He was thus clearly stating that non-material entities, such as communication, relations, and group and social processes were indeed real. Gregory Bateson (1972, 1979) would most certainly include them in his extended concept of Mind.

But this revolutionary stance of Foulkes coexisted, as Farhad Dalal (1998) has shown, with an unquestioned allegiance to Freud's theory and practice. Thus, although he conceived the group analytic process as derived from a free-floating conversation among the group members, in which the conductor's contribution, beyond establishing the group and providing the conditions for the process to develop, consisted in being present, and not in implementing technical interventions, such as interpretations (Tubert-Oklander, 2019c), in his actual clinical work, most of his interventions were interpretations, usually framed in terms of Freudian theory. This has been analysed by Dalal as a contradiction between a Radical Foulkes and an Orthodox Foulkes, which generates an inner tension in his work. It seems that revolutionary thinkers, such as Freud and Foulkes, cannot fully assume, or even recognise, the consequences of their rupture from the tradition in which they have been reared, and so need to keep a part of the latter side by side with the new ideas they are generating. This, of course, requires a split in their personality – what Freud (1940b) called *Spaltung* – that allows the coexistence of two different and mutually incompatible trends of thought, without experiencing or acknowledging the underlying contradiction, since they never come into contact with each other.[4]

The very same thing may be said about the present-day reality of group analysis. Most group analysts, who have had an extensive study of Foulkes's writings, seem to be only giving lip service to the principles of group analysis but work in the clinic under one or other version of orthodox bi-personal psychoanalysis. Hence, they assign an undue importance to the analyst's interpretations, framed in terms of the Oedipus complex or the mother-child relationship, and focus on the intrapsychic, rather than the interpersonal or social dimensions. Consequently, as pointed out by Dalal (1998),

> group events . . . are understood through the transference by reference to past history, and the history that is used is the *history of asocial individuals.* . . . This throws into relief the absence of a group-analytic paradigm, one that might take account of the *history of social groups.*
>
> (pp. 12–13)

This establishes a social fact: the subservience of the community of group analysts vis-à-vis their highly prestigious relative, which manifests itself both in the use of various orthodox psychoanalytic theories in the understanding and interpretation of the patients' behaviour and discourse, and in attitudes that mimic a stereotyped image of 'what an analyst should be', such as neutrality, abstinence, and anonymity (Tubert-Oklander, 2019c).

But the problem is even deeper, since a *Weltanschauung* – understood as a set of assumptions about reality and existence that underlies all our experiences, perceptions, thoughts, feelings, and actions – is derived from the earliest introjections of our primary personal relations and of the social context in which they occur. It is therefore mainly unconscious, unacknowledged, and unthinkable, since we tend to take it as 'just the way things are' (Hernández Hernández, 2010; Hernández de Tubert, 2004a, 2009a; Hernández-Tubert, 2011b; Tubert-Oklander, 2014; Tubert-Oklander & Hernández de Tubert, 2004). Hence, it is most difficult, or almost impossible, to modify. And the individual paradigm – that is, the belief that only individuals are 'real' and that our conscious experience of self and agency is what we actually are – is so ingrained in our experience and thought that any attempt to undermine it is felt as a threat to the stability to our experiential world and our sanity – what Bateson (1972) called an 'epistemological crisis' and Bion (1970) named 'catastrophic change'. Of course, such a rupture of the continuity of our mental processes can either be a calamity or a major opportunity for growth (Gaddini, 1981), but it is never an easy matter.

Consequently, we are in dire need to revise those aspects of our *Weltanschauung* (Conception of the World) and *Lebensanschauung* (Conception of Life) that precede and underlie all our theories and practice, and obstruct the development of the path opened by the emergence of both psychoanalysis and group analysis.[5] These constitute what we may call the Individual Paradigm, which needs to be transcended. Hence, we have to go 'beyond psychoanalysis and group analysis'.

But is this really necessary? I believe it is. If all that were required was to substitute a social paradigm for an individual one, it would be enough to 'take the group seriously', to borrow Dalal's happy expression, and the new group-analytic paradigm would replace the outdated one of orthodox psychoanalysis. Several of our most gifted colleagues are working along this line. Among them, to mention only those I know best and have had an influence on my own thought, are Farhad Dalal (1998), Earl Hopper (2003a, 2003b), and Malcolm Pines (1998). But we need much more than that.

Our present world is facing a major crisis, which threatens our very survival. Our contemporary society unreservedly endorses a view of human existence as a perpetual competition, a ruthless cannibalistic struggle for survival, prestige, power, pleasure, and wealth, in which there is only a place for winners and none for losers. This is fully consistent with the individual paradigm and with Freud's conviction, in consonance with his bourgeois conception of life, that the human being is primarily and essentially selfish, and that 'the motive force of all human activities is a striving towards the two confluent goals of utility and a yield of pleasure' (Freud, 1930a, p. 94). Such conception leaves out the traditional values of solidarity, compassion, and care for other human beings, and fosters a general attitude of selfishness and lack of concern for other people who are apart from one's inner circle of relationships – one's family and, to a much lesser extent, friends – thus bringing about a fracture in the very fabric of society (Hernández-Tubert, 2011a [Chapter 12]).

Of course, neither psychoanalysis nor group analysis can, by themselves, reverse or solve such a widespread social tendency, but their joint voices can contribute, if they stick to a social paradigm that endorses and promotes Pat de Maré's value of *Koinonia* (de Maré, Piper, & Thompson, 1991), to a collective effort, stemming from multiple and very different sources, to question our present conception of life and restore humanness to social life.

But that's not all there is to it. We need to transcend the fetters of materialistic metaphysics, in order to fully acknowledge the existence of non-material entities, such as thoughts, feelings, values, relations, meanings, and social processes. This in the field of *ontology*. In that of *epistemology*, we have to go beyond the empiricism, positivism, and rationalism of modern science and common thought, which view human knowledge exclusively as a product of the split-off intellect, rather than an outcome of our whole being's relation and belonging to the world. You do not need an evidence-based research or a complex logical proof in order to know whether your spouse loves you or not and, if you do know, this knowledge is an evidence in itself. Much in the same vein, a patient and an analyst, or a whole group, including the conductor, may reach a shared conviction about some conclusion they have arrived through their mutual relation and dialogue, of which they are quite sure, even if they may not be able to convince other people who have not been there. Indeed, the validity of the findings of our analytic enquiry is to be based on our experience of the process of reaching them (Tubert-Oklander, 2013b).

In the field of *axiology* and *ethics*, the fact that we have assigned an ontological status to values implies that neither science nor analysis can ever be neutral. The quest for knowledge is always intentional; hence it is necessarily motivated by personal or social interests and values. It is an attempt to solve a problem, and therefore, depends on the reasons the enquirer had for conceiving that *it is* a problem. This has been extensively studied by the sociology of knowledge, from Émile Durkheim (1912), through Karl Mannheim (1936) and Michel Foucault (1961), to Peter L. Berger and Thomas Luckmann (1966). In the field of psychoanalysis, Willy Baranger (1992) published an article called 'On the necessary indeterminacy of the psychoanalytic classification of mental diseases', in which he puts forward the idea that all diagnoses are relative, since they are constructed by the analyst, on the basis of a series of assumptions about the patient's suffering, held by the analyst, the patient, his or her relatives, and society. 'The "private" individual neurosis, in its concept, comes from an artificial dissection made by the psychopathologist' (p. 89, my translation). Consequently, any serious attempt at analysis should include a shared reflection on our respective values, including the patient's and the analyst's, and their ethical implications.

There is still another major aspect that should be a part of the development of a new paradigm, and this is the need to transcend the major split between mind and body that characterises Western thought since Descartes. Of course, this is an ancient problem, which has had several answers in the history of human thought. Such answers are either dualistic or monistic. *Dualism* maintains that the human being is made of two substances: Mind and Body. Its main problem is explaining how they influence each other. *Monism* claims that there is only one substance in the human being, and it may take one of three forms. *Materialistic monism*, also called *physicalism* affirms that only matter is real, and that 'mind' is just a particular form of its organisation; this is the view of contemporary natural science. *Idealism*, states that *Mind* or *Spirit* is the only reality, and that the material world is only an appearance; this was Plato's and Berkeley's conception, and also that of most religions. Finally, *neutral monism* is the idea that the reality of human existence is neither material nor mental but appears as one or the other in different contexts and depending on the observer's vantage point (Wisdom, 1934).[6]

All this seems to be too abstract and of interest only to philosophers, but this is not the case. Freud's discoveries called into question the traditional conception of the mind-body dualism, when he assigned to mental processes the status of causes of physical symptoms. Hysterical conversion became then the equivalent of an involuntary gesture. Hence, his clinical theories tended to be of a kind of interactive dualism. But in his more abstract theory, which he called 'metapsychology', he fully adhered to the physicalism and reductionism of his teachers of physiology, which implied a materialistic monism, in which mind was just an epiphenomenon of brain function. Thus, he wrote, in 'On narcissism: An introduction' that 'all our provisional ideas in psychology will presumably someday be based on an organic substructure' (Freud, 1914c, p. 78). Although his definition of instinct or drive (*Trieb* in German) as 'a concept on the frontier between the mental and the somatic' suggests neutral monism, his immediate statement that it is 'the psychical representative of the stimuli originating from within the organism and reaching the mind, as a measure of the demand made upon the mind for work in consequence of its connection with the body' (Freud, 1915c, pp. 121–122) is clearly dualistic.

These contradictions have remained in the later history of psychoanalysis. As far as I know, there has been no psychoanalyst holding an idealist view; most of them oscillate between a positivistic and a dualistic view, or simply ignore the problem. But this comes to the fore when dealing with psychosomatic disorders, which are clearly related to emotional and relational conflicts, but cannot be interpreted as symbolic gestures. Most psychoanalysts who have tackled the problem of psychosomatic illness have used some version of dualism: they start by analysing the meaning of their patients' conflicts, but at some point of their reasoning, they have to switch over to the functional language of medicine.

One special case is the work of Mahmoud Sami-Ali (2014; Tubert-Oklander, 2019a), an Egyptian physician who trained as a psychoanalyst in France and practised first in Cairo and then again in Paris. His novel theoretical approach, which he calls 'Relational Psychosomatics' is based on the dialectic between two different human processes, which he calls the *imaginary* and the *real* – both terms that usually refer to Lacan's work, and which are roughly equivalent to Freud's primary and secondary processes. But his concept of these is quite different from that of those two predecessors. The *imaginary* includes dream thoughts, but also drawing, painting, dramatising, dancing, singing, storytelling, relating, and play; in sum, everything that Winnicott (1971b) would have included in his 'intermediate area'. But there is a difference: Sami-Ali's concept includes the body. However, this is not the body one learns about in medical studies, a biological machine of sorts, made of functional structures that operate in terms of the laws of physics and chemistry. It is rather a living experiential body, an integral part of Mind, whose vicissitudes are expressed in forms that also make sense in the perspective and language of medicine. Human conflicts – whether personal, interpersonal, or collective – emerge in this core of a person's being that is this living body. They take shape through the imaginary, by being dreamed, drawn, painted, enacted, narrated, poetised, sung, danced, or played; and finally, they are put into words and become the stuff of dialogue and thought, in the realm of the real, and become a shared property of the group. This is the process of minding, which is always relational, since expression and language are necessarily intentional, in relation to other living beings. But when the imaginary is repressed – it is the function and the process that is repressed, not its contents – the conflict becomes stuck in an impasse, so that it can only be expressed by the body, as a symptom, a disturbance, or a disease; the real becomes devitalised and conventional, and existence becomes banal.

Our present society has banished the imaginary, shut off dreams, creativity, and play, and generated in most people a *pathology of banality* or *pathology of adaptation*, this being a perfect breeding ground for psychosomatic disturbances. But when therapy recoups the imaginary, by means of a new relational experience – usually by narrating, drawing, modelling, singing, or enacting dreams[7] – the real is revitalised, and eventually the conflict is negotiated by means of words and dialogue, and this solves the bodily disturbance. But the content of dreams or other imaginary expressions is not interpreted, but rather allowed to evolve and be expressed through dialogue and relation, both in therapy, with the analyst, and in everyday life, with one's network of relationships.

And how does this relate to group analysis? Although Foulkes did not write much about the theory of psychosomatic illness, his clinical approach was quite similar to Sami-Ali's. Foulkes and Anthony (1957–1965) clearly state that a great number of patients in their groups suffer from psychosomatic symptoms (pp. 43–44), and then they add, 'We believe that everything that happens in the human organism can be looked upon from both aspects: the physiological as well as the psychological or mental'. [p. 49]

In group-analytic therapy, this is worked-through by a process Foulkes (1957) calls *translation*, and this is how he explains it:

Group-analytic theory recognises this translation as a part of the process of *communication*. In a group-analytic group, all observable data are held to be relevant communications, whether they take the form of conscious or unconscious, verbal or non-verbal communications.

. . .

At one end of the scale is the inarticulate symptom: it may be biting, excessive blushing, palpitation of the heart or migraine headache; at the other end lies its representation in verbal imagery. Between these two must be cut an intricate sequence of steps leading to verbalisation. Many complex processes have to play their part before the mute symptom of a fellow member can attain linguistic expression and its meaning be grasped by the others.

It is the *process of communication* rather than the information it conveys which is important to us. In a group-analytic group, communication moves from remote and primitive levels to articulate modes of conscious expression and is closely bound up with the therapeutic process.

(p. 111)

We can well see how this conception of the process is similar to Sami-Ali's. The free-floating discussion in group analysis – which I prefer to call 'free-floating conversation', to emphasise its dialogic nature – can be seen as an equivalent of play, but Foulkes's emphasis on verbal means actually leaves out much of the deployment of the imaginary. Were we to include in our groups the practice of explicit dramatisations – which would draw us nearer to psychodrama – plastic or musical expressions, or play – which would be akin to child analysis – we would benefit from the direct expression of the imaginary, which most certainly is an essential part of the 'intricate sequence of steps leading to verbalisation'.

In any case, if we are to tackle the momentous task of constructing a new paradigm of the human being, we should indeed include in it the body and vital processes, as well as psychological and social processes. In Gregory Bateson's (1972) 'ecology of mind', all of these are deemed to be *mental processes*, since in them information and communication are the active causes, rather than the 'forces and impacts' of causation in natural science. This gives us an expanded concept of Mind, which allows us to integrate seamlessly the body, the psyche, and the social world.

Most relational approaches to analysis take exception at Freud's theory of drives. For many years, I shared this point of view. However, more recently, in a paper called 'The wind and the tide: On personal acts and impersonal currents in human life' (Tubert-Oklander, 2015 [Chapter 14]), I suggested that, even if Freud's attempt to explain the drives in terms of physical causality were discarded as inadequate, the concept still conveys a valid idea, an obscure intuition that human experience, thought, and behaviour are driven by impersonal currents that act beyond our personal intentionality, whether conscious or unconscious. Such currents can be conceived as either social or biological – and here by 'biology' I am referring to vital and bodily processes, and not to the theoretical discourse of the scientific discipline that attempts to explain them. The name of this paper, 'The wind and the tide', is derived from the metaphor of the wind, the tide, and the vessel. In this,

> The self is a sailing vessel with a structure, a captain, a crew, and a cargo; the weightless wind that blows the sails corresponds to the social currents, while the tide, deep, dark, and thriving with invisible life, corresponds to the ever-expanding forces of bodily existence. Life is a permanent negotiation of all these elements, in order to make the trip feasible, fruitful, and happy.
>
> (p. 192)

Psychoanalysis has always included the body in its psychological theory, albeit is has tended to ignore the social dimension, but this vital side of human experience has been obscured by Freud's project of basing it on a mechanistic metapsychology that would eventually be reduced to a positivistic biological discourse. This view has been firmly criticised by James Home (1966), who rejected the notion that psychoanalysis could or should be a science and affirmed that it is one of the Humanities, and Charles Rycroft (1966, 1985), who argued that psychoanalysis is not a natural science, but a semantic science, one that looks for meanings, not causes. But he qualified this statement by saying that it is 'a biological theory of meaning', one that 'regards the self as a psychobiological entity which is always striving for self-realization and self-fulfilment'. Hence 'it regards mankind as sharing with the animal and plant world the intrinsic drive to create and recreate its own nature' (Rycroft, 1966, p. 20). In other words, this is not a psychology that could or should ever be reduced to the discourse of positivistic biology, as Freud believed, but a psychology that includes the facts and experiences derived from the recognition that we humans are living beings, with a bodily existence and a vital cycle moved by specific needs, relations with other living beings, and belonging to an ecological environment. Such facts and experiences are birth, growth, aging, and death, as well as the need for contact and relating, and emotional, sexual, and social needs.

Consequently, our new paradigm of the human being should be a holistic one, in the sense of studying the global properties of any given situation, instead of fragmenting it and then studying the parts, as required by the analytic method of natural science (Tubert-Oklander, 2017c; see also Appendix III). In this, group analysis has a lot to give, since it was conceived by Foulkes, from the very beginning, as a holistic theory, in accordance with what he had learned through his relationship and work with Kurt Goldstein (Foulkes, 1990). (Here it should be noted that James Home, whose momentous paper 'The concept of mind' I have just quoted, was not only a psychoanalyst, but also and fundamentally a group analyst and a member of the Group-Analytic Society.)

It may be argued that these are only philosophical matters, which are of no interest to a community of practitioners such as ours. Analysts and psychotherapists are usually more interested in theoretical, technical, or clinical themes. But the focus of this presentation is epistemological, that is, metatheoretical; consequently, it must remain at the most abstract level, in order to expose the hidden assumptions that lie behind the manifest surface of our theories and practice. This, with the purpose of establishing that there is an urgent need to revise them.

Besides, our discipline cannot dispense with the so-called 'mere philosophy'. Ever since Freud, we psychoanalysts and group analysts have had to deal with and try to help people – our patients – who are struggling with the very same questions that philosophers have asked since the beginning of culture. Is life worth living? What is the meaning of life? What is good and what is bad? What should one do? Who am I? What is my place in the Universe? Who are other people and what do they mean to me? What is love? These are some of the questions that both we and our patients are trying to answer. So are the philosophers. But the difference is that, unlike them, we deal with these questions through the study of particular cases, and instead of engaging in an armchair abstract reflection, we carry our enquiry in the concrete practice of an exploratory dialogue with other human beings, which also includes affects and an intimate, intense, and enduring relationship. Our findings are valid for the particular cases we study, and yet give us an inkling of the universal problems of human existence. Hence, the practice of analysis may be conceived as a *field philosophy*.

You can well see that this project of developing a new paradigm of the human being is still on the making, and that I have neither put forward a version of it, nor have I claimed to have solved the problem, but rather concentrated on establishing the need for such a paradigm change and suggested some possible directions in which it may come about.

This idea is not new. Indeed, many people have attempted to formulate something similar along the history of human thought, but it is presently brewing, in the intellectual climate of our time, as a response to a major need. For me, it emerged in November 1992, in a long conversation I had with Reyna Hernández Hernández, a colleague who was soon to become my wife. This was her idea, and it put a name to some of my major concerns that have worried me from the beginning of my study of psychoanalysis. Ever since, we have worked together in thinking, discussing, writing, and teaching on the subject. This brought about a great many articles and book chapters, two doctoral theses, four published books and now the present one. The aim is much clearer now than it was twenty-eight years ago, but there is much more work ahead, and it cannot be done by any single person, group, or discipline.

This is a work in progress, which is being tackled by many people from different fields of human knowledge and practice, such as physical science, biology, neuroscience, psychoanalysis, group analysis, sociology, political science, philosophy, theology, hermeneutics, and the Humanities, among many others. Hence, it is an interdisciplinary enterprise, to which analysis may and should contribute, but only through an open dialogue with its peers in the field of human thought. There is, however, one major voice that stands out, for me, from this chorus, and this is that of Malcolm Pines, who has had a great influence on my thought and practice (Tubert-Oklander, 2010b). For many decades now, Malcolm has unobtrusively toiled towards the construction of a group-analytic conception of human life that integrates psychoanalysis, group analysis, biology, the social sciences, history, politics, the arts, myth, and philosophical and ethical concerns, thus being a major contributor to this collective endeavour.[8]

Nonetheless, even though we analysts cannot claim to be the bearers of an ultimate truth, we still hold a special position in the most difficult task of integrating these widely different approaches. The fact that we strive to deal with the whole human being, including body, mind, relationships, social participation, and thoughts, feelings, motivation, and experience, gives us an opportunity to bring together the various contributions and give them a more encompassing meaning that they would not attain if they stood by themselves. Of course, psychoanalysis and group analysis could not do it either, without the knowledge and ideas provided by all the others.

The very incompleteness of these ideas, which is unavoidable in process thinking, is bound to generate uneasiness in all of us, but that is as it should be, since such distress is the ferment that nourishes the emergence of new ideas. In this momentous enquiry, there are no definitive answers, but only an unending series of successive steps in the right direction. But this is precisely what brought us to analysis in the first place. As the Spanish poet Antonio Machado once wrote, *Caminante, no hay camino, se hace el camino al andar*, which means, 'Wayfarer, there is no road, it is walking that draws the path' (my translation).

Notes

1 See Appendix III on Holism.
2 See Appendix II on the Conception of the World.
3 See Tubert-Oklander (2016 [Chapter 7], on the concept of 'reality'.
4 In Chapter 3 (Tubert-Oklander, 2017d), I have argued that the same kind of split can be found in the work of Donald Winnicott.
5 See Appendix I on Analogical Hermeneutics.
6 This reference is to the British philosopher John Wisdom, of the University of Cambridge, not to be confused with his cousin, John Oultom Wisdom, of the London School of Economics, who significantly contributed to psychoanalytic theory from the philosophic vantage point.
7 This is, of course, more akin to Jung's approach to dreams than to Freud's.
8 Malcolm Pines died on June 31, 2021, at the age of 96.

Chapter 16

And what next? (2021)

Juan Tubert-Oklander and Reyna Hernández-Tubert

This book represents the evolution of our thought, since 1992, on the underpinnings of analytic theory and practice, but the texts that constitute its chapters were written and published during the past twelve years. We have argued that there is an urgent need for the development of a new paradigm of the human being, not only for the theory and practice of analysis – both psychoanalysis and group-analysis – but also for all the disciplines that study human nature, and for the survival and further development of our present culture. In tackling this task, we have relied on the tripod provided by three disciplines: *psychoanalysis*, *group analysis*, and *analogical hermeneutics*,[1] but we have also had recourse to the social sciences, the Humanities, and the more recent developments in biology, such as neurosciences, ethology, and ecology.[2]

This new paradigm is far from being fully developed, but we already have some idea of what its main features should be:

1 It is bound to be a *holistic* paradigm. This means that it should strive to enquire and understand complex entities, situations, and processes *in their wholeness*, instead of splitting them into artificially isolated 'parts', in order to study these fragments and their properties, and then try to reconstruct the already mutilated whole, as required by the analytic method.[3]
2 It should integrate the various dimensions of human existence: bodily, affective, cognitive, relational, social, cultural, political, ideological, spiritual, and ecological. All these are but aspects of a single totality, but they have been studied separately, due to our language and habits of thought, and also to the use of different methodologies, all of these leading to the misguided ontological conviction that they are actual separate entities, instead of facets of a single complex reality.
3 It should identify, enquire, question, and critically revise the Conception of the World (*Weltanschauung*) and Conception of Life (*Lebensanschauung*) that underlie all our theories, practices, and everyday common sense.[4]
4 It should strive to weave and integrate the Golden Braid of *thought*, *feeling*, and *action*, in order to attain a fuller, unmutilated view of the human condition.

DOI: 10.4324/9780429055287-20

5 All this implies transcending the inherent limitations of the split-off intellect, which has been hailed by Western tradition and thought as the only valid instrument for attaining knowledge.

6 Consequently, this new paradigm is based on a wider and deeper conception of knowledge, which goes beyond description, explanation, prediction, and manipulation of objects, human beings, and the world, as it is regularly done by science and technology. Such knowledge requires the confluence of mere knowing with feeling and being-in-the-world, thus becoming what has traditionally been known as 'wisdom'.

7 The approach to this knowledge is not antithetical (exclusive, either-or), but synthetic (inclusive, both-and), avoiding polar thinking and questions such as whether something is internal or external, social or natural, individual or collective, and replacing them by what is integral. In this approach, all questions are interrelated, thus making it possible for us to speak about our primary intuitions. The effect of all those questions framed in terms of oppositions is to obstruct the answer. This is so because the human being is a totality that cannot be split thus. Oppositional thinking impedes the answer, because the only viable answer is to include them all.

8 The *Lebensanschauung* in this new paradigm should not focus exclusively on psychopathology or what goes wrong in human relations and collective living, as classical psychoanalysis and many philosophical enquiries have done, but should also strive to include the best of human traits, those that constitute the ideal goal we are trying to attain and develop. Our picture of human life and condition should include both good and evil, creation and destruction, love and hate, solidarity and competition, generosity and meanness, health and sickness, charity and greed, altruism and egoism, all of these being contrasting aspects of Life.

9 Of course, it may be said that this duality is contained in Freud's (1920g, 1930a) conception of the Life and Death Drives, and this is most probably the basic intuition that underlay his second theory of drives.[5] Nonetheless, we still believe that his choice of language and perspective has been an unhappy one, since it places Life and Death on a same standing, albeit affirming the ultimate primacy of death and destruction. In our own view, Life is the central concept, the driving force, which always displays a dual nature of love and hate, creation and destruction, but it is a single ever-expanding principle. Of course, these are matters that cannot be elucidated by means of argument or experimentation since they are basic assumptions, part of our respective *Weltanschaungen*, which are previous to the starting point of our enquiries. But standing on one or the other position does have major consequences for our understanding and acting, so that choosing one of them is a major decision, which is surely related to our personal life experiences.

10 One final point that should be stressed is that this is an *ethical* paradigm. In this, there is no possible neutrality, since the understanding of the human being's existence, needs, and relations, demands from us a reflection about

right and wrong, good and evil, and a commitment to act in consequence. It is never enough to state things as they are, but we should also affirm how they should be and strive to attain this end. This is the basis of action in the various fields of personal and family living, relations, groups, politics (in its original sense of the *Polis*, the City – i.e., the affairs of the community), and ecology. One cannot be a good person, parent, spouse, or citizen, and at the same time abuse other persons, ill-treat animals, flout the rules of society, and destroy the physical and biological environment.

11   Of course, this commitment to developing people, groups, society, and the world depends on what one believes to be the right direction, and not everyone agrees on the desirability of any given course. This is the source of political and ideological conflicts. Hence, all this should be a part of the analytic enquiry, which should necessarily include an ethical and political reflection that explores the similarities and differences among everyone involved, patients and analysts, conductors and group members alike. This is, as we have seen, the gist of the work in the group-analytic large group.[6] But in any case, every kind of enquiry of human nature should include the ethical and political dimension.

The previous list is, of course, a rather hazy outline of a possible path for the development of a new paradigm, a sort of schematic road map. But there is need for a caveat here: this is the path we devised in terms of our starting point as psychoanalysts, but surely other students of human nature, starting from their own disciplines, will draw different courses. But in every case, the goal that sets our common direction would be the same: to recoup and enquire what is specifically human in our existence as living, sentient, and relational beings, in order to replace the previous attempts to explain the human being in terms of those sciences that study inanimate matter.

Notes

1   See Appendix I on Analogical Hermeneutics.
2   We have now had the fortune of being able to conceive, develop, and lead a new Doctorate on Psychoanalysis and Group Analysis at the Marista University of Merida (Yucatan, Mexico), based on this point of view.
3   See Appendix III on Holism.
4   See Appendix II on the *Weltanschauung*.
5   See Chapter 14.
6   See Chapter 11.

Appendices

Appendix I

Analogical hermeneutics

The concept of analogical hermeneutics is referred to in several chapters of the book. As it is a major feature in our conception and it is not well-known in the English-speaking world, we have provided a brief presentation of its meaning and applications.

Hermeneutics is the discipline that studies the theory and practice of the interpretation of texts. The word 'text' is directly related to language. It comes from the Latin *textus*, which means a tissue, something woven. The metaphor is that, once you have chosen your words, you must weave them together in order to form a tapestry, which displays an image or pattern. Although the word originally referred to speeches, in common parlance it usually applies to a written document. But in its hermeneutical technical sense, the concept of 'text' is not restricted to written documents, but has instead been extended to include discourse, dialogue (Gadamer, 1960), intentional action (Ricoeur, 1965), and every other form of expression, such as music, dancing, ritual, manners, customs, the plastic arts, and culture in general. Hence, the contemporary definition of hermeneutics is 'the theory of the rules that preside over an exegesis – that is, over the interpretation of a particular text, or of a group of signs that may be viewed as a text' (Ricoeur, 1965, p. 8).

There have been traditionally three forms of hermeneutics: *univocality*, *equivocality*, and *analogy*. *Univocality* – from 'univocal', which means 'only one voice' – asserts that, for any given text, there is one, and only one, correct interpretation, which is considered to be 'true', while all others are 'false'. This is the kind of understanding sought by natural science, and it may be identified with the spirit of Modernity. It provides us with a feeling of clarity and certainty, but unfortunately it also tends to foster rigidity and dogmatism.

Equivocality – from 'equivocal', meaning 'equal voices' – holds that, for any given text, there are multiple, perhaps infinite, interpretations, and that all of them are equivalent, so that personal taste and practical convenience are the only possible criteria for choosing one among them. This position came as a reaction against Modernity and characterises Postmodern thinking. Where univocality emphasises identity, equivocality highlights difference. Hence, it is particularly sensitive to the effects of history, context, and perspective on any interpretative activity, thus allowing a more varied and nuanced understanding of the text, but it breeds ambiguity, relativity, and uncertainty, as well as an abandonment of any concept of truth. For equivocality, there is no such thing as truth, but only opinions, and each one is entitled to have his or her own view of things.

The third form of interpretation is *Analogy* or *Analogism*. *Analogia* in Greek means 'proportion', hence, it implies finding a fair and balanced mean between opposites. In hermeneutics, analogism corresponds to an acceptance that there are more than one, albeit not infinite, possible interpretations for a given text, but that they are not necessarily equivalent; some of them are better, others not so good, others still are poor, and some are outright bad. The criterion for choosing among them is to take into account, not only *sense*, which derives from the inner logic of the symbolic systems used by the author and the interpreter, but also the *references* of the text and its interpretations – that is, the non-textual reality that they are talking about. The result is flexibility and a recognition of the difference in points of view, but without relinquishing the search for truth, a relative, partial, and humble truth, it is true, but good enough to go on thinking and acting. Paraphrasing Winnicott, we might say that, in the case of both hermeneutics and psychoanalysis, it is not a question of interpretations having to be 'true', but only 'good enough'.

In semiotics, meaning is derived from *reference* and *sense* (Frege, 1892). The *reference* of any given sign, statement or text is the non-semiotic or non-textual reality it refers to. In positivistic science and semiotics, meaning depends exclusively on the reference, so that expressions that refer to inexistent entities, like 'the present-day king of France', are considered to be meaningless. This is the basis of univocal hermeneutics.

Sense, on the other hand, is derived from the inner coherence of the whole text or expression and from the nature, properties, and tradition of the symbolic system or language in which it is formulated. Hence, in equivocal postmodern hermeneutics, which rely only on sense, there is no ontological basis for meaning and interpretation, but only points of view. This is clearly stated in Nietzsche's dictum, 'There are no facts, only interpretations'.[1]

Consequently, in univocal hermeneutics, there is only one valid interpretation for any given text, and this is the truth. In equivocal hermeneutics, there are infinite interpretations for a text, and there is no truth, only opinions.

Analogism strikes a balance between these two extremes. There are indeed numerous possible interpretations for a text (experience, perception, thought, or statement), but not all interpretations are equivalent: some of them are better, others not-so-good, poor, or even bad, and this depends on the reference (denotation) and the richness and depth of their sense (connotation). Hence, analogism retains a connection with ontology, albeit a weak one, and a concept of truth, although, as we have seen, a relative truth, quite unlike the overpowering and imposing Truth of Univocality.

Mexican philosopher Mauricio Beuchot proposed, in 1997, the introduction of Analogical Hermeneutics, which is a hermeneutical theory and practice based on analogy. This original approach to interpretation is related to and consistent with the contributions of Hans-Georg Gadamer (1960) and Paul Ricoeur (1965), albeit it has a particular Latin-American flavour, derived from the hybrid origins of our culture, based on mestization, both cultural and racial, which brings about the confluence and fusion of our Native American and European roots (Tubert-Oklander & Beuchot Puente, 2008).

This dual nature makes analogical hermeneutics particularly useful for clarifying the nature, aims, and methods of psychoanalysis, which is a hybrid of biology and psychology,[2] and group analysis, which combines psychology and social science, as well as the meeting and dialectical fusion of both disciplines.[3] In understanding, interpreting, and translating psychoanalytic and group-analytic texts, it gives us the opportunity of considering the various theoretical and clinical perspectives, without either claiming that only one of them is right – which would be a univocal interpretation that disqualifies all other points of view that differ from one's own – or that all of them are equivalent – an equivocal interpretation, for which all points of view are equally valid, which makes any rational discussion meaningless. There would still be, however, the possibility of evaluating them in terms of their comparative ability to identify, clarify, and account for the problems and experiences that they are trying to understand and solve.

Of course, analogical hermeneutics has been criticised by the other two polar conceptions of interpretation. Univocists resent its weakening of the absolute concept of truth and its acceptance of the existence of alternative, and perhaps complementary, interpretations of a same text or situation. Equivocists, on the other hand, utterly reject its use of ontology, through the reference, for choosing among the various interpretations, which they deem to be a relapse into the tyranny of an overpowering, dogmatic, and authoritarian metaphysics.

It is worth noting that the various psychoanalytic orthodoxies have used similar arguments against a hermeneutic conception of psychoanalysis as a hermeneutical science. Those psychoanalysts who adhere to Freud's conception of psychoanalysis as an empirical science feel this to be a regression to the ambiguity and arbitrariness of mysticism, while those of a humanistic postmodern bent, consider it a call for a linear and schematic type of interpretation, which ignores the polysemy of human expressions. It is obvious that the former understand hermeneutics, from their univocal stance, as an incurably equivocal and relativistic practice, while the latter view it as a univocal, positivistic, and unilateral approach. And none of them considers the option of an analogical hermeneutics.

Since analogical hermeneutics considers the possibility of having several alternative interpretations for a given text or situation, some of them equally valid, others less adequate, and yet others utterly unacceptable, it has to face the problem of finding a criterion for separating the chaff from the grain and rank them in terms of their validity and adequateness. This evaluation is done according to their inner coherence and capacity to depict and signify a relevant aspect of the complex entity it is trying to interpret – in other words, of its sense and its reference. And here we meet a difficulty, since the reference of the interpretation need not be a material entity or event, accessible by means of sensuous experience – the only kind of reality accepted by positivistic semiotics. The reference of the text may be yet another text, an utterance, a dialogue, an emotion, a relationship, an idea, a theory, a tradition, an experience, and anything that has a meaning for us. All of these are ontological realities, albeit not material ones, and therefore we need some way to access them by non-sensuous means. And here is where intuition comes into the picture. We need to start with a direct contact with things, what Maurice Merleau-Ponty (1945) described as a pre-verbal, pre-reflective experience of things, and use it as a guide for our interpretative dialogue with them.

This led Mauricio Beuchot to an expansion of his theory. Whereas his original formulation of 1997 was focused on analogy, which is primarily a verbal resource, in later works (1998, 1999, 2007), he introduced a new element, *iconicity*, which complements analogy. An icon is a representation that somehow reproduces the experience of what it is trying to represent, in sensorial terms, according to Charles Sanders Peirce, who described three kinds of icons: images, schemes, and metaphors. Iconic thinking allows us to have a perception of our primary intuition that serves as a guide for our analogical analysis (Tubert-Oklander, 2009, 2014; Tubert-Oklander & Beuchot Puente, 2008).

Ever since, Beuchot has changed the name of his theoretical and practical proposal to *Analogic-Iconic Hermeneutics*. This is in accordance with the psychoanalytic conception of thinking processes, in terms of a dual nature: *primary process* (which corresponds to iconic thinking) and *secondary process* (which is verbal thinking). Freud (1900a) conceived imaginary thought as being more primitive and inadequate for accessing knowledge, by comparison to verbal thought, which he saw as rational and scientific. However, more recent developments in psychoanalytic theory have considered them to be complementary (Rycroft, 1968, 1985). Ignacio Matte-Blanco (1988), who made an extensive study of the logic of the primary and secondary processes, posed that unconscious thinking has a *symmetric logic* (i.e., a reversible one), while conscious thought is ruled by an *asymmetric logic*, which is irreversible, and that the fullest and deepest form of thought is shaped by a *bi-logic*, which combines the other two. This is, of course, fully compatible with the principles of analogic-iconic hermeneutics (Tubert-Oklander, 2013c, 2014).

The fact that analogic-iconic hermeneutics strives to transcend the dilemmatic oppositions of either-or thinking, replacing it by both-and thought, allows us to go beyond the polarities that so often sterilise psychoanalytic controversies,[4] such as intrapsychic – interpersonal, instinctual drives – relationships, interpretation-relation, individual – society, or constitution – environment.

The conception of the world (*Weltanschauung*)

Another concept we use repeatedly is that of the Conception of the World or *Weltanschauung*. Since Freud explicitly rejected it, we deem it necessary to explain briefly what we mean by it and why we consider it to be a major concept for analysis – both psychoanalysis and group-analysis.

The concept of the Conception of the World – *Weltanschauung* in German – is not a term belonging to the vocabulary of psychoanalytic theory and it is not to be found in Laplanche and Pontalis's (1967) *The Language of Psychoanalysis*. It has also been mainly disregarded by psychoanalysts, ever since Freud (1933a) declared, in 'The question of a *Weltanschauung*' (pp. 158–182) that psychoanalysis,

> as a specialist science, a branch of psychology – a depth psychology or psychology of the unconscious – . . . is quite unfit to construct a *Weltanschauung* of its own: it must accept the scientific one.
>
> (p. 158)

However, Freud only considered one of the two possible meanings of the *Weltanschauung*: that of an intellectual system that proposes a formal theoretical reconstruction of everything that is, how it functions, and how we should think about it. This is certainly not a matter for psychoanalysis, but there is yet another meaning of the term, and a very important one, which refers to a rather indefinite and loose set of assumptions, beliefs, intuitions, values, habits, ideals, aspirations, and procedures, shared by a community and largely unconscious for the individuals who have internalised them during socialisation (Ferrater Mora, 1994, vol. 3, p. 2481; Hernández Hernández, 2010).

The first definition refers to a conscious, rational, and systematic intellectual construction, which can indeed be carried out as an armchair speculation. The second one corresponds to an empirical entity, a psychological highly complex dynamic structure. This includes the whole 'set of our assumptions in dealing with reality – prejudices, we might say, inasmuch they are judgements made before the fact, pre-conceptions that are usually unexamined by the subject' (Tubert-Oklander & Hernández de Tubert, 2004, p. 77), as well as values, emotions, and habits. The main part of this spontaneous *Weltanschauung* is unconscious, and this turns it into a subject matter for psychoanalytic enquiry (Hernández de Tubert, 2004a, 2004c, 2009a; Hernández Hernández, 2010).

Such empirical *Weltanschauung* is a real psychological structure, not a logical systematic reconstruction, like the formal *Weltanschauungen* contrived by philosophers like Hegel. Being largely unconscious, it is multifarious, highly complex, and frequently contradictory. It includes all the assumptions, feelings, yearnings, beliefs, values, vocabulary, and habits from which we build our image of the world, ourselves, and others. It therefore includes the natural, implicit, non-reflective, equivalents of an ontology, an epistemology, an axiology, a logic, a semiotics, a hermeneutics, an ethics, an aesthetics, and a procedural code for action. It is on this foundation and within this framework that all our perceptions, judgements, thoughts, valuations, decisions, relations, and actions take place.

This means that perception and experience are always a form of interpretation, constructed from a specific point of view – what Enrique Pichon-Rivière (1971a) used to call the CROS, an acronym for 'Conceptual, Referential, Operative Schema' (Tubert-Oklander & Hernández de Tubert, 2004).[5] (In Pichon-Rivière's original Spanish text, the acronym for the term '*Esquema Conceptual, Referencial y Operativo*' was ECRO.)[6]

This *Weltanschauung* is partly a personal construction, based on idiosyncratic experiences and early identifications. On this, psychoanalysis has a lot to say, since we are used to identifying and interpreting the patients' unconscious personal ontologies – something like private religions. But the main part of this conception of the world stems from the experience of participating in social life and incorporating the ideology that prevails in one's community and groups. These a priory assumptions, beliefs, and values are acquired with the earliest introjections of primary relations, this being the reason for their persistence and invisibility, as the subject does not even perceive them as assumptions or beliefs, but only as 'the way things are'. The internalisation of the social conception of the world, shared by the community and conveyed by the family, determines that culture becomes an essential part of the inner organisation of the personality and its mental processes. And the axis on which all culture revolves is, of course, language (Hernández de Tubert, 2004a, 2004c, 2009a).

This inner structure that determines a person's feeling, thoughts, aspirations, relations, and behaviour comes more readily to the fore in our work with groups, in which the contrast and conflict between the assumptions of group members becomes painfully explicit and becomes thus an object of enquiry. Nonetheless, it may also be explored in bi-personal psychoanalysis, if the analyst does not hide behind the shroud of neutrality (Hernández de Tubert, 2006d).

This subject deserves, of course, a much extensive treatment, which shall be the subject of a later publication.

Holism

Our understanding of analysis and human nature is based on a holistic point of view. *Holism* is a theory-building strategy that strives to understand complex wholes in their own dimension, instead of fragmenting them into 'parts', studying the properties of these artificially isolated fragments, and then try to reconstruct the wholes. Here we explain briefly the bases of this approach, which underlies ours.

A holistic theory is based on the assumption that systems should be viewed as wholes, and not as a collection of parts, and that the properties and behaviour of the system cannot be inferred from the study of the isolated parts. This implies a serious criticism of the research strategy of positivistic science of tackling the study of any complex entity or situation by splitting it into simpler parts, studying them in detail, and then reconstructing the original whole from the summation of the now well-known properties of the parts, which we usually call the 'analytic method'. Holistic thinking claims, on the contrary, that the so-called 'parts' are really created by such analytical splitting (whether it is a physical split or a conceptual dissection), as an artifact of the analytic technique. In actual reality, the nature, properties, and behaviour of the various elements that may be identified in a complex system, can only be fully understood in terms of the latter's global organisation and functioning. This is usually summarised by the aphorism '*The whole is prior to, more than, and more elementary that the sum of the parts*'.

Although the more ambitious holistic theories (such as David Bohm's conception that any collection of quantum objects constitutes an indivisible whole within an implicate and an explicate order) apply this view to the physical world and the Universe as a whole – a contention we shall not discuss here – the strongest support in favour of the holistic approach comes from the study of living systems – including human beings and their societies. This led thinkers like the British-born anthropologist, epistemologist, and systems theoretician Gregory Bateson (1972, 1979) to postulate a caesura between the study of inanimate systems and that of living systems – biological, psychological, social, and cultural. The inanimate world – which he calls (following Jung) the *pleroma* – which is set in motion by forces and impacts, can be studied by means of the analytic method and explained in causal terms. In this world there are no differences, everything is homogeneous, in terms of forces and impacts. Here, everything fits into Newton's conception of the Universe in terms of inert objects – called 'matter' – that are set in motion, deformed or destroyed by shapeless and massless forces – collectively called 'energy'. This was applied by Freud in his 'metapsychology', ever since his *Project for a Scientific Psychology* of 1895 (Freud, 1950a).[7]

But in the world of living beings – which he calls *creatura* (again following Jung) – everything happens in terms of differences – that is, information. This is 'the world of *form* and communication [, which] invokes no things, forces, or impacts but only differences and ideas. (A difference which makes a difference *is* an idea. It is a 'bit', a unit of information)' (Bateson, 1972, pp. 271–272). This idea he develops further, in the following terms:

> In the hard sciences, effects are, in general, caused by rather concrete conditions or events – impacts, forces, and so forth. But when you enter the world of communication, organization, etc., you leave behind that whole world in which effects are brought about by forces and impacts and energy exchange. You enter a world in which 'effects' – and I am not sure one should still use the same word – are brought about by differences. That is, they are brought about by the sort of 'thing' that gets onto the map from the territory. This is difference.
>
> (p. 452)

In the world of positivistic science (*pleroma*), causes must necessarily be 'real' (that is, either matter or energy), and nothing ever comes out of nothing. But in the world of *creatura*, something that does not exist may well determine events:

> [R]emember that zero is different from one, and because zero is different from one, zero can be a cause in the psychological world, the world of communication. The letter which you do not write can get an angry reply; and the income tax form which you do not fill in can trigger the Internal Revenue boys into energetic action, because they, too, have their breakfast, lunch, tea, and dinner and can react with energy which they derive from their metabolism. The letter which never existed is no source of energy.
>
> (p. 452)

The question is that inanimate objects – such as rocks, rivers, planets, or billiard balls – are inert, and this means that they cannot move or transform by themselves, and so they have to be pushed, pressed, deformed, or destroyed by outside forces. The situation is pretty much the same in the case of human-made machines, such as clocks, cars, or TV sets. So here the explanation of anything that happens to them must be framed in terms of forces and impacts – that is, causes.

But in the case of living systems, everything is different, since living beings are moved by their own inner energies and their behaviour vis-à-vis the different situations they face are regulated by their internal organisation and aimed at their goals. The latter is essential: the behaviour of living beings is always intentional, that is, it tends to attain certain ends. Hence, it always has a meaning and responds to some inner data processing. This is the reason why there is no direct relation between the input and the output. A living being's behaviour is not 'caused' because the input does not act in terms of forces and impacts; it is rather a *stimulus* – that is, a bit of information about the world that has to be processed by an inner mentation until it generates a reaction that serves its goals. Therefore, such behaviour has to be interpreted in order to be understood.

This is the reason why the analytic method of physical science does not fit the study of living beings. A clockwork may well be disassembled in order to study its parts, but if you intend to apply the same strategy to living beings, you have to kill them first or either mutilate them, so that you can isolate its so-called 'parts', and then you have lost sight of the unique characteristics of living systems.

This is what happens, for instance, in anatomy and physiology, which are basically an attempt to study the structure and function of living beings, including humans, as if they were machines. This whole research project is based on the metaphor of living organisms as biological machines. But machines have been created by human beings as a crude attempt to imitate the functioning of living beings; that is to say that they are analogues of some of their functions, devised in order to serve our goal, by amplifying our capacities. An analogy between two entities preserves and highlights what they have in common and omits their differences. So, when we reverse the analogy and try to conceive and treat living beings as if they were machines, we are bound to see in them only those features that can be found in our own contraptions. It is understandable that Nineteenth Century scientists, most of them male middle class Western Europeans, raised in the ethos of the Industrial Revolution, were so fascinated by the power of machines, that they tended to conceive, perceive, and understand living beings (and, in the case of Freud, mental processes) in mechanical terms. That was the physicalist ideology taught by Freud's mentors.

But at the same time, there was another current in European thought that also had an impact on the creator of psychoanalysis, and this was Romanticism. The Romantic thinkers emphasised the unique characteristics of Life and Nature, and their emotional and aesthetic connotations. In this line of thought, there was no gap or opposition between subject and object, as required by positivistic science and materialist metaphysics, but a deep and indissoluble relationship between them. Such an ethos had a major bearing on psychoanalytic practice and understanding, although it was clearly excluded from Freud's formal theory. And this is what a holistic approach strives to recover.

One perfect example of holism in biology is the work of the German neurologist and psychiatrist Kurt Goldstein on the nervous system and the organism as a whole. In his study of brain damage, based on the treatment of soldier casualties from World War I, he reached the conclusion that the nervous system always reacted as a whole, which is also a part of an even larger whole, which is the physical, ecological, and human environment. Hence, he defined the nervous system as a network of multifarious connections, in which individual neurons were just the focal points of the network – that is, those points in which a number of connections coalesce. But the nervous system is immersed in the larger network of the organism, and this is embedded in the network of connections that make up the environment. So, any disorder of the organism and the nervous system is the expression of a disturbance of this reticulum.

As we have seen in Chapters 13 and 15, Goldstein's ideas had a major impact on the founder of group analysis in Britain, the psychoanalyst S. H. Foulkes, who was his assistant for two years at the Neurological Institute in Frankfurt, between 1926 and 1928. Following his teacher's approach, Foulkes defined the group and society as a network of communications and relations, in which individuals are its focal points. He adopted Goldstein's holistic approach to neurology and biology to psychopathology and psychotherapy, and he adhered to his dictum that 'This kind of reciprocal relation between organism and environment we call the fundamental law of biology', which became the basic assumption for the development of his own psychoanalytic approach to the inquiry of human affairs, which he called Group Analysis (Foulkes, 1990).

This was the British root of group analysis. The other root was Latin American and emerged in Buenos Aires in the work and thought of Enrique Pichon-Rivière (1971a, 1979; Tubert-Oklander & Hernández de Tubert, 2004), who was the pioneer of psychoanalysis and group analysis in Argentina. Pichon-Rivière always emphasised, like Foulkes, the essential unity of the individual and the group, society, and the non-human environment. His main concept was that of the '*vínculo*', which may be translated as 'link' or 'bond'. This he clearly differentiates from the concept of 'object relations', which are conceived as an internal occurrence. The Bond, on the other hand, is intra-personal, inter-personal, and trans-personal. It includes the subject, the objects (which are really other subjects), their mutual relation, the group, and the whole social, cultural, political, physical, and ecological environment. In the ongoing dialectic interchange between the individual and the environment, the internal becomes external, the external becomes internal, and then external again, in a dialectical process which follows a spiral expanding and forward-moving course. And this is what happens in the psychoanalytic and group-analytic processes (Tubert-Oklander, 2017b).

Pichon-Rivière's conception was clearly holistic and it took the form of field and process concepts (Hernández-Tubert, 2017c; Tubert-Oklander & Hernández de Tubert, 2004). He took the field concept from Kurt Lewin, who had also been reared in the cradle of Gestalt Theory, and his dialectic spiral process concept had a distinct Hegelian and Marxist flavour. But he did not develop a formally structured theory, but rather followed – quite consistently with his avowed ethos – a dialectic path of theory building. Hence, his contributions were always in the nature of a work in progress; he did now write much, since he was passionate about teaching through dialogue, and a large part of his work was recorded by some of his students, as in the case of Harry Stack Sullivan.

It was then left to some of his disciples to spell out the consequences of his teachings. Two of them, Madeleine and Willy Baranger (2009), who were deeply influenced by him, turned his ideas into their own conception of the analytic situation as a dynamic field. They conceived the psychoanalytic situation as a whole, in which both analyst and analysand are embedded, and none of them can be fully understood without the other and the organisation and dynamics of the field. Nonetheless, the Barangers' field is more restricted than Pichon-Rivière's, since they focus on the two parties, their relation, and whatever emerges in the treatment situation, but they leave out the social, political, and ecological dimensions of Pichon-Rivière's thought. This is probably the reason why their contribution remained and eventually flourished in the psychoanalytic community, while Pichon-Rivière found it necessary to distance himself from orthodox psychoanalysis and the psychoanalytic institution that he had founded. It is only in recent years that there has been a revival of interest in Pichon-Rivière's pioneering contributions to psychoanalysis and group analysis – particularly as a forerunner of the contemporary relational approach – and his work has become more widely known since the publication of its French translation and the forthcoming English translation.

The Baranger's theory is one the three present-day psychoanalytic field theories, together with Antonino Ferro's Bionian approach and the interpersonal field theory derived from Sullivan's pioneering work. These have similarities and differences between them, but in any case, it is quite clear that any field approach must necessarily be thought as a holistic theory and practice. This is the case of the concept of the matrix, which is Foulkes field theory of individual, group, and social functioning.[8]

There are three kinds of holistic theories that have a bearing on psychoanalytic practice and thinking. The first one is, of course, the *field model*. This focuses on the simultaneous and mutual influences of everything that is present in the observational field at any given moment. It is therefore an *atemporal* construction of the analytic experience and events. The second is the *process model*, which studies the evolution in time of all events in the observational field during a certain period and projects its future course in terms of a given goal. Hence, it is a *temporal* construction of the events under study. A *process* is not just any sequence of events, and most certainly it is not a linear chain of cause-effect relations. A process, in this sense, is a highly complex evolving whole, self-organised around an *aim* or *goal*; it therefore has a *direction*, a *course*, and an *intentionality*, which give it a *meaning* that can be interpreted. This is, of course, a *teleological* understanding, in terms of what Aristotle called *final causes*, in sharp contradiction with the ethos of present-day natural science, which is inimical to teleological thinking, deemed to be mystical or religious, and demands that all explanations be strictly causal. Nonetheless, intentionality has been an essential underlying assumption of the practice of psychoanalysis from its very beginning, most probably derived from what the young Freud learnt from his philosophy teacher, Franz Brentano, as we have seen in Chapter 8.

The third kind of holistic theory in psychoanalysis is the *dramatic model*, which views mental events, whether intrapersonal, interpersonal or transpersonal, as the result of a complex interrelationship of personal characters that engage in dramatic relations, determined by an unconscious scenario (Pichon-Rivière et al. 1969). Even though this model was implicit ever since Freud's early works – as, for instance, in his description of the dynamics of the relation between the unconscious wish, the conscious ego, and the dream censorship – it was only in *Mourning and melancholia* (1917e) and *The ego and the id* (1923b) that it became explicit, thus paving the way for the development of object relations theory. In present-day psychoanalysis, such model is found in Thomas Ogden's (1994) concept of a third subject in the analytic relationship and in the ample literature on enactment.

These three models are not mutually exclusive, but fully complementary. Field theories are only atemporal in their theory-building strategy, which takes all events in a given lapse as if they were simultaneous, but they must necessarily include the evolution of the field, in order to account for the therapeutic process. Process theories are temporal in their strategy, but they need to consider the simultaneous disposition and mutual influence of all elements that are present at a certain moment, whether personal, interpersonal, cultural, political, physical, climatic, or ecological. And, as every human occurrence is always personal and relational, the view in terms of the dramatic model is also needed to complement the other two.

It is obvious that such holistic approach to the study of the human being is consistent with the theory and practice of analogic-iconic hermeneutics.

Thinking group or therapeutic group – a personal reflection on the large group experience

Reyna Hernández-Tubert

In 2008, after attending the Dublin European Symposium of Group Analysis and participating in the Large Group, I wrote this personal reflection on the experience, which was published in the newsletter of the Group-Analytic Society (Hernández-Tubert, 2009) and generated some controversy. As it relates to the position we put forward in Chapter 11, we felt that it would be pertinent to include it in the book.

These are the Christmas holidays. A few months have passed since last August, and I have been thinking all along about what happened at the Large Group in Dublin. I had wanted to write on the matter ever since, but it is only now, with the loving company of my husband, that I have finally made up my mind to do it.

When we arrived in Dublin, to participate in the 14th European Symposium of Group Analysis, my husband and I decided to attend the Large Group. We were especially interested in this experience, which in our own tradition we would have called a 'reflection group'. We had had the experience of conducting large groups, although none of them had been as massive as this one, and we were keen to observe the conductors' handling of a five-hundred-member group.

In the first session, on Tuesday, there was no introduction by the conductors. Indeed, we did not even know who they were, until their very brief interventions, from three different sides of the concentric circles of chairs. The idea was clearly to create a highly unstructured situation. We all remained silent. This unleashed an impressive schizoid-paranoid and sterilising climate. Nothing seemed to happen, except that one of the members left the group. The whole thing seemed to go far beyond the usual desultory beginnings of groups.

It seemed to me that the social and political context was very much present at the time. The theme of the Symposium was highly evocative[9] and I could not help thinking, when witnessing the group's response, about the wealth of information we have in our country on policies in the First World: the anti-immigrant legislation in Europe; the booking of all gipsies, including children, in Italy; the beatings of South Americans in Spain; the detention of undocumented Africans crossing the Mediterranean. But I also thought about my own country: the death of large numbers of Mexicans, when trying to cross the Northern border, their systematic abuse by the US Border Patrol and the many vigilante groups, and also the equal fate of the South and Central Americans who cross our Southern border into Mexico, on their way North. There we were, over five hundred people from thirty-seven countries, all of us highly qualified practitioners of the helping professions, and all we could think of was about how dangerous were the others. The complaints about the lack of technical facilities for communicating in such a large group were obsessive and excessive. Some said: 'It doesn't matter if your words cannot be heard, the emotional tone is nonetheless perceived. Speak, even if your English is poor, or even in your own language; whatever you wish to convey the others will pick out'. Would anyone dare to take the stage? I wondered. Everyone was inviting it, but I thought none of us would have the nerve – or the cheek – to go for it. We were all expectant. I later commented with my husband that we were wasting the opportunity to work together as a group, and I wondered whether the tensions generated by the internationalisation of the Group-Analytic Society were lurking in the background.

Thus, we came to the second session, with a recurrence of the previous day's emotional climate, albeit in an even more paranoid version: we were now the perfect target for a terrorist attack, where else would an evildoer have the chance to do away with five hundred group analysts in a single stroke? One of the members, who had mistakenly come an hour before the appointed time, even had the ominous fantasy that the whole group had vanished into thin air.

I wanted to participate, but I do not speak English, so I decided to dramatise my contribution, and asked my husband to translate for me. I have a powerful voice and decided to enter the central Ring. I knew that I could only plan and anticipate my own actions; the group's reaction was, of course, unpredictable, and would depend on the pervading fantasies. As I planned it, I thought: 'They can only cut down someone's head if she allows it, and it shall not be mine, though they will certainly try'.[10]

The response was immediate and fiery, even before I had finished: there were attacks and intolerance, what we usually project on those who are not like us. I was demanded, and even shouted at, that I shut up; they tried to silence me by means of infantile seduction, contempt, or outright aggression. They demanded that my participation be just like that of the imaginary 'us'. 'You may speak, as long as it is unintelligible and inaudible, or that you only utter loose phrases, in a fearful or aggressive tone'. The whole atmosphere was quite violent, and it focused on me.[11]

I sat down and shut up. Then, I observed. I saw with sadness how our assets and strengths withered away, while our liabilities, weaknesses, and meanness flourished. We could now listen each other a little bit more; the group obviously needed a scapegoat and I had received an invitation to play the role. I was beginning to feel as if I were Dr Thomas Stockmann, Ibsen's *Enemy of the People*.

Nonetheless, the other members' attitude towards me showed ambivalent traits. Many looked at me with curiosity, some seemed embarrassed, others were sympathetic and concerned. Fortunately, only a few stared at me with deep hate and contempt. There also were those who tried to soothe my wounds, although I did not need it. It is not that I am denying that I have them, but they were hardly the result of the present situation, but rather ancestral, historical wounds, that all of us share, the result of many generations having experienced this sort of rejection.

The third session started with an open invitation to those of us who had arrived early – the bulk of members were delayed – and who were sitting in or near the inner circle, to speak, since we surely would have much to say. Perhaps under influx of the group's paranoid climate, I felt this as if it were meant for me. Yet some of it must have been true; I had obviously taken a leading role with my impudence of the previous day, which did not fit with my present silence. At the same time, some had been wondering, in the aisles, about the apparent contradiction between my formal presentation of my paper, on Tuesday, and my irreverent participation in the Large Group, on Wednesday. Apparently, they were earnestly looking for some psychopathological explanation that would help them to eschew any responsibility for whatever had been done to the 'victim'.

On the other hand, as the session unfolded, there was an increasing verbalisation of conflicts derived from the perception of differences – generational, political, racial, national, ethnic, linguistic, or gender. Someone mentioned whether all this might be related to the recent rejection of the Lisbon treaty by the Irish,[12] but this was not pursued any further by the group.[13] A senior analyst reprimanded a younger colleague for not offering him his seat in the inner circle, the latter replied he had no intention of doing so, and a tense dialogue followed. Another hostile discussion also centred on the question of space, who owned the chairs, and if a newcomer was entitled to occupy a seat that had been reserved for someone else. There were several comments about gender differences, and the particular role played by women in the organisation of this Symposium. National and ethnic differences and prejudices were also very much present. An African colleague expressed feelings of isolation because no one else in the room spoke her native language. Someone suggested that we had been afraid all along that our differences might end up in a violent conflict. Someone else suggested that there might be envy of those couples that were both present and active, and our President, Gerda Winther, and her husband, Henning Green, were prompt to reply. I also wondered whether my own alliance with my husband, Juan Tubert-Oklander, might be at stake.

On the whole, it was a profitable session, in which many underlying conflicts were expressed, albeit haphazardly, but I sorely missed some recapitulation or integrating interventions on the part of our conductors.

The fourth session was the last one, and started with the announcement, by some of the members, that they had to leave early for the airport and wanted to bid farewell. The session then developed as an evaluation of the experience, mainly in a complimentary mood. Towards the end, I felt the need to share with the others my own working-through of the experience, and especially my interest in unravelling my own prejudices. I had them, of course, like everyone else. My prejudice was that the European colleagues should be far beyond the rest of us in the path of overcoming the everyday biases and discriminations of social life. I was wrong and, at the same time, I realised that this was an unfair demand, since prejudice cannot be solved by means of the social or economic development of a nation or community, but only through a shared personal endeavour to build understanding, hope, and tolerance, instead of prejudice, intolerance, and hopelessness, and this is where our profession should contribute. I felt that I could not miss the opportunity to share this quest with over 500 group analysts (568 minus quite a few who missed the closing session or had left early for their countries). This was my small contribution, an invitation to enquire into our hearts to find, understand, and question those prejudices that lurk in them. So, I once again spoke in Spanish, with my husband as interpreter. As I was communicating these reflections, one of the men interrupted me abruptly and violently, demanding that I stopped speaking and claiming that what I was saying was utterly irrelevant. I acquiesced to his command because I believed him to be one of the conductors and was therefore entitled to exert authority – an assumption that I later found out to be wrong (although he was indeed a member of the Society's Management Committee). So, I remained silent, but one of the women then denounced his behaviour, in no uncertain terms, and protested the intolerance towards a reflective thought that included the social and political dimension.

One very interesting comment, made by one of our Oriental colleagues, was the question of why is this called a 'European Symposium', when it assembles such a vast amount of people from the five continents? Should it not be called an 'International Symposium of Group Analysis'?[14]

As the closing time neared, many of us felt the need to express our satisfaction with the experience, not only of the Large Group, but also of the whole Symposium. I also shared these feelings and came back to Mexico with the hope that there may still be hope, and the reaffirmed conviction that trying to communicate with and understand each other is a worthwhile endeavour.

Nonetheless, I also pondered on the diversity of our traditions. My feeling that something was missing in the otherwise quite adequate conduction of the Large Group, was surely derived from the fact that I come from a different group-analytic tradition – that initiated in Latin America by Enrique Pichon-Rivière – one that highlights the importance of interpretation in the group process. I am fully aware that the conductors' systematic silence and sparse interventions were part of a conscious strategy, aimed at offering the group the widest possible breadth for the expansion of its own capabilities and resources. However, I still wondered whether such a large group – the largest I have ever participated in – would find the time it needed for carrying its process of working-through to a completion, in the four brief sessions it had at its disposal. Of course, this kind of reflection does not have an end, and it may well be argued that the individual members carried home with them the questions raised in the group, for their personal working-through – as I did – but I still feel that an attempt by the conductors to integrate and reflect upon the many themes that emerged during the sessions would have enriched the experience and made a further use of the group's resources to the advantage of its members.

This by no means implies adhering to a concept of interpretation that views it as a dogmatic or revealed truth. Quite on the contrary, in our own experience in conducting large groups, the conductors pick up the leads provided by the members' apparently disconnected contributions and try to articulate and construct them into a thought, which is then offered for them to play with, chew, refute, destroy, or build upon. This is quite different from our experience with therapeutic groups, since we consider the large group to be a privileged space for thought and reflection, specifically about the social and political context. In the case of this particular large group, we would probably have commented on the anxieties generated by the great number of participants, their many differences, the process of generational replacement that was taking place in the Society, the fact that both the Presidency and the Organizing Committee were in charge of women, and that they were not British, and the vertiginous growth and variegation of the Society. We would also have tried to identify the prejudices and defensive manoeuvres mustered against such anxieties, and the obstacles to communication that were thus generated. We would also have pointed out the impediments to the group's enquiring and thinking, derived from the fact that most members were striving to participate, not as individual human beings, but *as group analysts*, thus assuming the role of a professional identity, which barred the exploration of our participation in and responsibility for a social process. All of this, of course, would be based on the many expressions provided by the members during the sessions, and would be offered as a stimulus for further discussion.

Such differences in conception, theory, and practice may raise fears of a dilution and corruption of the Group Analytic tradition, as some colleagues expressed to Gerda Winther. However, I fully agree with her opinion – in the December 2008 issue of *Contexts* – that 'danger is not so big', as long as we try 'to keep the balance between new developments and contact with the original theory' (Winther, 2008, p. 5). It is the old dilemma of Continuity vs. Change, Identity vs. Difference, Creativity vs. Rigour; in other words, the same predicament faced by any national society, which is the bearer of a national tradition, when it mushrooms inordinately into an international association.

I know that this is really the subject for a wider discussion, and we are presently writing a paper on our own conception, understanding, and practice of the conduction of large groups, which we intend to submit for publication in *Group Analysis*, as a contribution to the dialogue between the different group analytic traditions.[15]

Notes

1 Nietzsche is usually seen as a full-fledged equivocist and as the founder of Postmodern relativism, but Mauricio Beuchot (2016) argues, in his recent book in Spanish, called *Facts and Interpretations: Towards an Analogical Hermeneutics*, that he has undoubtedly been misinterpreted. According to him, Nietzsche did not mean to say that only interpretations exist, and that they do not correspond to any fact, but that he could not side with interpretations only, without the facts. Thus, he was saying that facts need be

interpreted, in order to be known. 'That is, there are two things, the facts and the interpretations we make over them, without discarding neither one, nor the other. What we need is an inclusive hermeneutics' (p. 9, our translation). So, Beuchot refutes the usual interpretation of Nietzsche as a relativistic equivocist and presents him as an analogical hermeneut.

2 See Chapter 1.

3 See Chapter 15.

4 See Chapter 2.

5 The idea that facts can only be perceived and thought by means of interpretation has been dealt in note 1, in terms of Mauricio Beuchot's (2016) reading of Friedrich Nietzsche famous dictum, 'There are no facts, only interpretations'.

6 See Chapter 9.

7 See Chapter 1.

8 See Chapter 8.

9 'Despair, Dialogue and Desire: The Transformative Power of the Analytic Group in the Movement from Despair to Desire through Dialogue'.

10 I had also decided to wear a typical Mexican indigenous dress. This was indeed a provocative political statement, since it flouted the unwritten law that all participants in analytical conferences should disguise themselves as Europeans, no matter where they came from. Such convention, just as the demand that everyone should speak in English, is a present-day manifestation of colonialism, which is to be found in most international analytic conferences nowadays.

11 It is interesting to note that Teresa von Sommaruga Howard (2011), one of the three conveners of the Dublin large group wrote, commenting on this episode, 'When newcomers fight to be heard without conforming to the rules of the dominant culture, they are often labelled as terrorists' (2011, p. 334). In other words, when the members of the group share a 'large group etiquette', derived from the culture of the wider social and institutional environment in which this experience is inserted, they tend to react rather violently when others try to participate in any other way they see fit.

12 Which had been discussed and dealt with in the very same room in which we were now meeting.

13 Or interpreted by the conductors.

14 It is only fair to point out that this change of name was decided some time afterwards, perhaps, at least partly, as a result of the experience of this Large Group in Dublin.

15 This paper finally became our Belgrade lecture, which was published in *Group Analysis* in three parts (Tubert-Oklander & Hernández-Tubert, 2014a, 2014b, 2014c), which are reproduced here as Chapters 9, 10, and 11.

References

The following references are identified with the year of first publication and consecutive letters, whenever there is more than one reference to an author in the same year, except in the case of Sigmund Freud's writings. There, we have followed the standard academic practice in psychoanalytic publications of referring to Freud's works with the date of first publication and a letter that identifies its placing in the Freud Bibliography included in Volume XXIV of the *Standard Edition of the Complete Psychological Works of Sigmund Freud*. This does not apply to Freud's letters, which have been published in separate books.

Abraham, Karl (1924). A short study of the development of the libido, viewed in the light of mental disorders. In Douglas Bryan & Alix Strachey (trans.), *Selected Papers on Psycho-Analysis*. London: Maresfield, 1979, pp. 407–501.

Actualidad Psicológica (1977). E. Pichon-Rivière: el legado de un maestro [E. Pichon-Rivière: The legacy of a Master]. June, 3 (27): 1, 7.

Ahlin, Göran (2010). Notations about the possibilities in large groups. *Group Analysis*, 43 (3): 253–267. https://doi.org/10.1177%2F0533316410371782

Ahlin, Göran (2011). Response to von Sommaruga Howard's 'architecture of domination'. *Group Analysis*, 44 (3): 342–345. https://doi.org/10.1177%2F0533316411411804

Anthony, E. James (2010). My psychoanalytic and group-analytic life with S.H. Foulkes. *Group Analysis*, 43 (1): 81–85. https://doi.org/10.1177%2F0533316409357135

Aron, Lewis. (1996). *A Meeting of Minds: Mutuality in Psychoanalysis*. London: Routledge, 2001.

Assoun, Paul-Laurent (2000). *La metapsicología* [Metapsychology]. Mexico City: Siglo Veintiuno, 2002. [Spanish translation of *La metapsychologie*. Paris: Presses Universitaires de France].

Balint, Michael (1952). *Primary Love and Psycho-Analytic Technique*, second enlarged edition. New York, NY: Liveright, 1965.

Balint, Michael (1968). *The Basic Fault: Therapeutic Aspects of Regression*. London: Routledge, 2013.

Baranger, Madeleine & Baranger, Willy (2009). *The Work of Confluence: Listening and Interpreting in the Psychoanalytic Field*, Leticia Glocer Fiorini (ed.), H. Breyter & D. Alcorn (trans.). London: Routledge, 2018.

Baranger, Willy (1979). Spiral process and the dynamic field. In Madeleine & Willy Baranger (2009), pp. 45–61.

Baranger, Willy (1992). De la necesaria imprecisión en la nosografía psicoanalítica [On the necessary indeterminacy of the psychoanalytic classification of mental diseases]. *Revista de Psicoanálisis, 1992, Número Especial Internacional* [Special International Issue], 83–97.

Bateson, Gregory (1972). *Steps to an Ecology of Mind*. New York, NY: Ballantine.

Bateson, Gregory (1979). *Mind and Nature: A Necessary Unit*. New York, NY: Bantam.

Bendix, Reinhard (1966). A memoir of my father. *Canadian Review of Sociology and Anthropology*, 2 (1): 1–18.

Berger, Peter L. & Luckmann, Thomas (1966). *The Social Construction of Reality*. New York, NY: Anchor Books, 1967.

Beuchot, Mauricio (1985). Aspectos epistemológicos y hermenéuticos en el Proyecto de Freud [Epistemological and hermeneutical aspects of Freud's *Project*]. In Zarco, Miguel Angel (ed.), *En torno al Proyecto de Freud* [About Freud's Project], *Cuaderno de Filosofía* 9. Mexico City: Universidad Iberoamericana, pp. 9–36.

Beuchot, Mauricio (1997). *Tratado de hermenéutica analógica. Hacia un nuevo modelo de interpretación* [Treatise of analogical hermeneutics: Towards a new model of interpretation], fourth revised and enlarged edition. Mexico City: National Autonomous University of Mexico/Itaca, 2009.

Beuchot, Mauricio (1998). *Perfiles esenciales de la hermenéutica* [Essential profiles of hermeneutics], fifth revised and enlarged edition. Mexico City: Fondo de Cultura Económica/UNAM, 2008.

Beuchot, Mauricio (1999). *Las caras del símbolo: el ícono y el ídolo* [The faces of the symbol: The icon and the idol]. Madrid: Caparrós.

Beuchot, Mauricio (2003). *Hermenéutica analógica y del umbral* [Analogical hermeneutics and threshold hermeneutics]. Salamanca, Spain: San Esteban.

Beuchot, Mauricio (2004). *Antropología filosófica. Hacia un personalismo analógico-icónico* [Philosophical anthropology: Towards an analogic-iconic personalism]. Salamanca: Mounier.

Beuchot, Mauricio (2005). *Interculturalidad y derechos humanos* [Interculturalism and human rights]. México City: UNAM/Siglo XXI.

Beuchot, Mauricio (2007). Interpretación, analogía e iconicidad [Interpretation, analogy, and iconicity]. In D. Lizarazo Arias (ed.), *Semántica de las imágenes*. Mexico City: Siglo XXI, pp. 15–27.

Beuchot, Mauricio (2016). *Hechos e interpretaciones. Hacia una hermenéutica analógica* [Facts and interpretations: Towards an analogical hermeneutics]. Mexico City: Fondo de Cultura Económica.

Beuchot Puente, Mauricio (2008). La presencia de la hermenéutica en el discurso epistemológico de Freud [The presence of hermeneutics in Freud's epistemological discourse]. In Tubert-Oklander & Beuchot Puente, pp. 33–49.

Binswanger, Ludwig (1925). Letter from Ludwig Binswanger to Freud, February 15, 1925. In Fichtner (2003), pp. 175–178.

Bion, Wilfred R. (1952). Re-view: Group dynamics. In Bion (1961), pp. 139–191.

Bion, Wilfred R. (1959). Attacks on linking. *International Journal of Psycho-Analysis*, 40: 308–315. [Also in *Psychoanalytic Quarterly*, 2013, 82 (2): 285–300. https://doi.org/10.1002/j.2167-4086.2013.00029.x].

Bion, Wilfred R. (1961). *Experiences in Groups and Other Papers*. London: Routledge, 1991.

Bion, Wilfred R. (1962). *Learning from Experience*. London: Routledge, 1991.

Bion, Wilfred R. (1963). *Elements of Psycho-Analysis*. London: Heinemann.

Bion, Wilfred R. (1967). Notes on memory and desire. *Psychoanalytic Forum*, 2: 271–280. [Reprinted in E. Bott Spillius (Ed.), *Melanie Klein Today: Vol. 2: Mainly Practice*. London: Routledge, 1988, pp. 17–21].

Bion, Wilfred R. (1970). *Attention and Interpretation: A Scientific Approach to Insight in Psycho-Analysis and Groups*. London: Routledge, 2019.

Bleger, José (1961). Grupos operativos en la enseñanza [Operative groups in teaching]. In Bleger (1971), pp. 55–86.

Bleger, José (1967). *Simbiosis y ambigüedad* [Symbiosis and ambiguity]. Buenos Aires: Paidós, 1978. [English translation: *Symbiosis and Ambiguity: A Psychoanalytic Study*. Hove, East Sussex: Routledge, 2013].

Bleger José (1971). *Temas de psicología. Entrevista y grupos* [Psychological themes: The interview and groups]. Buenos Aires: Nueva Vision.

Bourdieu, Pierre (1972). *Outline of a Theory of Practice*. Cambridge, UK: Cambridge University Press, 1977.

Bregman, Rutger C. (2020a). *Humankind: A Hopeful History*. London: Bloomsbury.

Bregman, Rutger C. (2020b). The real Lord of the Flies: What happened when six boys were shipwrecked for 15 months. *The Guardian*, May 20.

Brierley, Marjorie (1944). Notes on metapsychology as process theory. *International Journal of Psycho-Analysis*, 25: 97–106.

Brierley, Marjorie (1951). *Trends in Psycho-Analysis*. London: Hogarth.

Burrow, Trigant (1927). The group method of analysis. *Psychoanalytic Review*, 14: 268–280.

Campos Avillar, Juan (1981). Postdata a una presentación y un prólogo póstumo [Postscript to a presentation and a posthumous prologue]. In *Psicoterapia grupo-analítica. Método y principios*. Barcelona: Gedisa, pp. 20–37. [Spanish edition of Foulkes, S.H. (1975). *Group-Analytic Psychotherapy: Method and Principles*].

Cappiello, A.; Zanasi, M. & Fiumara, R.S. (1988). The therapeutic value of the silent observer: Clinical experience in group analysis. *Group Analysis*, 21 (3): 227–232. https://doi.org/10.1177%2F0533316488213003

Carpintero, Enrique & Vainer, Alejandro (2009). Enrique Pichon-Rivière y la Experiencia Rosario [Enrique Pichon-Rivière and the Rosario experience]. In the Web Page of Topia.com (visited July 18, 2020). www.topia.com.ar/articulos/enrique-pich%C3%B3n-rivi%C3%A8re-y-la-experiencia-rosario

Civitarese, Giuseppe; Katz, Montana & Tubert-Oklander, Juan (eds.) (2015). Postmodernism and psychoanalysis. Thematic issue of *Psychoanalytic Inquiry*, 35 (6): 559–662.

Clarke, Graham S. (2014). John Padel's contribution to an understanding of Fairbairn's object relations theory. In Clarke & Scharff, pp. 295–308.

Clarke, Graham S. & Scharff, David E. (2014). *Fairbairn and the Object Relations Tradition*. London: Routledge, 2019.

Dalal, Farhad (1998). *Taking the Group Seriously: Towards a Post-Foulkesian Group Analytic Theory*. London: Jessica Kingsley.

Damasio, Antonio (1994). *Descartes' Error: Emotion, Reason, and the Human Brain*. London: Penguin, 2005.

Dellarossa, Alejo (1979). *Grupos de reflexión. Entrenamiento institucional de coordinadores y terapeutas de grupos* [Reflection groups: Institutional training of group coordinators and group therapists]. Buenos Aires: Paidós.

de Maré, Patrick; Piper, Robin & Thompson, Sheila (1991). *Koinonia: From Hate, through Dialogue, to Culture in the Large Group*. London: Routledge, 2019.

Diez, Tino (2010). Enrique Santos Discépolo. *Terapiatanguera.com.ar* (visited October 4, 2020). www.terapiatanguera.com.ar/Notas%20y%20articulos/tino_discepolo.htm

Dilthey, Wilhelm (1883). *Introduction to the Human Sciences*, Rudolf A. Makkreel & Fritjof Rody (eds.). Princeton, NJ: Princeton University Press.

Domenjo, Blanca Anguera (2000). Thoughts on the influence of Brentano and Comte on Freud's work. *Psychoanalysis and History*, 2 (1): 110–118.

Donne, John (1624). Meditation XVII. *The Literature Network*. Web Page (visited June 17, 2020). www.online-literature.com/donne/409

Durkheim, Émile (1912). *The Elementary Forms of the Religious Life*, Carol Cosman (trans.). Oxford: Oxford University Press, 2001.

Eco, Umberto (1990). *I limiti dell'interpretazione*, fourth edition. Milan: Bompiani, 2004. [English translation: *The Limits of Interpretation*. Bloomington, IN: Indiana University Press, 1994].

Eco, Umberto (1992). *Interpretation and Overinterpretation*. Cambridge, England: Cambridge University Press.

Elias, Norbert (1939). *The Civilizing Process: Sociogenetic and Psychogenetic Investigations*. Oxford: Blackwell, 2000.

Erikson, Erik H. (1950). *Childhood and Society*. London: Paladin, 1987.

Erikson, Erik H. (1958). *Young Man Luther: A Study in Psychoanalysis and History*. New York, NY: Norton, 1993.

Erikson, Erik H. (1969). *Gandhi's Truth: On the Origin of Militant Nonviolence*. New York, NY: Norton, 1993.

Esman, Aaron H. (1998). What is 'applied' in 'applied' psychoanalysis? *International Journal of Psycho-Analysis*, 79: 741–752.

Ezriel, Harry (1950). A psychoanalytic approach to group treatment. *British Journal of Medical Psychology*, 23: 59–74.

Fairbairn, W. Ronald D. (1929). Impressions on the 1929 international congress of psychoanalysis. In Elinor Fairbairn Birtles & David E. Scharff (eds.), *From Instinct to Self: Selected Papers of W. R. D. Fairbairn: Vol. II: Applications and Early Contributions*. Northvale, NJ & London: Jason Aronson, 1994, pp. 454–461.

Fairbairn, W. Ronald D. (1952). *Psychoanalytic Studies of the Personality*. London: Routledge, 1992.

Falk, Avner (1978). Freud and Herzl. *Contemporary Psychoanalysis*, 14 (3): 357–387. https://doi.org/10.1080/00107530.1978.10745545

Ferenczi, Sándor (1908a). The effect on women of premature ejaculation in men. In Ferenczi (1955), pp. 291–294.

Ferenczi, Sándor (1908b). Psychoanalysis and education. In Ferenczi (1955), pp. 280–290.

Ferenczi, Sándor (1909). Introjection and transference. In Ferenczi (1916), pp. 35–93.

Ferenczi, Sándor (1913a). Stages in the development of the sense of reality. In Ferenczi (1916), pp. 213–239.

Ferenczi, Sándor (1913b). A little chanticleer. In Ferenczi (1916), pp. 240–252.

Ferenczi, Sándor (1916). *First Contributions to Psycho-Analysis*, Ernest Jones (trans.). London: Routledge, 2019.

Ferenczi, Sándor (1924). *Thalassa: A Theory of Genitality*, Henry A. Bunker (trans.). London: Routledge, 1989.

Ferenczi, Sándor (1928a). The adaptation of the family to the child. In Ferenczi (1955), pp. 61–76.

Ferenczi, Sándor (1928b). The elasticity of psycho-analytic technique. In Ferenczi (1955), pp. 87–101.

Ferenczi, Sándor (1929). The unwelcome child and his death instinct. *International Journal of Psycho-Analysis*, 10: 125–129. [Reprinted in Ferenczi (1955), pp. 102–107].

Ferenczi, Sándor (1933). Confusion of the tongues between the adults and the child: The language of tenderness and of passion. *International Journal of Psycho-Analysis*, 1949, 30: 225–230. Also in *Contemporary Psychoanalysis*, 24 (2): 196–206. https://doi.org/10.1080/00107530.1988.10746234. [Reprinted in Ferenczi (1955), pp. 156–167].

Ferenczi, Sándor (1955). *Final Contributions to the Problems and Methods of Psycho-Analysis*, Michael Balint (ed.), Eric Mosbacher et al. (trans.). London: Routledge, 2019.

Ferenczi, Sándor (1985). *The Clinical Diary of Sándor Ferenczi*, Judith Dupont (ed.), Michael Balint & Nicola Z. Jackson (trans.). Cambridge, MA: Harvard University Press, 1988. [Originally written in 1932 and first published in French as *Journal Clinique (janvier – octobre 1932)*. Paris: Payot, 1985].

Ferenczi, Sándor & Rank, Otto (1924). *The Development of Psychoanalysis*, Caroline Newton (trans.). Mansfield Center, CT: Martino Publishing, 2012.

Ferrater Mora, José (1994). *Diccionario de filosofía* [Dictionary of Philosophy], new edition in four volumes, enlarged and updated by Josep-Maria Terricabras. Barcelona: Ariel.

Fichtner, Gerhard (2003). *The Sigmund Freud – Ludwig Binswanger Correspondence 1908–1938*. London: Open Gate Press, incorporating Centaur Press.

Foucault, Michel (1961). *Madness and Civilization*. London: Routledge, 2001.

Foulkes, Elizabeth T. (1984). The origins and development of group analysis. In Terence E. Lear (ed.), *Spheres of Group Analysis*. London: Group-Analytic Society, pp. 5–13.

Foulkes, S.H. (1946). On group analysis. *International Journal of Psycho-Analysis*, 27: 46–51. [Reprinted, in a slightly briefer version, in Foulkes (1990), pp. 127–136].

Foulkes, S.H. (1948). *Introduction to Group-Analytic Psychotherapy: Studies in the Social Interaction of Individuals and Groups*. London: Routledge, 2018.

Foulkes, S.H. (1957). Psychodynamic processes in the light of psychoanalysis and group analysis. In Foulkes (1964a), pp. 108–119. [Originally published as, Group-analytic dynamics with special reference to psychoanalytic concepts. *International Journal of Group Psychotherapy*, 7: 40–52].

Foulkes, S.H. (1961). The position of group analysis today, with special reference to the role of the Group-Analytic Society (London). In Foulkes (1990), pp. 145–150. [Paper originally written in 1955].

Foulkes, S.H. (1964a). *Therapeutic Group Analysis*. London: Routledge, 2018.

Foulkes, S.H. (1964b). A brief guide to group-analytic theory and practice. In Foulkes (1964a), pp. 281–298.

Foulkes, S.H. (ed.) (1967). *Group Analysis International Panel and Correspondence*, preliminary number. London: Group Analytic Society.

Foulkes, S.H. (1973). The group as matrix of the individual's mental life. In Foulkes (1990), pp. 223–233.

Foulkes, S.H. (1975a). *Group Analytic Psychotherapy: Method and Principles*. London: Routledge, 2018.

Foulkes, S.H. (1975b). Problems of the large group from a group-analytic point of view. In Lionel Kreeger (ed.), *The Large Group: Dynamics and Therapy*, London: Karnac, pp. 33–56.

Foulkes, S.H. (1990). *Selected Papers: Psychoanalysis and Group Analysis*. London: Routledge, 2018.

Foulkes, S.H. & Anthony, E. James (1957–1965). *Group Psychotherapy: The Psychoanalytic Approach*, second edition. London: Routledge, 2019.

Foulkes, S.H. & Lewis, Eve (1944). Group analysis: Studies in the treatment of groups on psychoanalytical lines. In Foulkes (1964a), pp. 20–37.

Frege, Gottlob (1892). On sense and reference. In Peter Geach & Max Black (eds.), *Translations from the Philosophical Writings of Gottlob Frege*, second edition. Oxford: Blackwell, 1960, pp. 56–78.

Freud, Sigmund (1883). Letter from Sigmund Freud to Martha Barnays, August 29, 1883. In Ernst L. Freud (ed.), Tania Stern & James Stern (trans.), *Letters of Sigmund Freud 1873–1939*. London: Hogarth, 1961, pp. 50–52.

Freud, Sigmund (1895). Letter from Freud to Fliess, May 25, 1895. In Jeffrey M. Masson (1985), pp. 128–131.

Freud, Sigmund (1895d). *Studies on Hysteria* (with Josef Breuer). S.E. 2. London: Hogarth.

Freud, Sigmund (1897). Letter from Freud to Fliess, September 21, 1897. In Jeffrey M. Masson (1985), pp. 264–267.

Freud, Sigmund (1898). Letter from Freud to Fliess, March 10, 1898. In Jeffrey M. Masson (1985), pp. 301–302.

Freud, Sigmund (1900a). *The Interpretation of Dreams*. S.E. 4–5. London: Hogarth.

Freud, Sigmund (1901b). *The Psychopathology of Everyday Life: Forgetting, Slips of the Tongue, Bungled Actions, Superstitions and Errors*. S.E. 6. London: Hogarth.

Freud, Sigmund (1904a). *Freud's Psycho-Analytic Procedure*. S.E. 7: 247–254. London: Hogarth.

Freud, Sigmund (1905d). *Three Essays on the Theory of Sexuality*. S.E. 7: 123–246. London: Hogarth.

Freud, Sigmund (1908d). *'Civilized' Sexual Morality and Modern Nervous Illness*. S.E 9: 177–204. London: Hogarth.

Freud, Sigmund (1909b). *Analysis of a Phobia in a Five-Year-Old Boy*. S.E. 10: 1–150. London: Hogarth.

Freud, Sigmund (1911b). *Formulations on the Two Principles of Mental Functioning*. S.E. 12: 213–226. London: Hogarth.

Freud, Sigmund (1912). *Recommendations to Physicians Practising Psycho-Analysis*. S.E. 12: 109–120. London. Hogarth.

Freud, Sigmund (1912–1913). *Totem and Taboo: Some Points of Agreement between the Mental Lives of Savages and Neurotics*. S.E. 13: 1–162. London: Hogarth.

Freud, Sigmund (1914c). *On Narcissism: An Introduction*. S.E. 14: 67–102. London: Hogarth.

Freud, Sigmund (1915c). *Instincts and Their Vicissitudes*. S.E. 14: 109–140. London: Hogarth.

Freud, Sigmund (1916–1917). *Introductory Lectures on Psycho-Analysis*. S.E. 15–16. London: Hogarth.

Freud, Sigmund (1917e). *Mourning and Melancholia*. S.E. 14: 237–258. London: Hogarth.

Freud, Sigmund (1918b). *From the History of an Infantile Neurosis*. S.E. 17: 1–124. London: Hogarth.

Freud, Sigmund (1920g). *Beyond the Pleasure Principle*. S.E. 18: 1–64. London: Hogarth.

Freud, Sigmund (1921c). *Group Psychology and the Analysis of the Ego*. S.E. 18: 65–144. London: Hogarth.

Freud, Sigmund (1923a). *Two Encyclopaedia Articles*. S.E. 18: 233–260. London: Hogarth.

Freud, Sigmund (1923b). *The Ego and the Id*. S.E. 19: 1–66. London: Hogarth.

Freud, Sigmund (1926e). *The Question of Lay Analysis*. S.E. 20: 177–258. London: Hogarth.

Freud, Sigmund (1927c). *The Future of an Illusion*. S.E. 21: 1–56. London: Hogarth.

Freud, Sigmund (1928a). *A Religious Experience*. S.E. 21: 167–172. London: Hogarth.

Freud, Sigmund (1930a). *Civilization and Its Discontents*. S.E. 21: 64–145. London: Hogarth.

Freud, Sigmund (1933a). *New Introductory Lectures on Psycho-Analysis*. S.E. 22: 3–182. London: Hogarth.

Freud, Sigmund (1933b). *Why War?* S.E. 22: 195–216. London: Hogarth.

Freud, Sigmund (1933c). *Sándor Ferenczi*. S.E. 22: 225–230. London: Hogarth.

Freud, Sigmund (1937a). *Analysis Terminable and Interminable*. S.E. 23: 209–254. London: Hogarth.

Freud, Sigmund (1937b). *Constructions in Analysis*. S.E. 23: 255–270. London: Hogarth.

Freud, Sigmund (1939a). *Moses and Monotheism: Tree Essays*. S.E. 23: 1–138. London: Hogarth.

Freud, Sigmund (1940a). *Some Elementary Lessons in Psycho-Analysis*. S.E. 23: 279–286. London: Hogarth.

Freud, Sigmund (1940b). *Splitting of the Ego in the Process of Defence*. S.E. 23: 271–278. London: Hogarth.

Freud, Sigmund (1950a). *Project for a Scientific Psychology*. S.E. 1: 281–391. London: Hogarth. [Written in 1885].

Fromm, Erich (1951). *The Forgotten Language: An Introduction to the Understanding of Dreams, Fairy Tales, and Myths*. New York, NY: Henry Holt, 1976.

Fromm, Erich (1956). *The Art of Loving*. New York, NY: Harper, 2006.

Fromm, Erich (1958). The Revolutionary Character. In *The Dogma of Christ and Other Essays*. London: Routledge, 2004, pp. 147–168.

Fromm, Erich (1975). La importancia del psicoanálisis para el futuro [The importance of psychoanalysis for the future]. In *Espíritu y sociedad* [Spirit and Society]. Barcelona: Paidós, 1996, pp. 155–187.

Gadamer, Hans-Georg (1960). *Truth and Method*, second revised English edition, translated from the fifth German edition, W. Glen-Doepel (trans.), Joel Weinsheimer & Donald G. Marshall (revs.). London: Bloomsbury, 2013.

Gaddini, Renata (1981). Bion's 'catastrophic change' and Winnicott's 'breakdown'. *Rivista di Psicoanalisi*, 27 (3–4): 610–621.

García Badaracco, Jorge (1990). *Comunidad terapéutica psicoanalítica de estructura multifamiliar* [Psychoanalytic therapeutic community of a multi-family structure]. Madrid: Julián Yébenes.

Ghent, Emmanuel (1990). Masochism, submission, surrender: Masochism as a perversion of surrender. *Contemporary Psychoanalysis*, 26 (1): 108–136. https://doi.org/10.1080/00107530.1990.10746643 [Reprinted in Mitchell, Stephen A. & Aron, Lewis (eds.) (1999). *Relational Psychoanalysis: The Emergence of a Tradition*. London: Routledge, 2015, pp. 213–239].

Golding, William (1954). *Lord of the Flies*. Herndon, VA: A & A Publishers, 2013.

Goldman, Dodi (1993). *In Search of the Real: The Origins and Originality of D. W. Winnicott*. Northvale, NJ: Jason Aronson.

Greenberg, Jay R. & Mitchell, Stephen A. (1983). *Object Relations in Psychoanalytic Theory*. Cambridge, MA: Harvard University Press.

Grinberg, León; Langer, Marie & Rodrigué, Emilio (1957). *Psicoterapia del grupo* [Psychotherapy of the group]. Buenos Aires: Paidós.

Guntrip, Harry (1961). *Personality Structure and Human Interaction: The Developing Synthesis of Psychodynamic Theory*. London: Routledge, 1977.

Hernández de Tubert, Reyna (1996). Racismo y trauma transgeneracional [Racism and transgenerational trauma]. Read at the 11th Monterrey Psychoanalytic Congress, Monterrey, Mexico, March.

Hernández de Tubert, Reyna (1997). Mentira y poder: sociogénesis de la enfermedad mental [Lies and power: The social genesis of mental illness]. *Cuadernos de Psicoanálisis*, 30 (1–2): 43–49.

Hernández de Tubert, Reyna (1999a). Identidad femenina y trauma transgeneracional [Feminine identity and transgenerational trauma]. In A.M. Alizade (ed.), *Escenarios femeninos. Diálogos y controversias* [Feminine scenarios: Dialogues and controversies]. Buenos Aires: Lumen, pp. 139–164.

Hernández de Tubert, Reyna (1999b). La regressione: espressione psicopatologica o fattore terapeutico fondamentale? [Regression, a psychopathological expression or a fundamental therapeutic factor?]. In Franco Borgogno (ed.), *La partecipazione affettiva dell' analista. Il contributo di Sándor Ferenczi al pensiero psicoanalitico contemporaneo* [The analyst's affective participation: Sándor Ferenczi's contribution to contemporary psychoanalytical thought]. Milan: Franco Angeli, pp. 186–209.

Hernández de Tubert, Reyna (2000). El principio de exclusión en el desarrollo del movimiento psicoanalítico [The principle of exclusion in the development of the psychoanalytical movement]. Read at the 8th International Meeting of the International Association for the History of Psychoanalysis, Versailles, France, June.

Hernández de Tubert, Reyna (2004a). Inconsciente y concepción del mundo [The unconscious and the *Weltanschauung*]. In Miguel Kolteniuk, Julio Casillas & Jorge de la Parra (eds.), *El inconsciente freudiano* [The Freudian unconscious]. Mexico City: Editores de Textos Mexicanos, pp. 63–78.

Hernández de Tubert, Reyna (2004b). Cuando el analista maltrata al paciente. Una perspectiva ética y epistemológica [When the analyst mistreats the patient: An ethical and epistemological perspective]. *Revista Latinoamericana de Psicoanálisis*, 6: 59–74.

Hernández de Tubert, Reyna (2004c). La concepción del mundo: una perspectiva psicoanalítica [The *Weltanschauung*: A psychoanalytic perspective]. Read at the 43rd International Psychoanalytical Congress, New Orleans, LA, March.

Hernández de Tubert, Reyna (2006a). Comentario al trabajo de Francisco Mancera 'Psicoanálisis, dialéctica de lo negativo y otros viajes' [Comment on Francisco Mancera's paper 'psychoanalysis, the dialectics of the negative, and other journeys']. Read in the Seminar 'Philosophy and? Psychoanalysis', Mexico City: National Autonomous University of Mexico, February.

Hernández de Tubert, Reyna (2006b). Social trauma: The pathogenic effects of untoward social conditions. *International Forum of Psychoanalysis*, 15 (3): 151–156. https://doi.org/10.1080/08037060500526037

Hernández de Tubert, Reyna (2006c). Los prejuicios de género en la interpretación de la teoría y la técnica psicoanalíticas. Su impacto en la transferencia-contratransferencia [Gender prejudices in the interpretation of psychoanalytical theory and practice: Their impact on the transference-countertransference]. *Cuadernos de Psicoanálisis*, 39 (1–2): 26–36.

Hernández de Tubert, Reyna (2006d). Más allá de la neutralidad. Los valores humanos que subyacen a la teoría y la práctica psicoanalíticas [Beyond neutrality: The values that underlie psychoanalytical theory and practice]. Read in the 19th Psychoanalytic Work Meeting, Guadalajara Psychoanalytic Association, Guadalajara, Mexico, November.

Hernández de Tubert, Reyna (2008). La antropología freudiana y la metasociología [Freudian anthropology and metasociology]. *Revista de Psicoanálisis*, 65: 29–56. [Chapter 5].

Hernández de Tubert, Reyna (2009a). Inconsciente y concepción del mundo. Implicaciones filosóficas y psicoanalíticas [The unconscious and the *Weltanschauung*: Philosophic and psychoanalytic implications]. In Ricardo Blanco Beledo (ed.), *Filosofía ¿y? psicoanálisis* [Philosophy and? Psychoanalysis]. Mexico City: National Autonomous University of Mexico, pp. 79–103.

Hernández de Tubert, Reyna & Tubert-Oklander, Juan (2005). Operative groups: A reply to Macario Giraldo. *Psychologist-Psychoanalyst*, 25 (1): 4–7.

Hernández Hernández, Reyna (1994). El mito del mestizaje. *Psicología Iberoamericana*, 2 (3): 5–13.

Hernández Hernández, Reyna (1994 [1999–2000]). El mundo del psicoanalista [The psychoanalyst's world]. Read at the 33rd National Congress of Psychoanalysis, Querétaro, Mexico, November. Published online in *Aperturas Psicoanalíticas*, October 1999–March 2000. www.aperturas.org

Hernández Hernández, Reyna (2010). *Inconsciente y concepción del mundo* [The unconscious and the *Weltanschauung*]. Unpublished Doctor in Psychotherapy dissertation, Centre for Graduate Studies, Mexican Psychoanalytic Association, Mexico City, June.

Hernández-Hernández, Reyna & Tubert-Oklander, Juan (1995). Del olvido a la violencia y de la violencia al mito. Reflexiones psicoanalíticas sobre el proceso político de nuestro país [From oblivion to violence and from violence to myth: Psychoanalytic reflections on the political process in our country]. *Subjetividad y Cultura*, (4): 71–79.

Hernández-Hernández, Reyna & Tubert-Oklander, Juan (1996). Poder y violencia en la matriz social [Power and violence in the social matrix]. *Psicología Iberoamericana*, 4 (3): 4–10.

Hernández-Tubert, Reyna (2009). A personal reflection on the large group experience: Thinking group or therapeutic group? *Group-Analytic Contexts*, June, 44: 27–32 [Appendix IV].

Hernández-Tubert, Reyna (2011a). The politics of despair: From despair to dialogue and hope. *Group Analysis*, 44: 27–39. https://doi.org/10.1177%2F0533316410390455 [Chapter 12].

Hernández-Tubert, Reyna (2011b). Hacia un nuevo paradigma del ser humano: la confluencia del psicoanálisis y la hermenéutica analógica [Towards a new paradigm of the human being: The confluence of psychoanalysis and analogical hermeneutics]. Read at the 47th Congress of the International Psychoanalytical Association, Mexico City, August.

Hernández-Tubert, Reyna (2012). Comentario sobre el trabajo de Eric Smadja "La noción de *Kulturarbeit* (trabajo de la cultura) en la obra de Freud" [Commentary on Etic Smadja's paper 'The notion of *Kulturarbeit* (the work of culture) in Freud's writings']. Read at the Mexican Psychoanalytic Association, Mexico City, February. [Chapter 6].

Hernández-Tubert, Reyna (2015). Inclusion and exclusion in psychoanalysis: From splitting to integration in our theory and practice. *Canadian Journal of Psychoanalysis/Revue Canadienne de Psychanalyse*, Spring, 23 (1): 179–186. [Chapter 2].

Hernández-Tubert, Reyna (2017a). El asesinato del alma de un pueblo [The soul murder of a people]. Read at the 50th International Psychoanalytical Congress, Buenos Aires, July.

Hernández-Tubert, Reyna (2017b). El papel fundamental de la agresión y el odio en el tratamiento psicoanalítico [The fundamental role of aggression and hate in the psychoanalytic treatment]. Read at the 26th Latin-American Meeting on Winnicott's Thought, Mexico City, November. [Chapter 4].

Hernández-Tubert, Reyna (2017c). Enrique Pichon-Rivière: Un faro orientador para el desarrollo del psicoanálisis [Enrique Pichon-Rivière: A guiding-light for the development of psychoanalysis]. In *E. Pichon-Rivière, Av. Santa Fe 1379, Buenos Aires G. Róheim, Hermina ut 35 b, Budapest, Nouveau Document*, 1. Paris: Nouveau Document. [Bilingual Publication; The present chapter is published in Spanish and French].

Hobbes, Thomas (1651). *Leviathan*. London: Penguin, 1982.

Home, H. James (1966). The concept of mind. *International Journal of Psycho-Analysis*, 47: 42–49.

Hopper, Earl (1982). Group analysis: The problem of context. *Group Analysis*, 15 (2): 136–157. https://doi.org/10.1177%2F053331648201500205

Hopper, Earl (1985). The problem of context in group-analytic psychotherapy: A clinical illustration and a brief theoretical discussion. In Malcolm Pines (ed.), *Bion and Group Psychotherapy*. London: Routledge & Kegan Paul, pp. 330–353. [Reprinted: London, Jessica Kingsley, 2000].

Hopper, Earl (2000). From objects and subjects to citizens: Group analysis and the study of maturity. *Group Analysis*, 33 (1): 29–34. https://doi.org/10.1177%2F05333160022 077209

Hopper, Earl (2003a). *The Social Unconscious*. London: Jessica Kingsley.

Hopper, Earl (2003b). *Traumatic Experience in the Unconscious Life of Groups*. London: Jessica Kingsley.

Hopper, Earl (2019). 'Notes' for my response to the Foulkes Lecture by Juan Tubert-Oklander on Friday 17 May 2019. *Group Analysis*, 52 (4): 427–433. https://doi.org/10. 1177%2F0533316419872861

Hopper, Earl & Kreeger, Lionel (1980). 'Report on the large group' of the Survivor Syndrome Workshop (1979). In Hopper (2003a), pp. 95–102.

Hopper, Earl & Weinberg, Haim (eds.) (2011a). *The Social Unconscious in Persons, Groups and Societies – Volume I: Mainly Theory*. London: Routledge, 2018.

Hopper, Earl & Weinberg, Haim (2011b). Introduction. In Hopper & Weinberg (2011a), pp. xxiii–lvi.

Hopper, Earl & Weinberg, Haim (eds.) (2016). *The Social Unconscious in Persons, Groups and Societies – Volume II: Mainly Foundation Matrices*. London: Routledge, 2019.

Hopper, Earl & Weinberg, Haim (2017a). Introduction. In Hopper & Weinberg (2017b), pp. xv–xxxv.

Hopper, Earl & Weinberg, Haim (eds.) (2017b). *The Social Unconscious in Persons, Groups and Societies – Volume III: The Foundation Matrix Extended and Re-Configured*. London: Routledge, 2019.

Horkheimer, Max (1937). Traditional and critical theory. In *Critical Theory: Selected Essays*, M.J. O'Connell (trans.). New York, NY: Continuum, 1975, pp. 188–243.

Isaacs, S. (1948). The nature and function of phantasy. *International Journal of Psycho-Analysis*, 29: 73–97. [Reprinted in Klein et al. (1952), pp. 67–121].

Jones, Ernest (1953). *Sigmund Freud Life and Work, Volume One: The Young Freud 1856–1900*. London: Hogarth, 1972.

Jung, Carl Gustav (1961). *Memories, Dreams, Reflections*, Aniela Jaffé (ed.), Richard and Clara Winston (trans.), revised edition. New York, NY: Vintage Books, 1989.

Kaës, René (1976). *El aparato psíquico grupal*. Barcelona: Gedisa, 1991. [Spanish translation of *L'appareil psychique groupal*. Paris: Dunod.]

Kaës, René (2007). *Un singulier pluriel. La psychanalyse à l'épreuve du groupe* [A singular plural. Psychoanalysis under the test of groups]. Paris: Dunod.

Kaës, René; Faimberg, Haydeé; Enriquez, Micheline & Baranes, Jean-José (1993). *Transmisión de la vida psíquica entre generaciones* [Transmission of psychic life through generations]. Buenos Aires: Amorrortu, 1996. [Spanish translation of *Transmission de la vie psychique entre générations*. Paris: Dunod, 2013].

Kahr, Brett (1996). *D. W. Winnicott: A Biographical Portrait*. London: Karnac.

Kaplan, Abraham (1964). *The Conduct of Inquiry: Methodology for Behavioral Science*. New York, NY: Chandler.

Katz, Montana; Cassorla, Roosevelt & Civitarese, Giuseppe (eds.) (2017). *Advances in Contemporary Psychoanalytic Field Theory: Concept and Future Development*. London & New York: Routledge.

Khan, Masud R. (1975). Introduction. In Winnicott (1958–1975), pp. xi–l.

Klein, George S. (1976). *Psychoanalytic Theory: An Exploration of Essentials*. New York, NY: International Universities Press.

Klein, Melanie (1946). Notes on some schizoid mechanisms. *International Journal of Psycho-Analysis*, 27: 99–110. [Reprinted in Klein (1975), *Envy and Gratitude & Other Works 1946–1963*. New York, NY: Delta, pp. 1–24.]

Klein, Melanie; Heimann, Paula; Isaacs, Susan & Riviere, Joan (1952). *Developments in Psycho-Analysis*. London: Routledge, 2018.

Klein, Melanie; Heimann, Paula & Money-Kyrle, R. (eds.) (1955). *New Directions in Psycho-Analysis: The Significance of Infant Conflict in the Pattern of Adult Behaviour*. London: Tavistock.

Kohut, Heinz (1982). Introspection, empathy, and the semicircle of mental health. *International Journal of Psycho-Analysis*, 63: 395–408.

Kohut, Heinz (1984). *How Does Analysis Cure?* Chicago, IL: University of Chicago.

Korzybski, Alfred (1941). *Science and Sanity*. New York, NY: Science Press.

Kuhn, Thomas S. (1962). *The Structure of Scientific Revolutions*. Chicago, IL: University of Chicago. [Reprinted, fourth edition, 2012].

Lacan, Jacques (1966). *Ecrits: The First Complete Edition in English*, Bruce Fink (trans.). New York, NY: Norton, 2006. [Original French publication: *Écrits*, Paris: Seuil].

Lacan, Jacques (1973). *Seminar of Jacques Lacan: The Four Fundamental Concepts of Psychoanalysis: Book XI*, Jacques-Alain Miller (ed.), Alan Sheridan (trans.). New York, NY: Norton, 1998.

Laplanche, Jean (1997). The theory of seduction and the problem of the other. *International Journal of Psycho-Analysis*, 78: 653–666.

Laplanche, Jean & Pontalis, Jean-Bertrand (1967). *The Language of Psycho-Analysis*, Donald Nicholson-Smith (trans.). London: Hogarth, 1973. [English translation of *Vocabulaire de la Psychanalyse*. Paris: Presses Universitaires de France].

Le Bon, Gustave (1895). *Psychologie des foules*. Paris: Retz, 1976. [English translation: *The Crowd: A Study of the Popular Mind*. Mineola, NY: Dover Books, 2002].

Levin, C. (2015a). Body, self, and society in psychoanalysis. *Canadian Journal of Psychoanalysis/Revue Canadienne de Psychanalyse*, Spring, 23 (1): 178.

Levin, C. (2015b). Discussion of 'body, self, and society in psychoanalysis'. *Canadian Journal of Psychoanalysis/Revue Canadienne de Psychanalyse*, Spring, 23 (1): 202–204.

Lewin, Kurt (1951). *Field Theory in Social Science*. New York, NY: Harper & Row, 1976.

Loewald, Hans W. (1951). Ego and reality. *The International Journal of Psycho-Analysis*, 32: 10–18. [Reprinted in Loewald (1980), *Papers on Psychoanalysis*. New Haven, CT: Yale, pp. 3–20].

Losso, Roberto; Setton, Lea S. de & Scharff, David E. (eds.) (2017). *The Linked Self in Psychoanalysis: The Pioneering Work of Enrique Pichon Rivière*. London: Routledge.

Mahler, Margaret (1968). *On Human Symbiosis and the Vicissitudes of Individuation. Vol I: Infantile Psychosis.* New York, NY: International Universities Press.

Mannheim, Karl (1936). *Ideology and Utopia: An Introduction to the Sociology of Knowledge,* Louis Wyrth & Edward Shils (trans.). Mansfield Centre, CT: Martino, 2015.

Marrone, Mario (1979). The development of group psychotherapy in Argentina. *Group Analysis,* 12 (3): 250–253. https://doi.org/10.1177%2F053331647901200313

Marx, Carl & Engels, Friedrich (1932). *The German Ideology.* Buffalo, NY: Prometheus, 2011. [Written in 1845].

Masson, Jeffrey M. (1984). *The Assault on Truth.* London: Fontana, 1992.

Masson, Jeffrey M. (1985). *The Complete Letters of Sigmund Freud to Wilhelm Fliess, 1887–1904.* Cambridge, MA & London, England: The Belknap Press of Harvard University Press.

Matte-Blanco, Ignacio (1988). *Thinking, Feeling, and Being: Clinical Reflections on the Fundamental Antinomy of Human Beings and World.* London: Routledge.

McDougall, William (1920). *The Group Mind.* New York, NY: Arno Press, 1973.

McGrath, William J. (1986). *Freud's Discovery of Psychoanalysis: The Politics of Hysteria.* Ithaca, NY: Cornell University Press.

Merleau-Ponty, Maurice (1945). *Phenomenology of Perception.* London: Forgotten Books, 2015.

Merriam-Webster (2002). *Webster's Third New International Dictionary, Unabridged* (electronic version). http://unabridged.merriam-webster.com

Mitchell, Stephen A. (1984). Object relations theories and the developmental tilt. *Contemporary Psychoanalysis,* 20 (4): 473–499. https://doi.org/10.1080/00107530.1984. 10745749

Mitchell, Stephen A. (1988). *Relational Concepts in Psychoanalysis.* Cambridge, MA: Harvard University Press.

Mitchell, Stephen A. (2000). *Relationality: From Attachment to Intersubjectivity.* London: Routledge, 2003.

Mojović, Marina (2015). The matrix disrupted: Challenges and changes. *Group Analysis,* 48 (4): 540–556. https://doi.org/10.1177%2F0533316415613484

Mojović, Marina (2016). Serbian reflective citizens' Matrix flourishing in leaking containers: Response to 40th Foulkes lecture. *Group Analysis,* 49 (4): 370–384. https://doi.org/ 10.1177%2F0533316416676449

Montevechio, Blanca (1999). *Las nuevas fronteras del psicoanálisis. Dionisio, Narciso, Edipo* [The new frontiers of psychoanalysis: Dionysus, Narcissus, Oedipus]. Buenos Aires: Lumen.

Montevechio, Blanca (2002). *Más allá de Narciso. La problemática de las identidades* [Beyond Narcissus: The problematic of identities]. Buenos Aires: Lumen.

Ogden, Thomas H. (1994). *Subjects of Analysis.* London: Routledge, 2019.

Olmsted, Michael S. (1959). *The Small Group,* second edition. New York, NY: Random House, 1978.

Ornstein, Robert E. (1972). *The Psychology of Consciousness,* 4th revised and enlarged edition. New York, NY: Penguin, 1986.

Orwell, George (1949). *1984.* London: Palgrave MacMillan, 2003.

Pascal, Blaise (1670). *Pensées,* A.J. Krailsheimer (trans.). London: Penguin, 1995.

Pichon-Rivière, Enrique (1951). Aplicaciones de la psicoterapia de grupo [Applications of group psychotherapy]. In Pichon-Rivière (1971a), pp. 75–81.

Pichon-Rivière, Enrique (1965a). Discépolo: un cronista de su tiempo [Discépolo: A chronicler of his time]. In Pichon-Rivière (1971a), pp. 161–168.

Pichon-Rivière, Enrique (1965b). Implacable interjuego del hombre y del mundo [Implacable interplay of man and world]. In Pichon-Rivière (1971a), pp. 169–172.

Pichon-Rivière, Enrique (1965c). Grupos operativos y enfermedad única [Operative groups and the single disease]. In Pichon-Rivière (1971a), pp. 121–139.

Pichon-Rivière, Enrique (1969). Estructura de una escuela destinada a psicólogos sociales [Structure of a school for social psychologists]. In Pichon-Rivière (1971a), pp. 149–160.

Pichon-Rivière, Enrique (1970). Concepto de E.C.R.O. [The concept of CROS]. *Temas de Psicología Social*, 1 (1): 7–10.

Pichon-Rivière, Enrique (1971a). *El proceso grupal. Del psicoanálisis a la psicología social (I)* [The group process: From psychoanalysis to social psychology (I)]. Buenos Aires: Nueva Visión.

Pichon-Rivière, Enrique (1971b). *La psiquiatría, una nueva problemática. Del psicoanálisis a la psicología social (II)* [A new problematic for psychiatry: From psychoanalysis to social psychology (II)]. Buenos Aires: Nueva Visión.

Pichon-Rivière, Enrique (1979). *Teoría del vínculo* [Theory of the bond]. Buenos Aires: Nueva Visión.

Pichon-Rivière, Enrique & Bauleo, Armando (1964). La noción de tarea en psiquiatría [The notion of task in psychiatry]. In Pichon-Rivière (1971a), pp. 33–36.

Pichon-Rivière, Enrique; Bleger, José; Liberman, David & Rolla, Edgardo (1960). Técnica de los grupos operativos [Technique of operative groups]. In Pichon-Rivière (1971a), pp. 107–120.

Pichon-Rivière, Enrique; Quiroga, Ana P. de; Gandolfo, Carlos & Lazzarini, Marta (1969). Grupo operativo y modelo dramático [Operative groups and the dramatic model]. In Pichon-Rivière (1971a), pp. 141–147.

Pines, Malcolm (1989). On history and psychoanalysis. In Pines (1998), pp. 167–181.

Pines, Malcolm (1998). *Circular Reflections: Selected Papers on Group Analysis and Psychoanalysis*. London: Jessica Kingsley.

Pinto, Rosa & d'Elia, Anna (1980). The therapeutic role of the observer. *Group Analysis*, 13 (1): 21–24. https://doi.org/10.1177%2F053331648001300107

Popper, Karl R. (1972). *Objective Knowledge: An Evolutionary Approach*, revised edition. Oxford: University Press, 1979.

Pribram, Karl H. & Gill, Merton M. (1976). *Freud's 'Project' Re-Assessed: Preface to Contemporary Cognitive Theory and Neuropsychology*. New York, NY: Basic Books.

Ragen, Therese & Aron, Lewis (1993). Abandoned workings: Ferenczi's mutual analysis. In Lewis Aron and Adrienne Harris (eds.), *The Legacy of Sándor Ferenczi*. Hillsdale, NJ: Analytic Press, pp. 217–226.

Remus Araico, José (1988). Algunas funciones de las estructuras psíquicas en las relaciones sociales, con algunos conceptos-puente con la etología [Some functions of psychic structures in social relations, with some bridge-concepts with ethology]. 10th Sigmund Freud Lecture, Mexican Psychoanalytic Association, Tequesquitengo, Mexico, May.

Ricoeur, Paul (1965). *Freud and Philosophy: An Essay on Interpretation*, D. Savage (trans.). New Haven, CT: Yale, 1970. [Original French publication: *De l'interprétation, essai sur Freud*, Paris: Seuil].

Rodman, F. Robert (ed.) (1987). *The Spontaneous Gesture: Selected Letters of D. W. Winnicott*. Cambridge, MA and London: Harvard University Press.

Rousseau, Jean-Jaques (1762). *On the Social Contract*. Mineola, NY: Dover Publications, 2003.

Roustang, François (1976). *Dire Mastery: Discipleship from Freud to Lacan*, Ned Lukacher (trans.). Washington, DC: American Psychiatric Association, 1986.

Rudnytsky, Peter L. (2019). *Formulated Experiences: Hidden Realities and Emergent Meanings from Shakespeare to Fromm*. London & New York: Routledge.

Rycroft, Charles (1962). Beyond the reality principle. *International Journal of Psycho-Analysis*, 43: 388–394. [Reprinted in Rycroft (1968), pp. 102–113].

Rycroft, Charles (1966). Introduction: Causes and meaning. In Rycroft (1966a), *Psychoanalysis Observed*. Harmondsworth: Penguin, pp. 7–21. [Reprinted as 'Causes and meaning' in Rycroft (1985), pp. 41–51].

Rycroft, Charles (1968). *Imagination and Reality*. New York, NY: International Universities Press.

Rycroft, Charles (1979). *The Innocence of Dreams*. New York, NY: Jason Aronson, 1996.

Rycroft, Charles (1985). *Psychoanalysis and Beyond*, Peter Fuller (ed.). Chicago, IL: University of Chicago.

Sabato, Ernesto (1941). *Hombres y engranajes* [Men and gears]. In *Hombres y engranajes. Heterodoxia*. [Men and gears. Heterodoxy]. Madrid: Alianza, 1998, pp. 7–94.

Sami-Ali (2014). *Convergencias. Ensayos de psicosomática relacional* [Convergences: Essays on relational psychosomatics]. Mexico City: Gedisa, 2018.

Sánchez-Darvasi, Marcela (2017). Habitar el espacio potencial de la lectura creativa [Inhabiting the potential space of creative reading]. Read at the 26th Latin-American Meeting on Winnicott's Thought, Mexico City, November.

Scharff, David (ed.) (2017). *Enrique Pichon-Rivière: Pioneer of the Link*. Chevy Chase, MD: International Psychotherapy Institute. Free e-book, available in the web page of the International Psychotherapy Institute (visited on June 9, 2020). www.freepsychotherapybooks.org/ebook/enrique-pichon-riviere-pioneer-of-the-link/

Scharff, David E.; Losso, Roberto & Setton, Lea S. de (2017). Pichon Rivière's psychoanalytic contributions: Some comparisons with object relations and modern developments in psychoanalysis. *International Journal of Psycho-Analysis*, 98 (1): 129–143. https://doi.org/10.1111/1745-8315.12496

Schoellberger, Roberto (2013). 1st International Median Group congress (Bolanzo, Italy) 18–19 June 2010: Welcome. *Group Analysis*, 46 (2): 116–119. https://doi.org/10.1177%2F0533316413483074

Scholz, Regine (2003). The foundation matrix: A useful fiction. *Group Analysis*, 36 (4): 548–554. https://doi.org/10.1177%2F0533316403364011

Scholz, Regine (2011). The foundation matrix and the social unconscious. In Hopper & Weinberg, pp. 265–285.

Scholz, Regine (2017). The fluid and the solid: Or the dynamic and the static: Some further thoughts about the conceptualisation of foundation matrices, processes of the social unconscious, and/or large group identities. In Hopper & Weinberg, pp. 27–46.

Scholz, Regine (2019). Sailing on an ocean of associations: Response to Juan Tubert-Oklander. *Group Analysis*, 52 (4): 434–440. https://journals.sagepub.com/doi/abs/10.1177/0533316419871398

Schorske, Carl E. (1974). Politics and patricide in Freud's interpretation of dreams. *Annual of Psychoanalysis*, 2: 40–60.

Schorske, Carl E. (1980). *Fin-de-Siècle Vienna*. New York, NY: Vintage.

Searles, Harold F. (1960). *The Nonhuman Environment: In Normal Development and Schizophrenia*. New York: International Universities Press.

Segal, Hanna (1964). *Introduction to the Work of Melanie Klein.* London: Routledge, 1988.

Sharpe, Meg (2008). Styles of large group leadership. *Group,* 32 (4): 289–301.

Slavson, Samuel R. (1964). *A Textbook in Analytic Group Psychotherapy.* New York, NY: International Universities Press.

Smadja, Eric (2008). The notion of the work of culture in Freud's writings. *Psychoanalysis, Culture & Society,* 13: 188–198.

Smadja, Eric (2012). La notion de *Kulturarbeit* (travail culturel) dans l'oeuvre de Freud [The notion of *Kulturarbeit* (the work of culture) in Freud's writings]. Read at the Mexican Psychoanalytic Association, Mexico City, February.

Soustelle, Jacques (1955). *La vida cotidiana de los aztecas en vísperas de la conquista.* México: Fondo de Cultura Económica, 1991. [English translation: *Daily Life of the Aztecs, on the Eve of the Spanish Conquest.* Palo Alto, CA: Stanford University Press, 1961].

Spielrein, Sabina (1912 [1994]). Destruction as cause of coming into being. *Journal of Analytical Psychology,* 39 (2): 155–186.

Spielrein, Sabina (1912 [1995]). Destruction as cause of becoming (S.K. Witt, trans.). *Psychoanalysis and Contemporary Thought,* 18 (1): 85–118.

Spielrein, Sabina (2019). *The Essential Writings of Sabina Spielrein,* R.I. Cape & R. Burt (eds.). London & New York: Routledge.

Stanton, M. (1990). *Sándor Ferenczi: Reconsidering Active Intervention.* London: Free Association Books.

Stern, Donnel B. (1983). Unformulated experience: From familiar chaos to creative disorder. *Contemporary Psychoanalysis,* 19 (1): 71–99. https://doi.org/10.1080/0 0107530.1983.10746593 [Reprinted in Mitchell, Stephen A. & Aron, Lewis (eds.), *Relational Psychoanalysis: The Emergence of a Tradition.* London: Routledge, 2015, pp. 79–105].

Stern, Donnel B. (1997). *Unformulated Experience: From Dissociation to Imagination in Psychoanalysis.* London: Routledge, 2015.

Stiers, Michael J. & Dluhy, Mary (2008). The large group and the organizational unconscious. *Group,* 32 (4): 251–260.

Strachey, James (1955). *Editor's note to 'From the History of an Infantile Neurosis'.* S.E. 17: 3–6. London: Hogarth.

Strachey, James (1961). *Editor's Introduction to 'Civilization and Its Discontents'.* S.E. 21: 57–63. London: Hogarth.

Sullivan, Harry Stack (1947). *Conceptions of Modern Psychiatry.* Whitefish, MT: Kessinger Publishing.

Szasz, Thomas S. (1960). The myth of mental illness. *American Psychologist,* 15: 113–118. Published electronically in the Web Page Classics in the History of Psychology (visited 16 Feb 2012). http://psychclassics.yorku.ca/Szasz/myth.htm

Szasz, Thomas S. (1961). *The Myth of Mental Illness: Foundations of a Theory of Personal Conduct.* New York, NY: Hoeber-Harper.

Szasz, Thomas S. (2003). The myth of mental illness: Transcript of a lecture, held at the UCE, Birmingham, 7 December. In the Web Page of Scribd.com (visited 16 Feb 2012). http://es.scribd.com/doc/4664008/thomas-szasz-The-Myth-of-Mental-Illness

Tubert, José Luis (2021). Email of February 19.

Tubert-Oklander, Juan (1997). El proceso psicoanalítico a la luz de la teoría de las relaciones objetales [The psychoanalytic process in the light of object relations theory]. *Cuadernos de Psicoanálisis,* 30 (1–2): 33–41.

Tubert-Oklander, Juan (1999). Sándor Ferenczi e la nascita della teoria delle relazioni oggettuali [Sándor Ferenczi and the birth of object relations theory]. In Franco Borgogno (ed.), *La partecipazione affettiva dell' analista. Il contributo di Sándor Ferenczi al pensiero psicoanalitico contemporaneo* [The analyst's affective participation: Sándor Ferenczi's contribution to contemporary psychoanalysis]. Milan: Franco Angeli, pp. 261–287.

Tubert-Oklander, Juan (2000). El psicoanálisis ante el nuevo milenio. Reflexiones sobre la epistemología del psicoanálisis [Psychoanalysis facing the new millennium: Reflections on the epistemology of psychoanalysis]. *Estudios sobre Psicosis y Retardo Mental*, 5: 275–295.

Tubert-Oklander, Juan (2002). Enrique Pichon-Rivière: Pioneer and outcast. In Tubert-Oklander & Hernández de Tubert (2004), pp. 25–36.

Tubert-Oklander, Juan (2004a). Dionisio y Narciso. La contribución de Blanca Montevechio al estudio del sincretismo [Dionysus and Narcissus: The contribution of Blanca Montevechio to the study of syncretism]. Read at the 43rd International Congress of Psychoanalysis, New Orleans, LA, March.

Tubert-Oklander, Juan (2004b). Mitología, desarrollo y proceso psicoanalítico [Mythology, development, and the psychoanalytic process]. Lecture delivered to the 44th National Congress of Psychoanalysis, Oaxaca, Mexico, November.

Tubert-Oklander, Juan (2004c). ¿Debemos creer en el inconsciente? [Should we believe in the unconscious?]. In M. Kolteniuk, J. Casillas & J. de la Parra (eds.), *El inconsciente freudiano* [The Freudian unconscious]. Mexico City: Editores de Textos Mexicanos, pp. 101–109.

Tubert-Oklander, Juan (2006a). The individual, the group, and society: Their psychoanalytic inquiry. *International Forum of Psychoanalysis*, 15 (3): 151–156. https://doi.org/10.1080/08037060500526045

Tubert-Oklander, Juan. (2006b). I, thou, and us: Relationality and the interpretive process in clinical practice. *Psychoanalytic Dialogues*, 16 (2): 199–216.

Tubert-Oklander, Juan (2008a). Las contradicciones de Freud y el carácter híbrido del psicoanálisis [Freud's contradictions and the hybrid character of psychoanalysis]. In Tubert-Oklander & Beuchot Puente, pp. 50–72. [Chapter 1].

Tubert-Oklander, Juan (2008b). ¿De qué verdad hablamos? [What truth are we talking about?]. In Marialba Pastor (ed.), *Testigos y testimonios. El problema de la verdad* [Witnesses and testimonies: The problem of truth]. Mexico City: National Autonomous University of Mexico, pp. 47–71.

Tubert-Oklander, Juan (2008c). An inquiry into the alpha function. *Canadian Journal of Psychoanalysis/Revue Canadienne de Psychanalyse*, 16 (2): 224–245.

Tubert-Oklander, Juan (2009). *Hermenéutica analógica y condición humana* [Analogical hermeneutics and the human condition]. *Analogía Filosófica*, Special Number 24, Mexico City.

Tubert-Oklander, Juan (2009–2014). El ícono y el ídolo: El lugar de Freud en la identidad y la formación psicoanalíticas [The icon and the idol: The place of Freud in psychoanalytic identity and education]. *Cuadernos de Psicoanálisis*, 42 (1–2): 7–47. [Reprinted in English in a revised and enlarged version as 'The icon and the idol: The place of Freud and other founding fathers and mothers in psychoanalytic identity and education'. In Tubert-Oklander (2014), pp. 113–155].

Tubert-Oklander, Juan (2010a). The matrix of despair: From despair to desire through dialogue. *Group-Analysis*, 43 (2): 127–140. https://doi.org/10.1177%2F0533316410363446 [Reprinted in Tubert-Oklander (2014), pp. 227–244].

Tubert-Oklander, Juan (2010b). A gentle revolutionary: The influence of Malcolm Pines on my thinking and practice. *Group Analysis*, 43 (3): 228–240. https://doi.org/10.1177% 2F0533316410371272

Tubert-Oklander, Juan (2011a). Lost in translation: A contribution to intercultural understanding. *Canadian Journal of Psychoanalysis/Revue Canadienne de Psychanalyse*, 19: 144–168. [Reprinted in Tubert-Oklander (2014), pp. 81–111].

Tubert-Oklander, Juan (2011b). Enrique Pichon-Rivière: The social unconscious in the Latin-American tradition of group analysis. In Hopper & Weinberg (2011a), pp. 45–67.

Tubert-Oklander, Juan (2013a). *Theory of Psychoanalytical Practice: A Relational Process Approach*. London: Routledge, 2019.

Tubert-Oklander, Juan (2013b). *Un estudio del tipo de conocimiento que nos brinda el psicoanálisis* [A study of the kind of knowledge provided by psychoanalysis]. Unpublished Doctor in Psychotherapy dissertation, Centre for Graduate Studies, Mexican Psychoanalytic Association, Mexico City, July.

Tubert-Oklander, Juan (2013c). Hermes en el diván. El encuentro del psicoanálisis y la hermenéutica analógica [Hermes on the couch: The confluence of psychoanalysis and analogical hermeneutics]. In Juan R. Coca (ed.), *Impacto de la hermenéutica analógica en las ciencias humanas y sociales* [The impact of analogical hermeneutics on the human and social sciences]. Huelva, Spain: Hergué, pp. 283–297.

Tubert-Oklander, Juan (2014). *The One and the Many: Relational Psychoanalysis and Group Analysis*. London: Routledge, 2019.

Tubert-Oklander, Juan (2015). The wind and the tide: On personal acts and impersonal currents. *Canadian Journal of Psychoanalysis/Revue Canadienne de Psychanalyse*, Spring, 23 (1): 187–194. [Chapter 14].

Tubert-Oklander, Juan (2016). The quest for the real. In Gabriela Legorreta & Lawrence J. Brown (eds.), *On Freud's 'Formulations on the Two Principles of Mental Functioning'*. London: Routledge, 2019, pp. 185–200. [Chapter 7].

Tubert-Oklander, Juan (2017a). The inner organization of the matrix. In Hopper & Weinberg, pp. 65–85.

Tubert-Oklander, Juan (2017b). Of links and bonds: The complex thought and practice of Enrique Pichon-Rivière. In Scharff (2017), pp. 28–34.

Tubert-Oklander, Juan (2017c). Field theories and process theories. In Katz, Cassorla & Civitarese (2017), pp. 191–200.

Tubert-Oklander, Juan (2017d). Donald Winnicott: un revolucionario a pesar suyo [Donald Winnicott: A revolutionary malgré lui]. Read at the 26th Latin-American Meeting on Winnicott's Thought, Mexico City, November. [Chapter 3].

Tubert-Oklander, Juan (2018). Is Fairbairn still at large? *Contemporary Psychoanalysis*, 54 (1): 201–228. https://doi.org/10.1080/00107530.2017.1422356

Tubert-Oklander, Juan (2019a). Presentation of Sami-Ali's book *Convergences*. Mexico City, Palace of Mines Book Fair, February.

Tubert-Oklander, Juan (2019b). Ferenczi and group analysis. *Group Analysis*, 52 (1): 23–35.https://doi.org/10.1177%2F0533316418764388

Tubert-Oklander, Juan. (2019c). Towards a full comprehension of our paradigm: A response to Mário David's article 'How to be a "good-enough" group analyst'. *Group Analysis*, 52 (2): 230–241. https://doi.org/10.1177%2F0533316419831105

Tubert-Oklander, Juan (2019d). Beyond psychoanalysis and group analysis: The urgent need for a new paradigm of the human being. *Group Analysis*, 52 (4): 409–426. https:// doi.org/10.1177%2F0533316419863037 [Chapter 15].

Tubert-Oklander, Juan (2020a). Beyond subject and object or why object usage is not a good idea. In Daniel Scharff (ed.), *The Use of an Object*. London: Routledge, pp. 101–117.

Tubert-Oklander, Juan (2020b). 'Every child that's born alive . . . ': Response to Regine Scholz and Earl Hopper. *Group Analysis*, 53 (1): 119–129. https://doi.org/10.1177% 2F0533316419880652

Tubert-Oklander, Juan (2020c). Mountain or river? A response to Emma Reicher's article 'Approaching the mountain: A journey into the wilderness of large group thinking'. *Group Analysis*, 54 (1): 129-142. https://doi.org/10.1177%2F0533316420955098

Tubert-Oklander, Juan & Beuchot Puente, Mauricio (2008). *Ciencia mestiza. Psicoanálisis y hermenéutica analógica* [Hybrid science: Psychoanalysis and analogical hermeneutics]. Mexico City: Torres.

Tubert-Oklander, Juan; Campillo, Athos; Rita, Zepeda G. & Ellstein, Irene (1982). Participación de las funciones paterna y materna en el proceso de semiotización temprana [Participation of the paternal and maternal functions in early semiotic development]. *Cuadernos de Psicoanálisis*, 15 (3–4): 93–117.

Tubert-Oklander, Juan & Hernández de Tubert, Reyna (1996). Psicoanálisis del poder y la violencia en el contexto social e institucional [Psychoanalysis of power and violence in the social and institutional context]. *Revista de Psicoanálisis, Número Especial Internacional 1996*, 5: 231–251.

Tubert-Oklander, Juan & Hernández de Tubert, Reyna (2004). *Operative Groups: The Latin-American Approach to Group Analysis*. London: Jessica Kingsley.

Tubert-Oklander, Juan & Hernández-Tubert, Reyna (2011). A conversation with Malcolm Pines: Part Two. *Group Analysis*, 44 (1): 3–26. https://doi.org/10.1177% 2F0533316410387744

Tubert-Oklander, Juan & Hernández-Tubert, Reyna (2014a). The social unconscious and the large group, Part I: The British and the Latin American traditions. *Group Analysis*, 47 (2): 99–112. https://doi.org/10.1177%2F0533316414523209 [Chapter 9].

Tubert-Oklander, Juan & Hernández-Tubert, Reyna (2014b). The social unconscious and the large group, Part II: A context that becomes text. *Group Analysis*, 47 (3): 329–344. https://doi.org/10.1177%2F0533316414541366 [Chapter 10].

Tubert-Oklander, Juan & Hernández-Tubert, Reyna (2014c). The social unconscious and the large group, Part III: Listening to the voices in the wind. *Group Analysis*, 47 (4): 420–435. https://doi.org/10.1177%2F0533316414550588 [Chapter 11].

Volkan, Vamik & Itzkowitz, Norman (1984). *The Immortal Atatürk: A Psychobiography*. Chicago, IL: University of Chicago.

von Sommaruga Howard, Teresa (2007). To stand sitting! Reflections on weaving our living stories: The NZAP conference in Napier. *NZAP Journal Forum*, 13: 92–113.

von Sommaruga Howard, Teresa (2011). The architecture of domination: Reflections on conducting the symposium large group in Dublin. *Group Analysis*, 44 (3): 328–341. https://journals.sagepub.com/doi/abs/10.1177/0533316411411803

von Sommaruga Howard, Teresa (2012). To stand sitting! Bi-cultural dilemmas in a large group in *Aotearoa* New Zealand. *Group Analysis*, 45 (2): 219–243. https://doi.org/10.1 177%2F0533316411408804

Weinberg, Haim (2015). From the individual unconsciousness through the relational unconscious to the social unconscious. *Canadian Journal of Psychoanalysis/Revue Canadienne de Psychanalyse*, Spring, 23 (1): 195–201.

Winnicott, Donald W. (1949). Hate in the countertransference. In Winnicott (1958c), pp. 194–203.

Winnicott, Donald W. (1950–1955). Aggression in relation to emotional development. In Winnicott (1958c), pp. 204–218.

Winnicott, Donald W. (1954). Metapsychological and clinical aspects of regression within the psycho-analytical set-up. In Winnicott (1958c), pp. 278–294.

Winnicott, Donald W. (1955–1956). Clinical varieties of transference. In Winnicott (1958c), pp. 295–299.

Winnicott, Donald W. (1956). Letter to W. Clifford M. Scott, 26 December. Quoted by Brett Kahr. In *D. W. Winnicott: A Biographical Portrait*. London: Routledge, 2019, p. 70.

Winnicott, Donald W. (1958a). The capacity to be alone. In Winnicott (1965), pp. 29–36.

Winnicott, Donald W. (1958b). Child analysis in the latency period. In Winnicott (1965), pp. 115–123.

Winnicott, Donald W. (1958c). *Through Paediatrics to Psycho-Analysis*, second edition. London: Routledge, 2019.

Winnicott, Donald W. (1959–1964). Classification: Is there a psychoanalytic contribution to psychiatric classification? In Winnicott (1965), pp. 124–139.

Winnicott, Donald W. (1960a). The theory of the parent-infant relationship. In Winnicott (1965), pp. 37–55.

Winnicott, Donald W. (1960b). Ego distortion in terms of true and false self. In Winnicott (1965), pp. 140–152.

Winnicott, Donald W. (1962). A personal view of the Kleinian contribution. In Winnicott (1965), pp. 171–178.

Winnicott, Donald W. (1965). *The Maturational Processes and the Facilitating Environment*. London: Routledge, 1990.

Winnicott, Donald W. (1967). Postscript: D.W.W. on D.W.W. In Clare Winnicott, Kay Shepherd & Madeleine Davis (eds.), *Psychoanalytic Explorations*. London: Routledge, 2010, pp. 569–582.

Winnicott, Donald W. (1969). The use of an object and relating through identifications. In Winnicott (1971b), pp. 86–94.

Winnicott, Donald W. (1971a). Creativity and its origins. In Winnicott (1971b), pp. 87–114.

Winnicott, Donald W. (1971b). *Playing and Reality*. London, Routledge, 2005.

Winnicott, Donald W. & Khan, M. Masud R. (1953). *Psychoanalytic Studies of the Personality*: By W. Ronald D. Fairbairn. *International Journal of Psycho-Analysis*, 34: 329–333.

Winther, Gerda (2008). President's page. *Contexts*, 42, December 2008, pp. 4–5.

Wisdom, John (1934). *Problems of Mind and Matter*. Cambridge, UK: Cambridge University Press, 2009.

Wolf, Alexander & Schwartz, Emanuel K. (1962). *Psychoanalysis in Groups*. New York, NY: Grune & Stratton.

Younge, Gary (2009). Interview: The secrets of a peacemaker. *The Guardian*, May 22. In The Guardian Web Page (visited June 4, 2019). www.theguardian.com/books/2009/may/23/interview-desmond-tutu

Zito Lema, Vicente (1975). Todos los viajes de Enrique Pichon-Rivière [All the journeys of Enrique Pichon-Rivière]. *La Opinión Cultural*, June 22: 2–3.

Zito Lema, Vicente (1976). *Conversaciones con Enrique Pichon-Rivière. Sobre el arte y la locura* [Conversations with Enrique Pichon-Rivière: On art and madness]. Buenos Aires: Ediciones Cinco, 1993.

Index

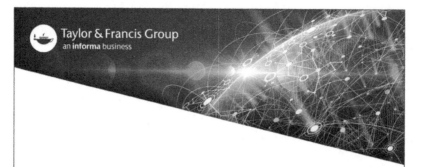

Made in the USA
Las Vegas, NV
11 November 2021